# Radio Content in the Digital Age

'Whenever one listens to the radio, he becomes part of the everlasting clash between ideas and icons, time and timelessness, the human and divine'

Herman Hesse: *Steppenwolf*

# Radio Content in the Digital Age
## The Evolution of a Sound Medium

Edited by Angeliki Gazi, Guy Starkey and Stanislaw Jedrzejewski

**intellect** Bristol, UK / Chicago, USA

First published in the UK in 2011 by
Intellect, The Mill, Parnall Road, Fishponds, Bristol, BS16 3JG, UK

First published in the USA in 2011 by
Intellect, The University of Chicago Press, 1427 E. 60th Street,
Chicago, IL 60637, USA

A catalogue record for this book is available from the
British Library.

Cover designer: Holly Rose
Copy-editor: Macmillan
Typesetting: Mac Style, Beverley, E. Yorkshire

ISBN 978-1-84150-423-0

Printed and bound by Hobbs, UK.

# Contents

# Acknowledgements

The conference Radio Content in the Digital Age was the first conference organized by the Radio Research Section of the European Communication Research and Education Association (ECREA). Hosted by the Cyprus University of Technology on their new Limassol campus from 14 to 16 October 2009, it was organized by one of the two Vice-Chairs of the section, Dr Angeliki Gazi. These separate section conferences are held every two years, and in cyclical fashion the whole of ECREA joins together in full, joint conferences of all the sections in another single location in each of the intervening years. So this was the first occasion on which the Radio Research Section could meet together in a dedicated context for a concentrated period of discussion of our research field: radio. With the full cooperation of the university and the magnificent assistance of Dr Gazi's colleagues in the Faculty of Applied Arts and Communication, the conference was a resounding success.

However, without Angeliki the conference would simply not have happened, so for her determination, her considerable organizational skills and her dedication to the task of making the conference not only successful but memorable, she deserves a particular mention here. It is those qualities, which are also to be found in our close colleague, the other Section Vice-Chair, Professor Stanisław Jędrzejewski of Kozminski University of Warsaw and the University of Minho, Portugal, which have made the job of being Chair so relatively easy and so rewarding. Despite Angeliki's gift for meticulous planning, it is worth noting that for the beautiful island of Cyprus to have experienced an early-Autumn heat wave that week, with temperatures in the mid-thirties, was an unexpected and very pleasant surprise for us all.

Prof. Guy Starkey
Chair, ECREA Radio Research Section

# Introduction: Radio and the Digital Age

Angeliki Gazi, Guy Starkey and Stanislaw Jedrzejewski

W hen the Canadian inventor Reginald Fessenden broadcast the first ever radio programme of speech and music in December 1906, he could not have imagined how pervasive radio would become. Guglielmo Marconi, indisputably a good European whether Italy or the United Kingdom would wish to claim him as their own, had already demonstrated the reach of broadcast radio signals over such great distances as span the Atlantic Ocean. His privately owned radio company later evolved into the BBC, and all across Europe a rich mix of commercial and public service broadcasters emerged – some aimed at domestic markets and others targeted worldwide as Europe sought to maintain its influence through the spoken word rather than the sword or the gun (Starkey 2007: 115–21). In 1964 the controversial media theorist Marshall McLuhan noted that it was radio that first shrank the world down to 'village size' (2001: 334). Yet there were many predictions in the last century of the demise of radio owing to increased competition, and there are those today who will suggest the same. The ECREA Radio Research Section gathered in Cyprus to discuss radio in its present form, fully conscious that at a time of great technological advance in production and distribution technology, radio is changing into a great medium of tomorrow. This is not unproblematic: one of our central concerns in examining radio today lies in predicting what will be the radio of tomorrow.

## Radio and new technology

Trends towards deregulation, the abolition of monopolies and decentralization of radio broadcasting, strong competition for public radio from commercial broadcasters, the dominant position of television, changes to modes of listening to radio and, finally, revolutionary changes in radio production and distribution technology have been the major driving forces behind changes to the medium of radio in recent years.

Traditionally, radio programmes have mainly been made available via dedicated terrestrial transmission networks, broadcasting to radio receivers. Typically, they have operated on AM and FM terrestrial platforms but, with some countries moving to digital broadcasting, today radio programmes are also available using digital transmission standards, including Digital Audio Broadcasting (DAB), Digital Radio Mondiale (DRM) and In-Band-On-Channel (IBOC). However, this paradigm is already changing. Radio programmes are increasingly available not only from terrestrial networks but also from a large variety of satellite, cable and wired telecommunications networks, including the internet. In many countries radio is added to digital television platforms. Radio 'receivers' are no longer only dedicated hi-fi tuners or portable radios with whip aerials in the traditional sense, but they are now also assuming the shape of various multimedia-enabled computer devices.

Technology is one of the most important factors in the development of radio. Technological advances accelerate with the growing use of digital technology. As the European Broadcasting Union (EBU) Digital Strategy Group II states: 'Digital technology makes possible new ways to produce and deliver media, and brings the wider use of ever more sophisticated multimedia, interactivity, the option of multichannel services, on-demand services, and the availability of different picture and sound quality options. Indeed, digitalization facilitates a transition of content provision, broadcasting and media consumption' (2006: 19).

Many radio analysts, such as the British radio theorists Crisell (1994), Lewis and Booth (1989) and Scannell (1996) located radio sound messages within a traditional model of communication. As a result radio content was defined through the traditional relationship between radio and the culture of sound. In the digital age this is evolving as new content is becoming located within visual paradigms (for example video, text and so on). Web radio has synergies with the visual images of other media, such as television. Through the web, radio that transmits sound and pictures can be characterized as being delivered with the additional power of given images.

The development of *audio* broadcasting via the web opens up the discussion about the implications that emerge from the convergence of technology, as we shift away from the sound to the image, and about the impact this new technological environment has on content. Sound already transforms voices, words, music into objects rich with representations. The disembodied voices of broadcasters already excite our imagination, curiosity and desire for more. They are related to the borders of sound that cannot become visible (Gazi, 2010). Web radio loses the sound-centric nature of traditional radio broadcasting and this kind of convergence raises issues about the quality and the type of content.

For Baudrillard (1988) the language of radio is not a direct reference to an external reality, but, instead, the imposition of an arbitrary web of signifiers. Traditional radio broadcasting has given birth and shape to its own sign system, and along with it to our expectations of the essence of radio. In that respect, any analysis of radio content in the digital age must begin from these first principles.

## The characteristics of radio

According to qualitative research (OFCOM 2005), for radio listeners the most important characteristics of the medium are now variety of music, localness in news and information about the weather, intelligent speech content and ease of access. These findings also confirm a survey conducted by a group of European experts in digital radio, Digital Radio Cultures in Europe (Ala-Fossi et al. 2008). The strengths of radio as a medium already migrating to new technological realities remain its mobility, easy access, its instant availability through real-time transmission, the ability to integrate with local communities, the personal appeal of presenters and a variety of programming genres including entertainment, traditional journalism and artistic programmes. The challenge for radio is how to transfer these characteristics to the digital environment which for the foreseeable future will be constantly evolving through developments in technology.

Before the arrival of the 'digital age', though, a key strength of radio in its original form was that it was distinguished from other media by its being invisible (Lewis & Booth 1989). That key characteristic of invisibility is even today almost certainly one of its strengths, but what does it mean? Put simply, the images created for us in, for example, radio drama, are not fully formed. As radio listeners, we have to complete them from the aural, technical, lexical and syntactical clues given to us, many of them formulated through codes and used in conventional ways for specific purposes: we are of necessity filling in the blanks from the deep resources of our own imagination, known in English as 'the mind's eye'. As radio producers, we have those techniques and the potential they unlock at our disposal in many exciting ways, some of which are explored later in this book. Not only, though, is that invisible content rich in potential, but the ways in which it is being created and consumed are going through a period of rapid change. We will read in the chapters that follow, some of the ways in which that change is already manifesting itself. Now even radio, once the invisible medium, can transmit fully formed, given images like television does, thanks to digital technology. Our focus on content, though, will remind us that changes in technology will alter only some of the essential characteristics of the medium, not all of them.

## New listening patterns – new audiences

The process of listening to that content often occurs alone. The portability of radio means it can accompany the listener almost anywhere. The secondary nature of the radio medium – meaning that it can be consumed while some other, primary activity is taking place – means the presence of other people at the point of reception is often a disadvantage (Crisell 1994). Driving a car or ironing clothes are just two such everyday activities that many people consider to be enhanced by the ability to listen to radio content at the same time. Being left alone to enjoy the radio without interruption must surely be one of life's greatest pleasures.

In recent years new listening patterns have been shaped by developments across all media – the press and television, for example, also have huge potential to exploit the internet and other new media. Undoubtedly, both access to the internet and the time devoted to it are increasing, as is the diversity of its different uses. However, unlike television or radio, the internet is characterized by a relatively equal distribution of public interest. It maintains the same high level of consumption throughout the day, with an increase in the afternoon and evening, as evidenced by research into internet usage in Poland carried out by Gemius (2008). These results derive from the multidimensionality of the internet, as it is used both for business purposes and for private use including study, entertainment, social networking and so on.

Time spent listening to the radio while surfing the internet is also increasing. According to the EIAA Report (2006) radio has the highest level of parallel media use, in comparison with other media, particularly the internet. Among those who 'mainly use' the internet, regardless of daypart, as many as 40% listen to the radio.

**Table 1**: Simultaneous use of media (percentage of time spent).

|          | Radio | TV | Internet | Press |
|----------|-------|-----|----------|-------|
| Radio    |       | 8   | 30       | 32    |
| TV       | 8     |     | 28       | 24    |
| Internet | 40    | 32  |          | 6     |

*Source*: EIAA Digital Generation Report 2006

According to ComScore MediaMetrix (2000) traditional radio listening decreases as online activities increase, and in some territories about one-fifth of listening may be via the internet. Some surveys report increases in the use of the radio, even to record levels, although – surprisingly – in the United Kingdom listening to the radio via the internet is comparatively low (Table 2).

Table 2: Weekly share of listening for the three digital radio platforms in the UK, 2007–09 (per cent).

| Year      | All platforms | DAB  | TV  | Internet |
|-----------|---------------|------|-----|----------|
| 2007 (Q4) | 16.6          | 10.0 | 3.1 | 1.9      |
| 2009 (Q2) | 21.1          | 13.1 | 3.6 | 2.2      |

*Source*: RAJAR 2007, 2009

Already almost 12 million adults in the United Kingdom, representing a quarter of the measured UK audience, listen to the radio through digital television platforms, including satellite and cable, other satellite transmissions and computer applications (RAJAR 2007, 2009). It is clear that in many markets, significant changes to patterns of radio listening are taking place. Currently, more and more listeners are turning to new modes of listening to enable them to decide how, when and where they will be using this medium.

## New radio as a participatory medium

Development in radio tends to be focused on relatively new technologies, which are opening up new opportunities for citizens to participate in the electronic communications environment. Initially, 'radio' referred to a mostly one-way communication system that was restricted to only those who could broadcast over the airwaves, and until recently,[1] a huge mass of largely uninvolved and mainly passive individuals who were receiving the communicative content each transmitter was sending out indiscriminately (in essence, 'broadcasting'). In representing this medium with the range of different characteristics we have already identified, communication through the radio has been defined as a strict linear model, whereby the receiver gets the transmitted message, yet remains relatively inactive in relation to the process of communication taking place. In the light of this 'linear' communication, the radio is defined as a one-way communicative medium. It allows each piece of information to be transmitted to people who are distant in space but not time, and the transmitter cannot hear the responses of those who listen.

Audience behaviour is changing as the radio succeeds in developing a form of communication that gives individuals a feeling of participation in a continual process. Because current technological developments have empowered the medium of radio to grow and diversify as a consequence of digital proliferation, it is important to problematize the actual uses people make of the interaction offered by radio stations.[2] They, in turn, have been explored through original research which is revealed in some of the papers which contribute to this book.

Radio transition in the digital age and its relationship to radio audiences lead us to define again the term 'participation' as some radio theorists and researchers believe that any engagement by, or involvement of, listeners with radio constitutes participation, no matter how fleeting, mediated or insignificant. On the other hand, it is indisputable that community radio groups are already exploiting the opportunities of participation in the digitization of radio. New communication technology that enables greater dialogue is available to broadcasters, but it is not yet being energetically explored for its potential to facilitate social change in the way that traditional community or local radio have been shown to be able to do. Radio now faces unprecedented challenges and opportunities, and the implications of further technological advance may be considerable for cultural diversity and citizenship in the future. As one major tendency in the world today is to retreat behind ethnic and community lines, it is important to investigate the situations in which culture encounters radio digitization.

Some issues with potential for framing further discussion of the relationship between the digitization of radio, audience participation and community groups arise from the use of control groups in research among listeners, as well as from inevitable new parameters such as the involvement of computers, user training and the availability of access to the internet, which are changing the traditional patterns of communication and with them the pre-established norms and models of communication which are mediated through the use of new technologies.

## Radio as a subject of research (towards practice and theory)

It follows that in an ever-changing communications world, one key concern of ours must be epistemological: what can we know about radio and how can we find appropriate sources to inform that knowledge? Just how does more generalizable knowledge about radio and its audiences emerge from specific research among listeners? What is the relationship between market research, ad hoc research and academic study? The methods used in research into radio for marketing purposes are broadly situated within quantitative and qualitative paradigms, often involving psycho-graphic and geo-demographic approaches.

Generally speaking, the application of research methodology is considerably more complicated in the new technological environment of the digital age. In terms of listeners, especially younger ones, who are either failing to engage with or departing from analogue technology, the difficulty of assessing this loss of audience has increased. In some markets radio is becoming increasingly popular and – in the United Kingdom and Denmark – DAB is gaining some momentum. Some users of digital radio benefit from an intense radio experience, given the presence of record and rewind, electronic programme guide and image functionality on some receivers. Market-orientated audience research to estimate radio audiences has acquired a new level of complication, in order to differentiate between listening by means of analogue or digital audio transmissions, digital television platforms and the internet. A major challenge remains measuring the use of online radio, although that does not mean that radio broadcasters are completely unable to measure the levels of engagement with such technologies as streaming and downloading, but that the comparability of such usage data is limited and reduced to the measurement of access to pages, sites or portals.

In this age we have seen fundamental shifts in society as well as in technology, and radio broadcasters are confronted with change on all sides, bringing both opportunities and threats provided by new digital media and increased competition within their traditional media markets. All of this adds up to uncertainty, and there is a massive demand for greater understanding of how these changes will impact on listeners' and users' behaviour, now and in the future. Moreover, in spite of the explosion in capacity resulting from the launch of new digital radio, television and web-radio platforms, one possibility is that a demand for greater diversity in content and thematic offering might still threaten to outstrip supply.

Many kinds of research findings serve to formulate current programme policies, to create the programme schedules of individual radio stations. The broadcasters should know –

perhaps this is a given – which audiences their programmes are reaching, in which dayparts and on which days of the week listeners prefer listening to which kinds of programmes. Finally, but not least, research into levels of audience appreciation produces data which might be useful for the working out of short-term programming decisions and long-term programming strategies, especially in relation to market competitors. Despite the fact that using research findings for specific decisions about programming is neither simple nor automatic, research findings can create an apparently robust rationale for such decisions.

In terms of academic research, the medium of radio is, relative to other media, undertheorized. Its implications for policy-making in Europe often remain unclear, and there has been little involvement of the European Commission with the radio industries and the state-owned radio broadcasters of the European member states. While Télévision sans frontières (Council of Europe 1989) and more recently the Audivisual Media Services Directive (European Commission 2007) established a Europe-wide policy for television, there was no corresponding initiative for radio, however prescriptive or permissive. Until recently little has been done to situate this important, popular medium in any wider contexts for the benefit of European citizens or their policy-makers. The potential of radio to reach beyond the frontiers of Europe, as evidenced by the appetite for international radio broadcasting during the Cold War, remains largely undiscovered. The Council of Europe acknowledged this need with the publication of *Promoting Social Cohesion: The Role of Community Media* (2008). The same problem, a lack of systematic analysis, besets radio broadcasting at international (external), national, regional and local levels, in the public and private sectors.

Academic approaches to radio have drawn on a number of different disciplines, including a growing body of medium-specific radio theory which uses sociological, political and economic perspectives, as well as certain cultural history paradigms. Broader approaches drawn from cultural studies, popular culture theory, linguistic analysis, psychology, business studies and marketing have each made a contribution. A new paradigm has emerged in the United Kingdom in the work of the Birmingham School into rejection hierarchies of high and low intellectual levels of culture, including radio.

In radio studies different research techniques have been used, including content analysis, experimental laboratory research, case studies, longitudinal studies and ethnographic studies. According to Hilmes (2002), 'Radio began to benefit from this historiographical shift – though slowly and more in some areas than others'.

## Some challenges for radio research

We are faced with a number of critical challenges for radio research:

1. Filling the information gaps. We need to provide an understanding not just of what people are doing, but of what they are like – their attitudes, values and behaviours, which may (directly or indirectly) affect their needs and behaviours related to media use.

2. Analysing the processes of communication through the medium (differentiating between types of radio stations, programming genres and the increasing choice of software services). The results of this kind of research are most often used for marketing and to measure the effects of ongoing changes in individual stations' programming offer.
3. Simultaneously, as radio researchers, we must address a third challenge – that of becoming predictors of behaviour as well as reporters. This is complicated as we have said, by the many uncertainties of the competitive environment, the penetration of hardware and the regulatory frameworks within which different countries' radio industries operate.

Another key question is, what should be done in the field, in the near future? There are two most important areas to explore which concern the social role of radio. One is the role of radio in everyday life. Most studies of public opinion and citizenship tend to eschew the fact that under the new conditions of the mediated public sphere, individuals build their opinions and participate in this public space from within the private space of their own homes. Meanwhile, the domestic sphere has become the launch pad from where individuals seek to bridge the great distance between their private space and the public sphere of the wider world. Listening, just like affecting public opinion, is situated somewhere on a continuum running between extreme active and passive levels of engagement with an external source, of appropriation, differentiated and located as it is, in distinct sociocultural and family contexts.

Another important area requiring further investigation is to examine and analyse the role of radio in mainstream culture and non-mainstream sub-cultures of the population (that is to say, minorities, countercultures, extremists and alternative-lifestyle clusters). It is important to understand and fully appreciate the way in which radio has operated and conducted itself concerning the fair and just treatment of different social groups at a time when cultural diversity and multiculturalism are generally recognized to be issues of great importance.

In this changing world, radio has been changing, too. Traditional media have already demonstrated a certain capacity to adapt and reconvert to a new climate. Despite any overall decrease in audience, audio messages probably still remain, for many people, the first and essential window to the world. In fact, some studies demonstrate the constancy of 'listening' even if digital platforms are taking an increasing share of radio listening (Radio Advertising Bureau and the Internet Adverting Bureau 2006). This means that listener-users are still listening to radio but in increasing numbers they are moving to the internet and are expecting to find there a new environment for radio genres: that is to say we are witnessing radio converging with multimedia interfaces despite the advantages of its own infrastructure.

As distribution platforms fragment, and radio research methodologies diverge, the next challenge will be how to develop some kind of holistic understanding of listeners. To what extent are listeners also viewers and online users, as well as readers of the press and books – and ultimately, prosumers (Toffler 1980)? Furthermore, how do these individual behaviours interrelate with consumption of other media? Even if we see technology as a decisive factor, it is impossible to ignore the way technical evolution has visibly forced us to make changes in terms of broadcasting in general and radio production in particular, having also created the potential for producers to draw upon an ever-expanding universe of sounds. Of course, transitions from analogue to digital environments lead to another main research challenge, namely to understand the future of radio as it adjusts to positive coexistence with the internet and continues to generate the new language and narrative of radio.

## Radio content in the digital age: selection and structure

While the quality of the papers presented at the conference was generally considered to be very high, the economics of book publishing demand an element of selection in compiling an edited collection of papers presented. Faced with a choice between prioritizing a representative sample of papers to be reproduced in full or severely abridging a larger number of contributions, the editors chose to adopt the former approach. Consequently, the book focuses on an intercultural dialogue about the important role that new technologies currently play – and will play in the future – in the different configurations of FM and digital sound broadcasting.

In order to present a coherent collection of contributions, the contents are divided into the following three parts:

I.  Convergence
II.  Content
III. Community

The first part, Convergence, comprises five thematically linked chapters presented at the Cyprus conference, which explore the intersections between radio and the web.

A discussion of the effects of media convergence on social change and audience behaviour begins with a chapter by Blandine Schmidt. She investigates the issue of interactivity in French radio broadcasts, being particularly interested in the emergence and the affirmation of the new digital ways of communication within the radio medium and its appropriation by the audience. Her field study is focused upon analysing comments left by listeners of France Inter (a public full-service French radio station) on the radio website during the programme *Service Public*. In her analysis she detects five types of listeners who are using new, interactive digital tools and she argues that the appearance and proliferation of such tools on radio websites induced modifications to the programmes by their interweaving or even inclusion within more traditional media forms.

This is followed by another case study, by José Luis Requejo Aleman and Susana Herrera Damas. They investigate Spanish talk radio and listener participation through the participative technologies of web 2.0. A content analysis of the main Spanish talk radio stations' websites is elaborated and the relationship between audience, participation and new technologies is re examined. They find that the listener seems to use these new technologies in order to communicate rather than to impact on the radio programme.

Pedro Portela, in his chapter, maps internet radio in Portugal over the period 2006–09. Using a methodology which has led to the classification of 318 Portuguese radio stations, he discusses the main evolutions in the use they make of interactive technologies. His argument opens up discussion of the issue of interactivity and audience behaviour in the digital age.

Carmen Peñafiel Saiz continues the discussion around listener participation, introducing the term 'citizen journalism' to the debate. It refers to a genre of journalism that recreates citizens as broadcasters, while engaging in conversations among them. Technological change seems to construct a different kind of audience behaviour, as the radio listener is able to receive and to create content at the same time. Through the internet the listener becomes the protagonist of information as new forms of participation and online content have emerged.

Maria Papadomanolaki rounds off Part I by introducing the relationship between radio art, interactivity and the community. She examines the use of radio in the context of performance and installation art. She argues that digital radio art enhances notions of locality, community and interactivity. In the projects she presents, radio intersects activism, architecture, music performance, film, site specificity, interactivity and locality, and through the challenge of the digital age surpasses what she calls the 'sterile' limitations of its role as a medium for the distribution of information.

The second part of the book, Content, also consists of five thematically linked papers, which consider how content may be evolving.

Tiziano Bonini explores the format of *Amnésia* and the way it blurred fiction with reality. *Amnésia*, described as a 'mockumentary', tells the story of a former presenter on Italian public radio, who suffered from a form of memory loss. Through the analysis of data derived from the use of a relatively new technological capacity, the ability to invite and to receive listeners' e-mails, audience reactions to this radio format are explored in detail.

Elsa Moreno, María del Pilar Martínez-Costa and Avelino Amoedo use as case studies the Spanish talk radio networks Cadena SER, COPE, Onda Cero, Punto Radio and Radio Nacional on the web. They investigate the way that the internet, as a platform, allows networks to enrich their relationship with the audience. Their research, based on a comparative tracking of the main pages of the websites during the period 2008–09 and their quantitative and qualitative analyses, provides a precise description of some news content strategies of Spanish talk radio.

Vesa Kurkela and Heikki Uimonen argue that radio broadcasting was more thoroughly influenced by the radical cultural transformations that occurred on the eve of the digital era. Concentrating on music listening and focusing on internet services such as Spotify, which supply music with financing from advertisers and users, they find that such developments are also challenging traditional and music radio content. Kurkela and Uimonen present and interpret findings around listening habits in Finland in 2009.

Josep Maria Martí, Xavier Ribes, Maria Gutiérrez, Luisa Martínez and Belén Monclús open a discussion about the format of music radio on the web, as the internet has altered most of the media consumption habits of broadcasters and listeners. Investigating the Catalan context they attempt to describe the affects of the internet on music radio and to answer questions which arise from the adaptation of audiences to the digital age.

Frank Byrne's polemic around 'Radio Content and Radio Audiences' attempts to address one aspect of the question, what are the main characteristics of today's radio content? The raw data of his research are drawn from the brief descriptors attached by RTE, the national Irish broadcaster, to the podcasts of each day's programme. Having categorized the topics covered in the programme over the previous two years, he extrapolates from them some insight into the anxieties attached to contemporary society as being a site of threat, risk and conflict.

The third and final part, titled Community, comprises five papers focused on radio communities in the digital era:

Pascal Ricaud analyses the characteristics and the new formats of the online community radio stations in France. Arguing that these new media contribute to the emergence of new forms of expression of citizenship, participation and social appropriation of mediatized public space, Pascal Ricaud takes on the issue of the new community forms of expression. He notes that participation in these forms of expression restricts public space without a deliberative approach and links with spaces of political decision.

Rosemary Day argues the case for participation in community radio. She presents a framework for participation in media and she distinguishes 'genuine' from 'pseudo' participation by investigating community radio stations and the new technologies they use. Her study explores twenty community radio projects in Ireland in 2009 and produces results which enhance the discussion about the definition of participation in community radio.

Hilde van den Bulck and Bert Hermans investigate the way Flemish local community radio is represented on the internet. Quantitative content analysis and semi-structured interviews are used in order to map the Flemish local radio stations and to examine radio producer practices in the new digital media applications. There are points in Hilde van den Bulck's and Bert Hermans's argument which open up a discussion about the range of possibilities of new media tools and their application to the problems local community radio faces today.

Mojca Plansak explores community radio, its current role and the issue of participation in Slovenia. She points out that new technology brings to community radio opportunities and threats, as it has the potential to re-establish the composition and power of the message. However the changes in the media industry are an integral part of the global transition from an industrial society to an information society.

Finally, Etienne L. Damome explores the challenge of new technologies in African community radio. He focuses on an investigation of the changes that convergence and digitization are promoting in the new patterns of production and in the relationship between radio and its audiences. His research raises questions about the opportunities or otherwise of the new information and communication technologies, and is partly based on a field survey conducted among a radiophonic community in Togo.

It should be noted that because the official lingua franca of ECREA is English, as was that of the conference, a number of the contributors to this volume have been asked to express themselves in a language which is not their mother tongue. Because the focus of both the conference and this edited collection has been the content of the papers rather than any niceties of linguistic expression, in terms of style the editors have restricted themselves to only a little light editing of the submitted texts, hoping to preserve in each case the authors' original meaning. We hope that they will be read in the spirit of inclusiveness and linguistic tolerance which nonetheless characterises both ECREA and the Radio Research Section.

## Notes

1. It was especially at the end of the 1970s that the audience's ability to form its own social reality was recognized (McOuail 1997).
2. Audience behaviour seems to be defined through two stages of web development which affect radio communication: Web 1.0 (e-mail, forum, chat, SMS, online interviews, online surveys) and Web 2.0 (blogs, wikis, content voting systems, social networks, etc.).

## References and further reading

Ala-Fossi, M., Lax, S., O'Neill, B., Jauert, P., Shaw, H. 'The Future of Radio is Still Digital – But Which One? Expert Perspectives and Future Scenarios for Radio Media in 2015', in *Journal of Radio and Audio Media*, London: Taylor and Francis, 15:1, 2008, pp. 4–28.

Arbitron/Edison, *The Infinite Dial 2010: Digital Platforms and Future of Radio*, Dallas: Arbitron/ Edison, 2005.

Arbitron/Edison Media Research, *Internet and Multimedia: On-Demand Media Explodes*, Dallas: Arbitron/Edison Media Research, 2006.

Baudrillard, J., *Selected writings*. Cambridge, UK: Polity, 1988.

Comscore, *Media Metrix*, Virginia, 2000.

Council of Europe, *Television without Frontiers Directive* (89/552/EEC), Brussels: Council of Europe, 1989.

Council of Europe, *Audiovisual Media Services Directive* (2007/65/EC), Brussels: Council of Europe, 2007.

Council of Europe, *Promoting Social Cohesion: The Role of Community Media Report prepared for the Council of Europe's Group of Specialists on Media Diversity (MC-S-MD)*, Rapporteur Peter M. Lewis for the Media and Information Society Division, Directorate General of Human Rights and Legal Affairs, 2008 http://www.coe.int/t/dghl/standardsetting/media/Doc/H-Inf(2008)013_en.pdf. Accessed 21 October 2010.

Council of Europe, *Promoting Social Cohesion: The Role of Community Media*. Brussels: Council of Europe, 2008.

Crisell, A., *Understanding Radio*. London: Routledge, 1994.

DCMS/DBIS, *Digital Britain*. London: Department for Culture, Media and Sport; Department for Business, Innovation and Skills, 2009.

DRWG, *Interim Report for the Secretary of State for Culture, Media and Sport*, London: Digital Radio Working Group, 2008.

EIAA *Digital Generation Report*, London: EIAA (European Interactive Advertising Association) 2006.

Ellis, M. 'New Age, New Media, New Researchers? The BBC experience', in *European Radio Broadcasting*, SIS EBU Briefings, 7 January 1998, London: UBS Warburg, 2000.

ETSI, *Radio Broadcasting Systems; Digital Audio Broadcasting (DAB) to mobile, portable and fixed receivers*. Sophia-Antipolis: European Telecommunications Standards Institute, http://www.etsi. org, 2006. Accessed 21 October 2010.

European Broadcasting Union, *Public Service Media in the Digital Age*, Digital Strategic Group II Report, Geneva: EBU, 2006.

European Broadcasting Union, *Public Radio Study*, Geneva: SIS EBU, 2007.

Fornas, J., Becker, K., Bjurstrom, E., Ganetz, H., *Consuming media*. Oxford/New York: Berg, 2007.

Gazi, A. 'The Image of the Sound: The Radio Case', in I. Vovou (ed.), *The World of Television: Theoretical Approaches, Programs Analysis and Greek Reality*, Athens: Herodotos, 2010.

Gemius, S. A., *Internet research in Poland*. Warszawa: Gemius SA, 2008.

Hilmes, M., 'Rethinking Radio' in M. Hilmes, J. Loviglio (eds), *Radio Reader*, London/New York: Routledge, 2002, pp. 1–20.

Lewis, M. P. and Booth, J., *The invisible medium*. London: Macmillan Press, 1989.

McLuhan, M., *Understanding media* (Routledge Classics), London: Routledge, 2001 (first published 1964).

McQuail, N., *Mass communication theory: An Introduction*. London: Sage Publications, 1995.

OFCOM, *Radio – Preparing for the Future Phase 2: Implementing the Framework Consultation*, London: OFCOM, 2005.

O'Neill, B., Ala-Fossi, M., Jauert, P., Lax, S., Nyre, L., Shaw, H., *Digital Radio in Europe: Technologies, Industries and Culture*. Bristol: Intellect Press, 2010.

Radio Advertising Bureau and the Internet Adverting Bureau, *Using radio with online: How radio and online combine to fulfill brand interactions*. London: Radio Advertising Bureau and the Internet Advertising Bureau, 2006.

RAJAR, *Quarterly Summary of Radio Listening*. London: Radio Joint Audience Research Limited, 2007, 2009.

Scannell, P., *Radio, television and modern life*. Oxford: Blackwell, 1996.

Starkey, G., *Balance and Bias in Journalism: Representation, Regulation & Democracy*. London: Palgrave Macmillan, 2007.

Starkey, G., 'The Quiet Revolution: DAB and the Switchover to Digital Radio in the United Kingdom', in *Revista ZER*, Bilbao: University of the Basque Country, 13:25, 2008, pp. 163–78.

Toffler, A., *Third Wave*. London/NY: W. Morrow Edition, 1980.

Winocur, R. 'Radio and Everyday Life: Uses and Meaning in the Domestic Sphere', in *Television New Media*, 6:3, 2005, pp. 319–32.

# Part I

Convergence

# Chapter 1

Interactivity on Radio in the Internet Age: A Case Study from France

Blandine Schmidt

Interactivity, a ubiquitous phenomenon in contemporary media, is much appreciated by radio professionals. In France, radio is the one traditional medium which invites its audience to participate in the creation of content on air. Far from being a recent phenomenon, interactive radio broadcasting has been an important part of radio programmes on various themes, including many issues concerning society. By empowering the public through direct democratic participation, radio broadcasting often makes claims to freedom of expression on air. However, media making such claims based on interactions with their audiences are often accused of manipulating people's voices in a way that is utilitarian or commercial or both.

Communication can be summarized as the transmission of a message between a transmitter and a receiver. Further research allows us to add detail and complete this basic outline. Norbert Wiener's (1943) notion of feedback in his text titled 'Behavior, purpose and teleology', written with Arturo Rosenblueth and Julian Bigelow, is an important source. They are of the opinion that behavioural analysis can be applied to both machines and living organisms. Wiener (1948) considers cybernetics as the science of 'control and communication of the animal and of the machine'. It was with the appearance of a new type of machine (the 'informative machine') that a theoretical framework was built, involving all the phenomena around mechanisms of information treatment (Meunier 2003). The mathematician Claude E. Shannon completed Wiener's work in *The Mathematical Theory of Communication* in 1949. A *protégé* of Wiener, Shannon proposes a conceptual framework to define and characterize notions of information and communication. Nowadays, these theories are used and widened in the social sciences. Therefore, sociology uses the concept of feedback in the field of interpersonal communication. Sociologists show interest in the exchange of messages between two sources of information, taking for granted that every sent message results in another received message in response. Even if feedback seems to be missing, it has to be supposed. Cybernetics opens up new horizons to discuss the qualities and specificities of transmitters and receivers.

The term 'interactivity' was first used in information technology and in the study of relationships between humans and machines. Today its meaning has widened; it has become a plural notion in numerous fields like information and communication sciences. To achieve interactivity, a transaction has to be established and maintained by two actors exchanging elements of equal, active and mutual participation. Interactive radio broadcasting has changed the foundations of the relationship between a medium and its audience. Listeners can break their earlier silence by contributing to a broadcast. This brings about a modification in their status as receivers; they become 'transmitters' themselves.

There are several approaches to interactivity in radio that enable various kinds of listener participation. We must say that these approaches have multiplied over the past few years. Indeed, the creation and the democratization of these new communication technologies (such as the internet or mobile phones) were considered and appropriated by the radio medium, resulting in the development of new means of interaction. In this chapter we will focus on the emergence and the re-enforcement of these new digital ways of communication by the medium of radio using the internet. The main questions we try to answer are, firstly, in terms of the appropriation of communication tools by the public, what does the use of these new technical interactions allow and involve? And secondly, what changes have been brought about by such interactive relationships today? Our work focuses on a common type of interactive radio programme in France: the advice line. Many radio stations claim to support, help and accompany listeners in their private lives. This help, more or less personalized to individual cases, is proposed in several fields: legal, emotional, familial, sexual, consumer-related, etc. Advice lines use different strategies to stimulate interactivity. To get answers to our questions, we will first consider the existing duality in the interactive radio relationship. Then we will talk about the internet tools radio stations provide to their listeners to interact with and participate in the content. Finally, we will describe the results of our field study of comments made by listeners of a French advice line programme.

## The duality in radio interactive relationship

Indeed, interactivity in radio is very attractive to radio professionals because it ensures dynamism on air while establishing a relationship of proximity with the listener. This can build up a loyal audience, which can lead to an increase in the number of listeners. Consequently, it is important for a radio station to become more accessible to people. To achieve this, the radio station multiplies platforms through which the listener may contact it. On air, the type of content provided by the listeners is varied and induces a duality to the interactive relationship.

The research is firmly rooted in information and communication sciences. The idea is to study the nature of interactive communication established between a medium and its audience. On air, we distinguished two types of interactive relationships that take place in the broadcasts: direct interactive relationships, where listeners express themselves, and indirect interactive relationships in which listeners' words are relayed. In order to establish the theoretical context, we will explain this duality in detail.

## Direct interactive relationships

These are the most widely used approaches to interactivity in the broadcasts. Listeners talk on air and contribute more or less autonomously and independently to the creation of content. Their voices are used to embellish and revitalize the programme, making it more appealing. The nature of their contributions depends mostly on the kind of broadcast and the radio station. However, some elements are common to all of them: letters, opinions, questions and reactions with regard to what is said on air. Using the telephone, listeners can interact with the presenter, or even with other people in the studio. The live dialogue takes place according to an implicit and pre-defined contract (Schmidt 2008). It is possible that 'liveness' is feigned during sessions of 'as-live' recording. This allows the station to maintain professional standards set for listeners without letting them talk unconstrained on air. Furthermore, the radio producer has the possibility and prerogative to edit material by cutting some parts of the listeners' contributions. It is however important to indicate that, when live, the listener is not protected from being cut by the presenter, either verbally or by deft use of the fader. They are generally unaware of this method of controlling access: it is common for them to be cut while they are still talking.

## Indirect interactive relationships

This is the oldest way of communication between a radio station and its public. In France, the first listeners were quick to write to their radio station to take part in games or to express their opinions and wishes about the programmes (Huth 1937). Later, listeners' letters were discussed during the broadcast. Menie Grégoire, through her programme which ran for over fourteen years (1967–81), developed a very intimate relationship with her audience. She read listeners' handwritten letters and gave them personalized answers on air. Besides being a success in terms of audience loyalty, the radio station received many thousands of letters concerning listeners' private, family or professional lives, involving topics which were still taboo at that time.

Today, listeners' letters have almost disappeared from radio stations' mailboxes. However, new communication tools such as cell phones and the internet have partially replaced the more traditional approaches. So listeners now have several ways of contacting the radio station and even of contributing indirectly to the programme, using:

- messages left on a telephone answering machine (Schmidt 2008);
- messages left with the radio station's switchboard operator;[1]
- text messages managed by a proprietary platform;
- e-mails sent directly to the presenter.

These letters and/or questions are precious material to radio producers. The broadcasters can claim that this represents interactivity because it puts listeners' contributions on air. However, this indirectness also allows them to control content submitted by the public and intercept all attempts to subvert their output and any other possible drift that might otherwise occur during a live contribution (Schmidt 2008). However, presenters can liberate themselves from this 'frightening speech', as Christophe Deleu (2006) calls it, by pre-selecting from indirect contributions listeners who each have a good point to make and letting them express it live on air. This process is sometimes used effectively by listeners who cannot reach a busy radio station switchboard.

Inevitably, there are more and more interactive tools inviting listeners to change their position as passive receivers to become active participants. Radio stations are increasingly turning towards their public, even putting them at the centre stage of the programme. These new tools are also a new source of finance in order to make profits out of their activities or even to reap profits by charging the cost of sending of text messages or from the presence of advertising banners on their websites.

## The appropriation of the web by traditional radio stations in France

Radio stations have had to react and adapt themselves to the democratization of the internet in French homes. Indeed, whereas less than 10% of households had internet access in 1999 (Frydel 2005), this rose to 48.5% by 2007.[2] More than simple shop windows on the web, radio stations' websites give internet users several functionalities which add to or even support programmes such as podcasts, access to archives and presenters' blogs. Radio websites also offer listeners specific platforms for them to interact not only with the media but also with other internet users. In this way, these websites contribute to the affirmation of what has become known as web 2.0 (Polomé 2009). Chat rooms, e-mails, comments or online polls provide important data to the media. The messages can be used in-house for the preparation of the broadcast or they can contribute to live content creation. For example, the presenter can read on air a part or the totality of an e-mail, which can be a link to some other content. After reading the message, the radio station can decide if it wants to call the person and let him speak on air about his experience. In order to better understand the importance of these new digital interactive tools, we will focus on a particular type of message sent live by listeners which are known as 'comments'.

## Towards a new interactive relationship

Our field study focuses on analysing comments left by listeners of France Inter (a public, 'full-service' French radio station) on its website during the programme *Service Public*, which translates into *Action Line* in English. This programme, which is broadcast every morning, targets the citizen living in a mass consumer society. It informs, advises, questions and alerts listeners about topics linked to consumerism while giving listeners the chance to intervene live or by sending e-mails and posting comments. Interactivity is an important source for presenter Isabelle Giordano, who states:

"I believe that the listener's participation is essential because it's a particular point of view. Generally, people whom I have in the studio are experts who have their views, their own vision about the subject and the listeners will have a more daily and convenient vision. I find that their point of view counterbalances and sometime contradicts what is being said in the broadcast. Therefore it is also a counter-power."[3]

However, it is important to point out that the presenter favours indirect contributions on air. Indeed, only 33% of the listeners are able to express themselves on the airwaves (Schmidt 2008). For the presenter:

"It takes much more time to let someone speak [on the air]. When I quote [listeners], it goes faster. So this is a time-management problem. But I try to let a maximum of people speak, to play interactivity by different manners by quoting them or letting them express themselves directly."

That approach can also be justified by the informative nature of the programme, which promotes a common awareness compared to individual treatment. The contributions of listeners corroborate what is said on air. Thus, the presenter controls content while promising free expression. But what is the nature of the messages posted on the web? What is their impact? Is an interactive relationship made easier by these new tools?

## The results of the fieldwork

To answer these questions, we will explain the preliminary results of our fieldwork carried out during the week between 4 and 8 May 2009 on the *Service Public* website. We made a qualitative and quantitative study of 261 comments posted by listeners during the hour-long broadcast everyday. Only a small number of listeners get past the hurdles posed by interactivity in order to participate in the broadcast. From the increasing number of interactive platforms available on the web, we can assume that the number of listeners who take the initiative to make contact with the radio station may be increasing. Indeed, in comparison to the difficulty of contacting a switchboard, which most of the time is overwhelmed by calls, the time and commitment needed to leave a comment are minimized. The procedure for sending a comment is simplified if the person has some prior knowledge of surfing the web. Here, no registration is required, and even if the listener is required to give a name or a nickname and an e-mail address, that information is not made public. Simple, but also fast, comments are written in a concise and strict editorial style. In contrast with e-mails, comments do not include such classic polite phrases as 'hello' or 'goodbye'. To ensure that the listeners' messages are not too long, the platform limits the number of characters to 1500. Aware of this message limit, listeners do not even use all the space granted to them. Indeed, over the studied period, messages did not exceed 900 characters. On average, comments totalled 301 characters, illustrating the brevity of the listeners' expression. Generally, the contemporaneousness of comments and the broadcast is high, insofar as listeners can react on the website only during the duration of the broadcast, so immediacy rules. However, since comments are archived and available on the web afterwards, their status can be modified.

Once the message is written and sent, it is validated by a moderator so that it can be published. During our visit to the radio station, a trainee,[4] who managed the electronic mailbox surveillance service, told us:

> "I am in charge of receiving the listeners' mail, both on the inbox of *Service Public*, and on the France Inter website. For comments, I accept them all. We make no censorship, except for the abusive or racist ones. […] Everything will depend on the type of language used. If it is rude or brutal, we delete it."[5]

In France, what is said on the web is subject to the same rules as for editing. Although the writer is responsible for the content of a message,[6] the broadcasting producer can also be prosecuted if a reprehensible speech is disseminated. Less important slips (mostly in terms of language) can occur, but only a part of the audience might be shocked by them. This remains quite hard to deal with because the degree of acceptance evolves with society. Our fieldwork considered comments posted on the broadcast website, allowing us to update the various ways identified for listeners to express their voices.

## An active and reactive listener

Throughout the broadcast, the presenter stimulates an interactive relationship by inviting listeners to call the switchboard or send messages on the website. In this way, the audience becomes active, or at least has the potential to be active. As we noted before, the platform for posting messages is only accessible during the broadcast. This affects the nature and the content of the messages. Since the listeners are reacting to the content of the broadcast, their messages must be understood in that context. At first, they express their opinion upon the subject of the day or the choice of guests. These contributions, which mainly occur during the first part of the broadcast, are expressed in general terms because the debate is just starting on air. The listeners claim their desire to contribute to the dialogue by giving their own opinion. Later, the content evolves, becoming more precise. As the broadcast continues, more and more people react to what is said by both the presenter and the guests present in the studio. This proves that they listen to the programme while being connected to its website. Thus, the comments reply to the programme; they depend on the broadcast.

## Listeners focused on themselves

During our analysis, we identified a recurring theme in the content of messages, which referred to the personal experience of the writer, considered here as a witness of reality. This is the main distinction between the experts, who base their knowledge upon the 'objective' study of a global phenomenon, and the listeners, who justify and legitimate their speech and opinions by their experience. The notion of authenticity differentiates listeners' words from those of the experts. In this way, the listeners each use a discourse focused on themselves, illustrating a thirst for personal expression in a public space. According to Anne Cauquelin (2003), spaces of expression on the web permit a search for identity, a quest in which the exposition of 'oneself' is dominant. Despite this obvious need to assert their own identity, most of the listeners write messages anonymously. Only three per cent of the audience leave their entire name. Of the rest, 67% give their first name and 30% use a nickname. This kind of behaviour can be explained by the approach of the presenter who never reveals the complete identity of the listeners, normally generalizing from any single event. From a holistic point of view, these personal testimonies can be considered as representing society, of course, but most of all reflecting the nature of the radio audience.

## A watchful and demanding listener

Listeners, who are aware of what is being said on air, critique the presenter's mode of expression, on the information she gives out on the show and on her acts of mediation in debates. Listeners can also critique the choice of guests and the way the topic of the day or the programme is treated. They make known their requirements of robustness and quality towards the broadcast. We need to remember that we are considering a public radio station that is in part financed by a tax called the audiovisual licence fee. Moreover, France Inter keeps alive a very close relationship with its public. As consumers, its listeners must be satisfied by the product for which they pay a subscription fee. For this reason, in a more or less sophisticated way, they express their complaints in this virtual space. Fundamentally, the latter is dedicated to the expression of the audience with regard to the topic of the programme, to help sustain the broadcasts by airing the audience's point of view. In practice, many listeners seize this opportunity to change the subject. Initially invited to take part in the content of the broadcast, such listeners free themselves from the parameters set by the broadcaster.

## A curious listener in need of answers

This radio programme, which promotes itself as working in the interests of citizen consumers, wants to help them by providing information on various subjects. The fact that experts are present in the studio justifies this intent. Conscious of this, the listeners use the radio website to put across their questions to the presenter. More or less precisely, every question concerns the theme of the day and/or something said on the air. The audience shows its interest in the topic under discussion and allows the broadcast to justify its existence. Radio provides this support and fully plays its mediating role between people in need and experts who can provide some sort of answers. But not every question posted on the website obtains answers on the air. The presenter has to judiciously select from the available messages, so in practice only few messages actually get through. In order to increase the value of interactivity, the presenter often quotes listeners' questions, making her interview seem more representative.

## A grateful listener

Several comments are posted to the presenter to thank her for the information given on air, or in a more global way, to congratulate her on the quality and usefulness of the broadcast. Radio exists partially as a support, or as an advisor, by treating topics directly concerned with the daily lives of people. Until now media were a part of the public scene, informing citizens so that they could be fully conscious of their civic duties. The appearance and increasing number of broadcasts offering a service allow radio to take an increasingly active part in people's everyday lives. Furthermore, this kind of broadcast stimulates the creation and assertion of a close relationship with the audience, playing an important role in our understanding of society. Media assume a noble status when helping people in trouble. Nevertheless, there is no need to exaggerate the altruistic nature of these broadcasts which, in a very competitive field, are there to attract the largest possible audiences.

## Conclusion

Such interactive programmes as this, in France, are not a minor phenomenon, in terms of their ubiquity and their contribution to the expression of public opinion. Reinforcing the separation between the private and public spheres, these programmes redefine the use, role and function of media in society. On radio, listeners have moved on from their passive receiver role to fully contribute to the content creation, even if the presenter, in most cases, remains at the centre of programmes. The appearance and progressive expansion of new digital tools on radio websites have brought about changes to the programmes through their interweaving with, or even insertion within, more traditional media forms. The dual role of direct and indirect contributions of listeners has become stronger on the radio. Moreover, we can see the development of a pseudo, non-broadcast programme that exists in parallel to the original through the web. Even if, as we have already seen, the web content is directly linked to what is said on air, it has a tendency to become more autonomous. The appropriation of this online space by listeners takes effect because their contribution surpasses limits originally established by the medium. As regards comments left on the web, listeners find there a space where they are allowed to express their opinions, to evoke topics which are not discussed on the air or to send critiques of the programme. The parallel pseudo-programme can have repercussions on the air because the presenter can read messages during the broadcast. However if messages are not chosen, they will still have a public impact through the web. Today, public participation in radio is no longer confined to the live broadcast.

Finally, according to our research, interactive tools available on radio websites will continue to evolve. The media must know how to renew themselves in order to satisfy public demand. We also consider that, increasingly, in future even newer ways of accessing radio will appear on mobile internet devices, in order to fit audiences' developing expectations.

## References and further reading

Cauquelin, A., *L'exposition de soi, du journal intime aux webcams*, Paris: Eshel, 2003.

Deleu, C., *Les anonymes de la radio*, Paris: De Boeck, 2006.

Frydel, Y., 'Un ménage sur deux possède un micro-ordinateur, un sur trois a accès à internet', *INSEE Première*, 1011, 2005, http://www.insee.fr/fr/ffc/docs_ffc/IP1011.pdf. Accessed 29 March 2011.

Huth, A., *La radiodiffusion, puissance mondiale*, Paris: Gallimard, 1937.

Meunier, J-P., *Approches systémiques de la communication: systémisme, mimétisme, cognition*, Paris: De Boeck, 2003.

Polomé, P., *Les médias sur Internet*, Toulouse: Milan, 2009.

Rosenblueth, A., Wiener, N., & Bigelow, J., 'Behavior, Purpose and Teleology', *Philosophy of Science*, 10, 1943, pp. 18–24, http://www.scribd.com/doc/946095/Behavior-Purpose-and-Teleology-Rosenblueth-Wiener-Bigelow. Accessed 29 March 2011.

Schmidt B., *Radiographie de L'interactivité radiophonique*, Mémoire de Master en Sciences de l'Information et de la Communication, sous la direction de Jean-Jacques Cheval, Bordeaux, Université Michel de Montaigne Bordeaux 3, 2008, http://www.scribd.com/doc/9097285/Radiographie-de-l-interactivite-radiophonique-Bs. Accessed 29 March 2011.

Wiener, N., *Cybernetics or control and communication in the animal and the machine*, New York: J. Wiley, 1948.

## Notes

1. This situation can be desired both by listeners who want to testify without speaking on the air and by those who do.
2. INSEE, Équipement des ménages en biens durables selon le type de ménage en 2007, http://www.insee.fr/fr/themes/tableau.asp?reg_id=0&ref_id=NATnon05155. Accessed 29 March 2011.
3. Interview with Isabelle Giordano, radio presenter and producer at France Inter, 21 June 2009.
4. Despite its precarious professional status, the broadcast uses trainees every year.
5. Interview with Laurie Madile, trainee at France Inter, 20 June 2009.
6. This sentence relates to the statement on the website: 'Comments published here may reflect only the personal views of the author'.

# Chapter 2

Convergence in Spanish Talk Radio Stations' Websites with the Participative Resources Provided by web 1.0 and 2.0

Jose Luis Requejo Aleman and Susana Herrera Damas

Although interactivity is not new in radio, the arrival of the internet has multiplied the possibilities for listeners to get in touch with the medium by opening up a wealth of new opportunities for participation. A whole new range of possibilities can be added to the traditional letters, telephone, voice mailbox and vox pops, thanks to the use of e-mail, chat, SMS, forums, digital interviews and surveys. In the last few years, this catalogue has also expanded, thanks to the participative technologies made possible by web 2.0. This concept represents the evolution of new web applications directed at a final user who need not be tech-savvy. In this sense, web 2.0 would not be so much a new product or a new technology as the second generation of the web based, in this case, in users' communities and in a special range of services that promote collaboration and an active exchange of information among its users. In particular, blogs, wikis, folksonomies, or the possibility for users to vote for their favourite content or to take part in personal or professional social networks are some of the participative modalities allowed by web 2.0.

This chapter will focus on an analysis of the ways these new possibilities are being incorporated into the Spanish talk radio stations' websites.

According to research undertaken upto the end of 2008, these participative resources were most enthusiastically received by music radio stations directed at young audiences. This might be explained by the preference that this type of radio stations have for innovation and for new technology. These results showed that the approach of Cadena SER was turning out to be very innovative in comparison with that observed in the rest of the Spanish stations. Now, it is interesting to analyse whether this situation remains the same or if, on the contrary, these new resources are being adopted more by *most* of the talk radio stations and not only by one of them. To this end, a content analysis of the leading Spanish talk radio stations' websites (www.cadenaser.com, www.cope.es, www.rne.es and www.ondacero.es) was carried out in September 2009. We shall discuss the results of that analysis in this chapter, and they are summarised in Table 2.1.

## www.cadenaser.com

Cadena SER's approach is ambitious, revolutionary, complete and path breaking, although it is no longer the only station that promotes the incorporation of new ways of audience participation. The website provides e-mail access to the various programmes, but does not provide direct access to the editors. It also includes e-mails from different stations across the Spanish territory. In the first week of September 2009, the site included a total of seven forums: five of them pertain to programmes, while the other two have a more generic character – one for news and the other one for sports. Although it is possible to access the full content of every forum, one needs to register to participate in them.

The site has five chat rooms and each of them relates to a specific programme. One can participate in these chat rooms merely by entering a nickname; registration is not mandatory. All the chatrooms allow the exchange of private messages and use of emoticons and colours. As in the forums, it is possible to know the number and identity of people who are connected because, chatting is a synchronous communication system in which communication is possible only between users connected at the same time.

Other features include the opportunity to participate in digital surveys and in digital interviews. In the first week of September 2009, the survey question was 'Do you think Nadal will be able to win the U.S. Open?' The options were:

(a)  Yes, he has recovered.
(b)  No, not yet.

By 8 September 2009 there were 906 responses. Each of the surveys was accompanied by two or three response alternatives, which could only be voted for once. Interim results could be viewed at all times and every survey is somehow related to current affairs. Moreover, the frequency of these surveys is still irregular; it depends on the rhythm of the news. The site also provides access to other surveys which are already closed; it also shows that up to 8 September 2009 there had been a total of 457 surveys.

On an average the site features between one and three digital interviews per day, depending on the news. On 8 September 2009, the audience could pose their questions to Julian Coca, Inversis analyst, regarding the best options for investment. The site also offers digital interviews with Carlos Miquel, sports journalist of *AS Daily*; with Molly Malekar, director of the NGO Daughters of Peace; with Alfredo Relaño, editor of *AS Daily*; with Tomas Guasch, deputy director of the same newspaper; with Carlos Boyero, film critic; and with Manolete, also editor of the *AS Daily*. In some sections, especially sports and economics, interviews are regular *rendezvous* that take place once a week. In the review period, these digital interviews are used to promote synergies with other media in the group. All digital interviews are accompanied by a picture of the interviewee and a small caption stating their credentials. These meetings are announced a couple of days in advance, so that users can pose their enquiries to the provided address. As in the surveys, it is also possible to access the entire content of the digital interviews. To facilitate navigating on the site, the interviews are arranged by topic-wise: international (162), opinion (85), Spain (344), society (188), culture (632), sports (698), economics (214) and technology (56), although it is not always easy to ascribe an interview to a single theme, given the excessively general character of some of them.

As for participation through blogs, it is remarkable that although it was common practice in 2007, in the survey period, only one of three announced blogs were still running. This helps us conclude that different radio networks seem willing to accept the users' participation as long as this does *not* involve extra cost, something we found to be common to the rest of the sites.

In essence users are offered two additional spaces for participation: one of them asks users to comment on current issues. In order to do this, users can choose the programme or the subject they want to comment on. They could also send their pictures, choosing from a range of topics and the active themes were 'This is my town' (128 photos), 'Spring' (21 pictures), 'Summer 2009' (122 photos), 'From my window' (33 pictures), 'My Pet and Me' (24 photos) and 'Madrid is yours' (77 photos). The identity of the photographers was provided below the pictures.

Two other features also require user participation. The first allows users to vote on news content, both in open and closed systems. In open systems, the news can be 'up' to the various web 2.0 applications that exist to rate the content (e.g. Digg, Inc.). In closed systems, users can vote by rating the news item on a scale of 1 to 5 stars. The more the stars, the higher the position in which the news item appears in the list of the 'most voted'. News items can be inserted into different social networks like Facebook, MySpace or in personalized pages like My Yahoo, My Live or iGoogle. Users are also allowed to comment on news items, often the most controversial one. Thus, it is mandatory to include one's name and e-mail address and accept the privacy clause.

The two most important participative resources recently taken on by www.cadenaser.com continue to strengthen the community of listeners and provide a space for participative journalism. The community is defined as

'a place where users can freely create and maintain their personal pages. The address is: http://lacomunidad.cadenaser.com/nombre-del-blog and it allows the user to have a place to write, and share his pictures, video or audio with other Internet users'.

SER Periodista offers the opportunity to practise participatory journalism. In it, users can publish their information and news in five formats: text, photo, video, audio and downloadable files. The main topics that feature in this space are

| | | | |
|---|---|---|---|
| (a) | Local problems | (i) | International |
| (b) | Citizens' achievements | (j) | Photocomplaint |
| (c) | Accidents | (k) | Housing |
| (d) | Demonstrations and protests | (l) | Health |
| (e) | Meteorological disasters | (m) | Education |
| (f) | Corruption | (n) | Sports |
| (g) | Environment | (o) | Culture |
| (h) | Urbanism | | |

The rest of the information can be placed in the 'General' category. Its description emphasizes the fact that it is is a place where one can provide information and not opinion. The information is published provided it is truthful, clearly written and not abusive of other people. News can also be posted through the internet or a mobile phone. However, it is mandatory for users to identify themselves and take responsibility for the accuracy of the submitted material.

So far, these are the most commonly used modalities for participation. All of them are grouped in the channel 'Participate' within the portal. We must also note the existence of some other smaller spaces like the one that lets users e-mail their letters to the editor of one of the programmes. Furthermore, Cadena Ser which is also present on Facebook had 7292 fans as of 8 September 2009.

## www.cope.es

Cadena COPE, whose internet approach used to be very modest until recently, has made great efforts to modernize its digital proposal and its incorporation of participative resources. The site provides a generic address for participation and also offers the addresses of different programmes. Participation is also possible via SMS, with a different direction for each of the different programmes. The digital interviews are shared with Popular TV although the running is still precarious.

In the first week of September 2009, the site introduced voting on the news, using both closed and open systems. Users can also take sides on articles thrown open for debate, comment on news items once they were willing to accept the privacy and standards-of-use clause.

Moreover, www.cope.es is the network that incorporates participation the most through blogs. In the first week of September 2009, there were a total of 100 blogs, on different subjects, most of which were linked with the ideals of the network and held a daily poll.

Users can e-mail letters to the editor and vote in both open and closed systems However, resources such as forums, chats, the possibility of sending pictures, phrases or recording messages are not available. No space was allocated for the practise of participatory journalism nor was there a community. Nevertheless, there has been a great change compared to that recorded in September 2008.

## www.rne.es

Until June 2007, Radio Nacional – the talk radio channel of the public network Radio Nacional de España – only used the internet to offer a live stream of the broadcast output. Options like chat, SMS, forum, digital interviews, polls or blogs were absent. This changed in the first week of September 2009, when the site included the generic e-mail addresses for the main programmes and the publication of thirteen blogs to which listeners could send their comments. In all cases, these blogs present internal aspects of the programmes and there are no social or political comments – as at least theoretically required, in a public network. However, this shows a significant attempt to make space for the audience.

Apart from blogs, the site also contains surveys that ask for listeners' feedback on controversial topics and current events. The site provides access to the latest polls. There is also a chance to comment on a survey topic and share it in open web 2.0 systems such as Delicious, Digg, Fresqui or Facebook.

In addition, users can also share news in open voting systems like Digg, Menéame or Fresqui and in social networks like Facebook. There are no other participative resources. For instance, news cannot be commented on or voted in closed systems. Nor are there any forums, chatrooms or communities. Digital interviews are also absent, although it is likely that this method will soon be incorporated. The site does not offer the possibility of posting comments, uploading pictures or recording messages.

## www.ondacero.es

Although the design of this site is clean and modern, the style of the new forms of participation is modest and austere. The site provides the generic e-mail for each programme but does not feature forums or chats.

From www.ondacero.es it is possible to access the forums and chatrooms of Antena 3 TV, but technically these are not forums or chatrooms in the Onda Cero network. News can be voted on in open systems like Digg, Menéame and Technorati or can also be discussed. There are no polls or digital interviews. One can access the podcasts of the entire content of a large number of traditional interviews, but there are no digital interviews.

Blogs seem to be the strongest element in the digital approach. In the survey period the site had 14 blogs. All of them were public, open to participation and visitors had to observe certain rules of conduct. For example, advertising was forbidden and so was disclosure of personal data (phone numbers, addresses, e-mails, etc.), uploading pornography, whether image or text, posting comments in defence of any terrorist group or organization and, broadly speaking, any content that violates the law.

There is no participation via SMS or through surveys. Users cannot send statements or photos, record messages, practise participatory journalism or join communities. However, they have recently integrated some programmes on Facebook. The www.ondacero.es site is conservative in its policy regarding the incorporation of new modalities for participation. The network is more determined to introduce other dimensions of interactivity, especially through the podcasting system.

**Table 2.1:** Summary table showing the incorporation of the new participative resources by the main Spanish talk radio stations' websites (September 2009).

| | Thematic forum | Programme forum | Thematic chat | Programme chat | E-mail | Participation through sms | Digital polls | Digital interviews |
|---|---|---|---|---|---|---|---|---|
| www.cadenaser.es | 2 | 5 | 0 | 5 | Yes, each programme and radio station has its own address | Just to send news to SER Periodista | 2 or 3 per day, according to current affairs. Access to all the closed polls | 1 or 3 per day, according to current affairs and to the availability of the interviewees. Access to the full content of every interview |
| www.cope.es | No | No | No | No | Yes, each programme has its own e-mail address | Yes, each programme has its own number | No | Shared with Popular TV, although its running is still precarious |
| www.rne.es | No | No | No | No | Yes, a generic address is offered. Each programme has also its own address | No | Yes, aprox 1 per day. Access to the content of every poll | No |
| www.ondacero.es | No | No | No | No | Yes, each programme has its own address | No | No | No |

*Source*: Own

| ...logs | Commenting the news | Voting the news | Sending messages | Recording messages | Sending pictures | Participative journalism | Community | Others |
|---|---|---|---|---|---|---|---|---|
| announced but ...st 1 running | Yes, in all of them by accepting the privacy clause | Yes, in closed and open systems (Digg, Menéame, Fresqi) | Yes, to different programmes or thematic sections | No | Yes, to every category of the section | SER Periodista | Yes | Integration of some programmes in social network like Facebook or My Space or in personalized pages like My Yahoo, My Live or I Google |
| ...00 | Yes, in all of them by accepting the privacy clause and the standards of use | Yes, in closed systems and in open systems like Menéame | No | No | No | No | No | Possibility of sending and commenting letters to the editor and voting opinon articles. Integration of some programms in social networks like Facebook |
| ...4 | No | Yes, in open systems like Digg, Menéame and Fresqui | No | No | No | No | No | Integration of some programmes in social networks like Facebook |
|  |  |  |  | No | No | No | No |  |
| ...4 | No, there is no news | Yes, in open systems like Digg or Menéame | No | No | No, just to one programme | No | No | Integration of some programms in social networks like Facebook |

## Conclusion

After analysing the ways in which the leading Spanish talk radio stations' sites incorporated new participatory resources provided by the two generations of the internet, we can offer the following conclusions:

(1) Gradually, all networks are incorporating new participatory approaches into their sites. There are obvious differences in speed and approach between the networks but all of them are betting on at least one of these new possibilities, apart from the use of e-mail which now seems fully assimilated into facilitating interactivity.

(2) Though Cadena SER is no longer the only network that advocates the incorporation of new modalities for participation, it remains the leader in the variety and number of spaces.

(3) In the past year, Cadena COPE has made a great effort to modernize its digital approach and has incorporated new resources for participation, especially through blogs. Other resources remain unexplored.

(4) Radio 1 and, especially, Onda Cero continue with their rather conservative approach as far as incorporating participatory resources is concerned. Both sites also seem to find blogs a quick and efficient way to capitalize on the involvement of users. Yet both networks are reluctant to integrate other resources.

(5) All networks show a special predilection for the first generation modalities while their engagement with the web 2.0 resources is rather guarded. Among these are the presence of some programmes on Facebook and the opening of several news sites to content voting systems like Digg, Menéame or Fresqui.

(6) Finally, it should also be noted that, unlike what happened with the 'traditional' possibilities, these new resources for participation often do not have a direct impact on programming. That is, it is true that more users have new technological opportunities to engage among themselves and with professionals. However, this does not ensure that their interventions have a direct impact on programming. Thus, the differences between media are diluted, at least in regard to their digital approaches.

## References and further reading

Bordewijk, J., & Kaam, B. Van, 'Towards a New Classification of Tele-Information Services', *Intermedia*, XIV:1, 1986, pp. 16–21.

Herrera, S., 'Tipología de la participación de los oyentes en los programas de radio', *Anàlisi*, 30, 2003, pp. 145–66.

Herrera, S., 'Las nuevas modalidades para la participación de los jóvenes en la radio', *Trípodos*, 1:20, 2007a, pp. 171–88.

Herrera, S., 'La radio española y su apuesta por las nuevas modalidades para la participación de los oyentes', in I. Egúzquiza, and V. Vidal (coords.), La ética y el derecho de la información en los tiempos del postperiodismo, Valencia, Fundación COSO, 2007b.

Fumero, A., & Roca, G., *Web 2.0*, Madrid: Fundación Orange, 2007.

Nafría, I., *Web 2.0. El Usuario, el Nuevo rey de Internet*, Barcelona: Gestión 2000, 2007.

Orihuela, J. L., La revolución de los weblogs. Cuando las bitácoras se convirtieron en el medio de comunicación de la gente, Madrid: La Esfera de los Libros, 2006.

Wu, W., & Weaver, D., 'On-Line Democracy or On-Line Demagoguery: Public Opinion "Polls" on the Internet', *Harvard International Journal of Press/Politics*, 2:4, 1997, pp. 71–86.

# Chapter 3

Portuguese Internet Radio from 2006 to 2009: Technical Readiness
and Openness to Interaction

Pedro Portela

The advent of the internet raised questions about the role of radio in a fast-changing media environment. Many voices forecast its end but in the summer of 2008 the Swedish Radio and TV Authority published a study named *The Future of Radio*, which clearly opposed the pessimism of recent analysis. While the study anticipates the exhaustion of the FM model, it clearly broadens perspectives for DAB and internet radio, highlighting digitalization as the key element for the future relevance of radio.

The Portuguese researcher and radio professional João Paulo Meneses states that 'the future of radio relies upon the internet', calling the broad service offerings of the net the pathway for the survival of radio from the threats to its two essential aspects: mobility and accumulation (Meneses 2008). Accumulation is radio's capability to be used in a non-exclusive manner, which means that a listener can use the radio while performing other activities, like cooking, sewing, reading, writing or jogging.

Even if we have the perception that internet users and computer users in general tend to 'accumulate' activities with a certain ease, in what concerns mobility there are some technical progresses that seem to confirm Meneses' conviction. If the transistor and the so-enabled miniaturization, mobile transmission and reception it allowed were radio's responses to the growth of television, it seems that the answer to the impact of the internet relies on the search for technical solutions that guarantee its relevance.

Two recent innovations are relevant here: firstly, internet-car-radio, which the Audi, BMW, Ford and Mercedes automobiles are equipped with, enable its users to access 30,000 internet radio stations (Moses 2009); secondly, the Olinda prototype, developed and already presented by BBC Audio & Music Interactive R&D, which consists of a DAB-based technology with interactive network-relationship capabilities (Ferne 2008).

These two devices may neutralize radio's loss of reach among itinerant users, who are seduced by iPod and MP3-capable car-radios, which also offer social networking – the hallmark of web 2.0 and contemporary internet use.

Mariano Cebrián Herreros (2007) reckons that radio has been able to mark its presence in all spaces of media consumption (at home, at work, in the car, on the move) and thus offers itself as an omnipresent option, while facing growing competition. This means that it must constantly re-position itself to sustain its relevance.

This focus on change is already propelling radio towards incorporating languages that are not part of its own tradition – such as video, image or written text – and pushing further its historical willingness to interaction, expressed by a tradition of 'inviting anonymous people to express themselves' (Becqueret 2006) either by phone or via vox-populi testimonials.

*The Future of Radio* shows that people are interested in interactivity and value-added services. While 36% showed interest in getting traffic information with text, maps and pictures, 33% were interested in accessing their favourite shows in a time-independent manner, 31% would like to have access to more radio channels and 23% expressed their willingness to programme the radio flow themselves (Swedish Radio and TV Authority 2008).

These types of services demand great efforts by radio stations, which need to adopt new ways to communicate and interact. According to Portela (2006):

'In these times, radio is asked a new hard-to-reach dynamic, because it needs to address the traditional listeners, maintaining their familiar expression through the airwaves – even though it has to be revised in order to Compete with the numerous alternative options – but also it needs to renew its language and social role, as the progressive individualization of communication processes and internet interactivity request a capable answer'.

All these facts suggest that interactivity is at the core of the new demands on radio stations, not only as a historical component of its expression but also because it is at the centre of new digitally mediated social relationships.

## Portuguese web-radio in 2006: a brief overview

We've observed how Portuguese radio stations were using digital interactive technologies in 2006 and how this reflected a willingness to seek new forms of relationships with its listeners/users. We also found that 30.8% of Portuguese radio stations did not have a website or a streaming system that could transmit their programmes to the whole world (Portela 2006). In that study it was also pointed out that 'the vast majority (73.4%) of radio stations with online presence don't reflect an interaction-stimulation behaviour'. In terms of technical readiness, only 8.4% of the stations with an online presence were using the available technical potential. Furthermore, despite being online, 62.9% of the stations didn't appeal to their listeners to interact or to establish contact using the internet. Finally, another interesting finding of this research was that 97.5% of online stations were not using web 2.0 (Portela 2006).

All these data suggested that radio was not capable of meeting its 'obligation to resituate itself in the media panorama' (Rodero Antón & Sánchez Serrano 2007).

The continuous loss of advertising revenue might explain the lack of investment in new technologies by small stations and may constitute, in itself, a bigger threat to their subsistence than competition posed by the internet.

From our research it was also clear that big national stations, with accompanying bigger budgets, were far more likely to adapt to change than smaller local ones. It was also noted that internet-only stations were, in their overwhelming majority, amateur initiatives (41.2% of cases were the work of a sole individual), exhibiting technical problems with their streaming systems, and did not have the essential resources to survive (Portela 2006).

## Current research course

According to our 2006 study, Rádio Renascença, RDP-rádio and TSF, the three key players who define the future of radio in Portugal, have upgraded significantly their online presence and have embodied in their websites forms of expression that are not part of the radio traditional language, taking more noticeable advantages from digital interactivity.

Other positive signs come from a recent French monitoring study that underlines the comfortable lead radio has in credibility as a source of information, as perceived by media consumers, ahead of newspapers, television and the internet, respectively (Petit & Afota 2009).

Furthermore, available data reinforce our conviction that radio should find a powerful ally in the internet. The *Barómetro Media e Comunicação: tendências 2008/2009* research by Obercom that collected and analysed answers given by the directors of several Portuguese media companies predicted that the internet would be an important source of revenue for radio stations in the next five years, providing profit by means of online advertising and value-added digital services (Obercom 2009).

Evidently the onus is now on radio to search for new pathways for its own future, using creativity and addressing the main needs of the target of its actions: the listener.

Taking into account that 'media [...] are being shaped at the intersection of new technological potentials, cultural traditions, and institutional circumstances' (Jensen 2006), it is necessary for radio to find a renewed identity, capable of understanding and integrating the new forms of online relations, while avoiding the trap of media standardization that might originate from the ongoing dynamics of media-convergence. Bruhn Jensen suggests 'redifferentiation' – the divergence in convergence – as a path for media to follow to avoid unification and find its own place, despite some degree of technological convergence (Jensen 2006).

Thus, the listener should have a crucial role in this dialogue between the medium in need of transformation and the ultimate beneficiary of its message, so that change occurs in a meaningful manner. It is true that 'the study of audiences has been a constant concern since the inception of mass communication research' (Pinto 2000) but it makes more sense now when radio is at the crossroads and is unsure of the course to follow in future.

A perspective expressed by Schramm et al. (cited in Pinto 2000) is pertinent here when one also considers that the present technological development empowers radio with a large set of digital tools. These in turn have been the object of research in recent times, so it is fundamental to raise some questions about the actual use people make of interactive tools offered by radio stations and what their particular framework is in respect to how, when and where they use it.

We share Finnemann's view that 'internet enables users to act and interact, not just with each other and at a distance, but with the system of communication in ways that may significantly reshape the very system' (Jensen 2006). Thus a better knowledge of radio's audiences and the type of interaction they maintain or wish to maintain with the stations and, eventually, with the community established amongst all listeners will definitely contribute to radio's correct positioning.

The urgency of this subject is reinforced by the realization that the youth audience, the one that can guarantee radio's future, does not seem to be interested in this medium but shows a high percentage of internet use. In Portugal, 81% of the people aged 15–24 are internet users (Obercom 2008), but when asked about their online radio listening habits 61% of the children aged 8–18 answered that they never do it (Obercom 2009b).

Therefore, it is clear that radio should charter its own course in the dynamic confluence of the three main vectors: technical change and radio digitalization; interactivity and its own redefinition brought in by the internet; and the role of listeners (conscious or not) in these changes.

In this chapter we discuss Portuguese online radio stations' technical readiness and their interactive positioning, identifying the main changes that have occurred since 2006 and attempt to establish a basis to undertake a deeper and more focused research and analysis.

## Portuguese internet radio in 2009: focussing on change

Firstly, let us consider how the big stations were reacting to technological change, and whether the internet-born stations were still active. Our 2006 study showed these to be two main indicators of the process of change, and by observing them three years later, we are able to identify the main changes taking place.

By doing this, we were left with a sample of 26 stations, 17 of which were web-only and the remaining 9 national[1] in terms of frequency coverage. We have analysed their websites between 31 August and 2 September 2009.

Amongst internet-only stations, we were not able to identify a single one that did not exist in 2006, and while back then 70.6% were undoubtedly active, now only 23.5% are transmitting. This means that in 2009 only four web-only radio stations were operative. Of these, one station belongs to a political party (that transmits only an hour per week), one university station and the remaining two are commercial stations. In other words, web-only stations in Portugal closed probably because they were unable to come up with a proper business model.

This further narrows down the number of stations analysed in this study to thirteen.

The situation is totally different when we look at national stations, since not only are all of them working but there is an extra radio bitcaster (Rádio Sim). While in 2006 only three of the stations mentioned above were broadcasting more than one streaming channel (two music-only streams and one all-speech stream), now this number is as high as seven, offering a total of nineteen extra streaming channels, thirteen of which include some speech and the remaining six work in the 'jukebox' mode. A clear increase in the use of the potential of the internet can be seen here.

Other positive signs include an increased use of podcasting, there are eight stations offering podcasts (one web-only and seven national), which means that there is one station more than there were in 2006 there. There are 279 channels now as against 168 which were there earlier, which is a growth of 66%.

The number of programmes available for streaming is also much bigger now. From 98 programmes in 2006, available from seven different stations, the number has now risen to 316 shows from eight stations that one can tune into in a time-independent manner.

The use of video and small flash interactive animations in radio-stations' websites has also increased as of 2009. Eight stations use video and seven exhibit interactive animations, whereas back in 2006 these figures were, respectively, one and four stations.

Listeners were more interested to interact with the station than in 2006, since there is now just one station more that invites the listeners/users to establish electronic contact. All stations provide e-mail addresses so that one can contact presenters, journalists and directors.

E-mail newsletters are increasingly being employed to contact listeners; whereas only one station used them in 2006, the number has risen to four in 2009.

In terms of comments on news stories, the approach remains practically the same; the dominant attitude is of reluctance to indulge the opinion of the users/listeners , since only three stations are inclined to publish people's written opinions on their websites (back in 2006 there was only one station). This attitude opposes Berthold Brecht's (2005) branding of the radio as a democratic media Only one station offers online discussion forums. The year 2009 saw a rise in radio's use of blogs for communication, when there were eight stations as compared to four stations in 2006.

The last relevant issue observed is that more than half of these stations – seven out of thirteen – do not use (or at least do not reveal the use at their website) social-web tools such as MySpace, Facebook or Twitter. Though there is more scope now than in 2006, when only one station used such tools, most of the radio stations are yet to be popular among the youth.

Chart 3.1 below shows that Twitter is the most used social-web tool, since there are six stations using it. One may consider that this is probably in line with short and simple messages that are constitutive of radio's linguistic essence, but no conclusion should be arrived at without further research.

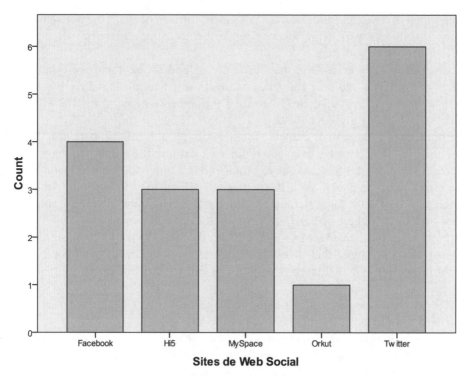

**Chart 3.1:** Radio's social web.

## Conclusion

If we group the data gathered using the same criteria as in the 2006 study (Portela 2006), we come to the conclusion that stations have been technically upgraded. The two national broadcasters classified as 'medium' users in 2006 have now been classified as 'advanced' users.

Chart 3.2 demonstrates that nationwide stations are using technical resources to a higher degree. The unique national station classified as a 'medium' user is Rádio Sim, which started its activities recently and did not exist at the time when the 2006 study was undertaken.

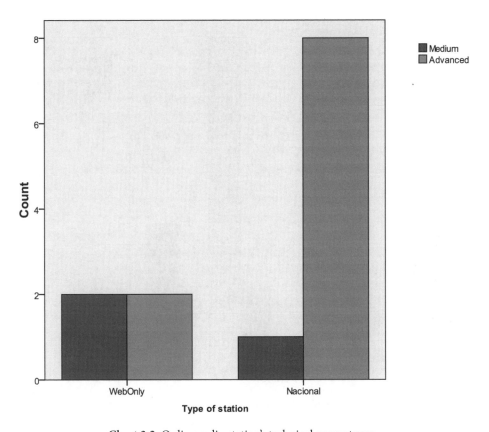

**Chart 3.2:** Online radio station's technical promptness.

The two web-only stations classified as 'medium' and also the ones classified as 'advanced' show exactly the same level of technical readiness when compared to those of 2006. This means that the thirteen stations of this type that ceased activities were the ones that then showed less technical development.[2]

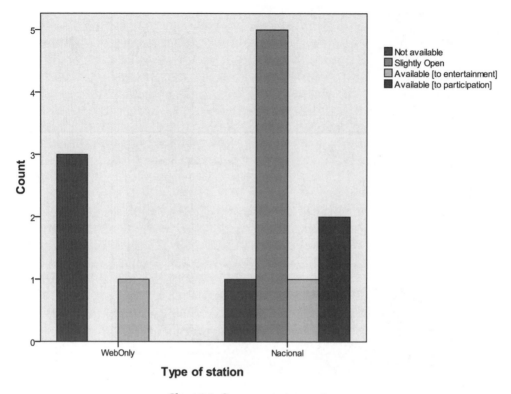

**Chart 3.3:** Openness to interaction.

Four stations are not available for interactivity with their listeners/users on the internet and five seem to distrust the power of interaction. The remaining four stations are already seeking interaction, although they seem to pursue different objectives. Two stations use interaction for entertainment, while the remaining two are willing to empower citizen participation in the public sphere.

In sum, these findings contribute to a better understanding of the internet's interactive potential for radio, indicating that the transformation of this medium is looking up to the net as the tool for change.

The slow pace of these transformations shows that radio is on the verge of carving out its niche in a fast-changing media environment and forecasting the right course is nearly impossible. It seems that there is still a long way for radio to go to *redifferentiate* itself and reinforce its appeal to future generations.

## Note

1. Given the changes in RCP (Rádio Clube Português) since 2006, we now consider this station as being countrywide in coverage.

## References and further reading

Becqueret, N., 'Un Modéle d'Analyse du Discours dês Emissions Intéractives Radiophonique', *Recherches en Communication*, 26, 2006, pp. 203–23.

Brecht, B., 'Teoria do rádio (1927–1932)' in E. Meditsch (ed.) *Teorias do Rádio – Textos e Contextos*, Florianópolis: Insular, 2005, pp. 35–45.

Cebrián Herreros, M., *Modelos de radio, desarollos e innovaciones*, Madrid: Editorial Fragua, 2007.

Ferne, T., 'Olinda – A New Radio', in *BBC Radiolabs* [Online], 2008, http://www.bbc.co.uk/blogs/radiolabs/2008/05/olinda_a_new_radio.shtml. Accessed 8 January 2009.

Jensen, K. B., 'Sounding the Media – An Interdisciplinary Review and Research Agenda for Digital Sound Studies', in *Nordicom Review*, 27 – 2: 7–33 [Online], 2006, http://www.nordicom.gu.se/common/publ_pdf/242_bruhn_jensen.pdf. Accessed 29 January 2009.

Meneses, J. P., *O consumo activo dos novos utilizadores na Internet: ameaças e oportunidades para a rádio musical (digitalizada)*, Ph.D. thesis, Universidade de Vigo, 2008.

Moses, A., 'Internet Car Radio a World First', in *The Age* [Online], 2009, http://www.theage.com.au/articles/2009/01/07/1231004091554.html. Accessed 8 January 2009.

Obercom, *A Sociedade em Rede em Portugal 2008* [Online], 2008, http://www.obercom.pt/client/?newsId=548&fileName=fr_sr_2008.pdf.Accessed 4September 2009.

Obercom, *Barómetro Media e Comunicação: tendências 2008/2009* [Online], 2009, http://www.obercom.pt/client/?newsId=25&fileName=barometro_2008_2009.pdf. Accessed 4 September 2009.

Obercom, *E-Generation 2008: Os Usos de Media pelas Crianças e Jovens em Portugal* [Online], 2009b, http://www.obercom.pt/client/?newsId=29&fileName=rr8.pdf. Accessed 4 September 2009.

Petit, G. & Afota, M. C. *Barometre de Confiance dans les Medias*, Montrouge: TNS Sofres, 2009.

Pinto, M., *A Televisão No Quotidiano das Crianças*, Porto: Edições Afrontamento, 2000.

Portela, P., *Rádio na internet em Portugal : a abertura à participação num meio em mudança*, Master Thesis, Braga: Universidade do Minho [Online], 2006, http://hdl.handle.net/1822/6251. Accessed 9 February 2009.

Rodero Antón, E. & Sánchez Serrano, Ch, 'Radiografía de la radio en España', in *Revista Latina de Comunicación Social*, 62 [Online], 2009, http://www.ull.es/publicaciones/latina/200714RoderoySanchez.htm. Accessed 9 February 2009.

Swedish Radio and TV Authority, *The Future Of Radio*, The Swedish Radio and TV Authority [Online], 2008, http://www.rtvv.se/_upload/Publikationer/The%20future%20of%20radio.pdf. Accessed 15 December 2008.

# Chapter 4

Radio and web 2.0: Direct Feedback

Carmen Peñafiel Saiz

## Background and current status of the issue

In the past ten years, the radio, like other social media, has undergone major transformations. We have gone from tuning into a conventional, traditional analogue radio to an internet radio characterized by interactivity in a multimedia system with new languages, new formats and new services. Linear programmes of the traditional radio waves are still on air but new possibilities have been added for those who want to search for their own content on the internet, finding specialized programmes and content on the new internet radio spectrum, all of which is directed to a diverse audience that shows more interest in the programme schedule. Thus emerges a new model of communication with even more identity (Cebrián 2008; Peñafiel 2007).

The consolidation of internet radio is seen as a dynamic model that is evolving constantly with a hypertext structure (audio, images, animation), an 'on demand' radio which marks a qualitative leap forward from the traditional radio model and which is more direct and participatory.

Academics and professionals study the technological changes that conventional radio is undergoing today in the sphere of communication in order to understand the essence of a new radio journalism in transformation. However, traditional, analogue radio still has a considerable presence in society. Different radio models coexist with their differences and interrelationships among the general, thematic radio that is convergent with the internet. Now that radio has delved into the workings of this convergence, it does not mean that current radio innovation turns off the previous radio rather it accumulates and forces new adjustments in their mutual relations. Internet radio is presented as a part of the internet world.

Mariano Cebrián sums up the transition from traditional radio to internet radio, as follows:

'The jump is momentous, as it changes to a model based on dialogue between users in the role of listeners, for they are the drivers of the communication process they undertake. Of course while the station has also designed another process as is the organization of the web, programming and providing tools so that users can then start the process. Users are freed from the bondage of live broadcasting and can access at other times and, most of all, develop personal strategies for use and consumption.'

(Cebrián 2008)

The socialization of technology, particularly the internet, gives the individual an unprecedented role insofar as participation in the process of creating and handling content (Turkle 1997; Vittadini 2002) is concerned. This technological revolution has produced a new type of individual who is the sender and receiver of the message (Burnett & Marshall 2003) and who becomes what might be called a selective user (Toral & Murelaga 2007). Radio programmes are presented in different sound environments. Firstly, traditional, analogue stations simulcast over the internet, creating their websites simply to accommodate the programming broadcast over the airwaves. Secondly, the internet offers tools such as surfing, hypertext and hypermedia links, interactivity to traditional radio. These possibilities can be made throughout the programming or at at certain times or only in programmes of particular genres. Thus internet radio came into being. Internet radio stations develop programmes exclusively for internet radio. Also, there is experimentation with other forms or extensions from internet radio, such as innovations using RSS, exchanges on P2P networks and the incorporation of VOIP, podcasting and audio blogs. Internet radio opens up a whole new vista (Cebrián 2008).

Moreover, the methods of journalism practice have radically changed. Mobile phones which not only offer voice services but also radio, music, databanks, internet, photo and video conferencing, thanks to applications of third-generation systems (UMTS and HSDPA [Universal Mobile Telecommunications System and High-Speed Downlink Packet Access]), have substantially changed business strategies and have led to some media groups using all possible options for disseminating the same content. Radio, like other media, is part of the future of multimedia convergence of systems and media integration, profound transformations in the role of informants, expansion of services, niches of audiences, unlimited supply, customized software, interactive media, active users and so on. So, we are witnessing the shaping of a new culture characterized by 'the global village' and the era of online interactive communication. This is encouraging mobile digital journalism which has blazed a trail towards what we call 'conversational journalism', a trend already publicized by web 2.0 proponents such as Tim O'Reilly and John Battelle.

## Objective

This chapter is the result of an investigation into technological change in the medium of radio, programming and the structure of radio. Here we analyse the technological changes that conventional radio has undergone in the sphere of communication in order to understand the key elements of a new radiophonic journalism. Research into radio led us to question whether we now have a new model of communication in which the approach of traditional radio in its various aspects is changing (Starkey 2007a). All the changes observed during the research programme cannot be addressed here; therefore we will concentrate on three key axes which coincide with a real transformation:

- the different forms of listener participation in the different radio formats;
- participative journalism developed in radio which presents itself through new formats and content via web 2.0 and 3.0;
- radio in virtual worlds with 'avatars' as protagonists of a radio station in the network of networks.

The last item on the list is a new formula which has already been used by one of the major commercial networks in Spain (Cadena SER), in which the analogue broadcaster transmits simultaneously over the airwaves and also in the 'virtual world' that is Second Life.

## Methodology

We worked using direct observation at the radio stations; we studied different radio websites; and we explored the opinions of radio professionals, also using questionnaires covering questions about before and after the advent of the internet as a universal information and communication platform.

## Analysis

Because of space constraints, we will focus on three areas that are clearly innovative: citizen journalism and mobile journalism; interactivity in radio programming and, finally, the virtual worlds of radio.

### *Citizen journalism and mobile journalism*

Mobile journalism has come to attain a place of importance within news organizations. With hi-tech phones which can record and even edit, people can write and send information to the radio instantly. Bloggers have been the first to use the possibilities of technology to support the immediacy of information. This model of journalism is based on the mobility of reporters with laptops, MP3 recorders and digital cameras, sending information to websites while helping members of the community to contribute reports to those same sites. In the evolution that has taken place in journalism in recent years on internet platforms, three major events coincide with three different versions. Journalism 1.0 consists of posting analogue content on the internet. This kind of journalism does not look forward to the possibilities of a new medium and is simply relayed on the internet. Journalism 2.0, on the other hand, comes with its own content creation for the internet because it is consumed by internet users. This is where information for the internet dissociates itself from the analogue version.

Journalism 3.0 has consolidated the internet, thanks to web 2.0 in blog format. It is a participatory journalism that socializes content and the medium itself. It is conversational and creates more and more broadcasters as they engage in conversations among themselves. Also, there is no need for a newsroom as the news usually comes from bloggers who need to further expand their content. One of the most important characteristics of this type of journalism is mobility. Nowadays mobility does not require a big investment, and reporters can attain it through a smart phone or a hi-tech phone with advanced audiovisual capabilities (Peñafiel & Palazio 2008).

Over the past decade, radio has made a qualitative leap forward. From offering programmes through conventional and traditional means it has gone to developing a participatory journalism of conversational information. This is called 'citizen journalism', a term which leads defenders and detractors alike to support or to question the concept. This concept has considerable advantages in instantaneity as it picks up interesting topics or discussion, and, users can receive news alerts on their mobile phones. Mobile phones and digital cameras have contributed to the development of this new specialized area of 'mobile digital journalism' and 'citizen journalism'. In citizen journalism, supported by almost all radio station websites, citizens are invited to send in news, videos, photos or images which demonstrate fact or substantiate criticism with the aim of dissemination and putting on the record news which comes from someone who is not a professional journalist. This type of information can then be transmitted by radio, television or the internet. The era of proliferation of broadcasters and ever smaller audiences has now arrived. This reinforces the importance of neutrality of platforms which will have to generate confidence in citizen journalists: platforms which give a voice to citizens who can publish and consume their own news, together and often as a form of dialogue.

All this brings risks, too, as noted by Starkey (2007b). Communication media needs to verify the public relevance, quality, presentability, veracity of the news items they receive from citizen journalists. Citizen journalism emerges strongly from this and its presentation of news in real time is what is making it more popular with the audiences. As a result citizen journalism is gaining importance in the broadcasting and consumption of news. Professional journalists are hesitant to accept the term 'citizen journalism' since journalism is a professional and academic discipline. Others see in citizen journalism a great leap forward for society in the sphere of news and perceive it to be a democratization of power in mass media. What we do know is this phenomenon is not developing uniformly. Citizen journalism is only two years old. It uses web 2.0 and 3.0 tools such as automatic moderation of content, blogs, videos, photographs and audio. And it is growing exponentially in the global village.

## Interactivity in radio programming

Interactivity and participation on internet radio is a dialogue between the radio station and internet users exclusively for those who want to interact. The station offers information, comments, interviews, reports and users can contribute their opinions and personal comments.

Listeners become the protagonists of information through the internet which assures us of the following:

- a visual configuration of the radio that is created by a symbolic-iconic language or website where users can manage messages and information in an intuitive way which creates an interactive model of selection – a new perspective of multiplication of messages that the user can enjoy through interactive sharing mechanisms;
- the proliferation of content, with no visible mass audiences and therefore the need to disseminate the content differently needs to be re-thought, creating new narrative and expressive forms;
- added services radio – internet radio offers a variety of *push* services which represent a set of mechanisms and information that stations offer for sale or for downloading of tangible and intangible products.

Technological changes directly affect the composition and disposition of the audience. We are heading towards custom radio, almost individual, emancipated by the multiplicity of options and by the mechanisms for managing on-demand information.

The interactivity of internet users depends on the communicative process and model. In his work 'La radio en Internet', Mariano Cebrián distinguished between the various characteristics of interactivity according to:

- the network model used;
- the time followed;
- the linking with products;
- the approach of the networks and stations;
- the type of production;
- the services offered to users;
- the general information on the website;
- the links between the expressive systems.

(Cebrián 2008)

Traditional radio incorporates some information and opinions from e-mails, chat rooms, forums, through reading, summarizing or reviewing them. It turns the listener into a parallel broadcaster along with the host. Interactivity also exists on radio websites with comments included and put on the internet so that other users can see them and expand upon them. Apart from these written forms, there are podcasts which users can download and regular feeds they can subscribe to. With the introduction of interactivity in internet radio, new genres appear based on dialogues which are sources of information that are introduced during a programme through the mediation of another person and, secondly, as the development of interest in the internet radio station that they want to encourage through the participation of their followers. They include:

- voice e-mail;
- phone chats;
- phone forums;
- others (voice mail for opinions and suggestions, oral conversations and online audio conferencing).

(Cebrián 2008)

Other forms of interactivity could also be added, such as surveys conducted via the website, polls, charts of hit songs, contests and sweepstakes. Alternatively, transactional interactivity includes viewing of advertising, timeless advertising and custom advertising. Finally, interactive groups open up possibilities for creating virtual communities and circles of people with similar interests.

## Second life radio

In addition to this citizen activity in today's radio, new forms of participation and online content have emerged. Other ways of presenting news became apparent in the study carried out. Recently, we have seen a veritable boom encouraged by the internet and web 2.0, such as the integration of virtual worlds in commercial radio broadcasting. This model belongs to young people and stems from the consumption of video gaming. Cadena SER, one of the most listened to broadcasters in Spain, together with Radiocable.com, has broadcast a Second Life radio programme simultaneously with its analogue broadcast. This has created possibilities for a new form of radio through virtual worlds and with the same people behind it, with the same voices in the Madrid Studios and with other virtual personalities as 'avatars'. It is the first programme in Castilian in the history of Spanish radio to have introduced a Second Life through the integration of virtual worlds. The model is interesting considering that there is a community of two million virtual inhabitants.

## Findings

A whole series of findings can be summarized in a single sentence: the concept of radio has changed. Our findings are as follows:

1. the relationship between the broadcaster and the audience has changed substantially;
2. the linearity of traditional radio has been broken by internet radio;

3. the participation of the audience is much more active (as users and also, in many cases, as broadcasters);

4. the listening and broadcasting places (virtual worlds) have changed; the concept of programming (on demand radio) has changed;

5. the formats, genres, etc. have changed;

6. cyberspace is a universe for radio where interactivity, innovation and creation are the pillars of the new model of communication, because it has been shown that radio is constantly changing;

7. we have internet radios with low levels of hypertext, multimedia and interactivity;

8. traditional broadcasters have developed their websites to enhance their radio broadcast and as a complement to their on air broadcasting as a value added service to their listeners or as a means to connect with their audience and thus obtain information or facilitate their participation;

9. many stations have not yet evaluated the actual capacity of the internet to broadcast journalistic content;

10. internet radio as a component of cyber media sets itself apart from traditional radio as it absorbs the contributions of the internet in their programmes and on the web and, on the other hand, is similar to the written press in its inclusion of writing, its forms of expression, its genres and narrative.

(López & Otero 2007)

In conclusion, we concur with Mariano Cebrián in his belief that

'technological innovation must be fuelled by the transformation and creation of additional content and services and other forms of expression. There is no other way but by the reinforcement of experimentation, imagination and creativity by professionals. Only with these injections can the radio, internet radio, and its extensions invigorate its significant presence in the new communicative ecosystem of the Society of Information and Knowledge as a driving force behind social dialogue'.

## References and further reading

Amohedo, A., 'Tecnología, especialización y creatividad en el nuevo sonido para los nuevos tiempos', in *Reinventar la Radio*, Pamplona: Eunate, 2001.

AA.VV., *Blogs, weblogs, bitácoras*, in Telos, Fundación Telef.nica, N 65, Oct-dic, Madrid, 2005.

Bustamante, Enrique (Coord.) *Hacia un nuevo sistema mundial de comunicación. Las industrias culturales en la era digital*, Barcelona: Gedisa, 2003.

Burnett, R. & Marshall P. D., *Web theory: An introduction*. London: Routledge, 2003.

Castells, M., 'La sociedad red', in *Teorías para una nueva sociedad*, Madrid: Fundación Marcelino Botín, 2002.

Castells, M., *La era de la información. Economía sociedad y cultura*, Madrid: Alianza, 1998.

Cebrián, M., *La radio en Internet*, Argentina: Icrj'inclusiones, 2008.

Cebrián, M., *Modelos de radio, desarrollos e innovacione. De la participación a la interactividad.* Madrid: Fragua, 2007.

Consell de l'Audiovisual de Catalunya, "Tema monogràfic: La ràdio, un mitjà en transformació", Barcelona : *Quaderns Del Cac*, 2004, n 18, gener-abril.

Flores J., Cebrián M. Y Esteve (eds) *Blogalaxia y periodismo en la Red. Estudios, análisis y reflexiones.* Madrid: Fragua, 2008.

Franquet, R., "La radio ante la digitalización: renovarse en la incertidumbre", in *Hacia un nuevo sistema mundial de comunicación. Las industris culturales en la era digital,* Barcelona: Gedisa, 2003.

López, Xosé & Otero, M., *Bitácoras. La consolidación del ciudadano*: netbiblo. La Coruña, 2007.

Meso, K., *Introducción al ciberperiodismo*: UPV/EHU, Bilbao, 2006.

Ortiz, Miguel Ángel y Cuesta, Juan, *La radio digital. Nuevos perfiles profesionales,* Madrid: Ed. Consejería de Trabajo de la Comunidad de Madrid y RTVE, 2003.

Peñafiel, Carmen & Palazio, Gorka, "El periodismo digital en la época de la multiplicidad de emisores", in Estudios de Periodística XIV. *Periodismo ciudadano: posibilidades y riesgos para el discurso informativo*, Salamanca: Sociedad española de periodística, 2009.

Peñafiel, Carmen (ed.), *Transformaciones de la radio y la televisión en Europa,* Bilbao: UPV/EHU, 2007.

Peñafiel, Carmen & López, Nereida, *Claves para la era digital. Evolución hacia nuevos medios, nuevos lenguajes y nuevos servicios,* Bilbao: UPV/EHU, 2002.

Toral, Gotzon & Murelaga, Jon, "Radio en Internet, emisoras personales y nuevas redes emergentes", in *Transformaciones de la Radio y la televisión en Europa,* Peñafiel, Carmen (Coor.) Bilbao: UPV/EHU, 2007.

Starkey, G., "Democratización de los mass-media por la proliferación de las nuevas tecnologías", in *Transformaciones de la Radio y la televisión en Europa,* Peñafiel, Carmen (Coor.), Bilbao: UPV/EHU, 2007a.

Starkey, G., *Balance and bias in Journalism: Representation, regulation and democracy.* London: Palgrave Macmillan, 2007b.

Turkle, S., *Life on the screen.* New York: Touchstone, 1997.

# Chapter 5

Radio as the Voice of Community: Locality, Interactivity and Experimentation

Maria Papadomanolaki

This chapter examines the use of radio in the context of performance and installation art. It aims to establish a clear connection of the medium to its grassroots, as a tool of community, locality and interaction. A brief study of free-radio initiatives from the second half of the twentieth century such as the Italian Radio Alice, the Japanese Mini FM and the American Radio Free Berkley, WTRA and free103point9, demonstrates with clarity the point that low-powered radio (micro-radio) was used as a vital tool for survival, creative dialogue and organic re-construction of communities, neighbourhoods and activist groups. Subsequently, it moved beyond the rigidity of the content politics and propaganda of the commercial radio giants. It is from that point on that radio vindicates the values of free-expression, re-contextualization and interaction with the everyday listener. Contemporary artists like Hildegard Westerkamp, neuroTransmitter, Max Neuhaus, Anna Friz among others place the radio visions of Futurism and the Weimar era in a new framework incorporating live interaction with the environment and the audience, physical performance and critical participation. In that sense, radio reflects and re-establishes our relation with nature and life. Most importantly radio eludes the physical space of a studio and becomes part of a live performance in projects like free103point9's *Tune(In)))* and *Radio 4x4* or merges with the public space in projects like Elvin's *Public Radio*, Neuhaus's *Drive In Music* and neuroTransmitter's *Branching to Broadcast*.

The spirit of free-form radio is apparent in projects that involve digital streaming technologies. The digitization of transmission brings about a challenging new spectrum of possibilities. When applied in the context of locality, community and site specificity, streaming and digital communication technology can consolidate the argument that new technologies facilitate the mediation of dialogue and broaden the methods of accessibility and participation to the creation of an artwork. In that framework analogue and digital transmission can co-exist and assist us in re-evaluating the relationship between artist-artwork-environment-audience.

## Medium versus content

The sociopolitical turbulence between the labour-committed communists and the young leftwing radicals (Autonomists), which occurred in mid-1970s Italy, began a series of low-powered free-radio initiatives, the most influential being Radio Alice in Bologna in 1976. The mission of Radio Alice was to create a democratic and open source network of free interlocutors. The radio station would function as the communicational spine of the collective and would overlook the language and monopolized repertoire of mainstream and 'institutionalized' media. Radio Alice amplified and unified the voices of the demonstrators and the listeners by relaying all the activities without intervention or censorship. Franco 'Biffo' Berardi, founder of Radio Alice, envisioned a functional system where listeners could not only express themselves but could also become part of it (Walker 2001). Radio Alice's repertoire of programmes included live phone-in coverage of street riots and demonstrations, experimental sound art shows, pure silence and radio static, cooking and yoga lessons as well as poetry and political discussions.

Inspired by the Italian free radio scene, Tetsuo Kogawa and other Japanese micro-radio luminaries picked up the idea of low-power, narrowcast transmission and developed a legal transmitter system. From 1981 onwards the 'Mini FM' boom had established a new fashion of door-to-door communication between family members, members of a community or even between the clients of a coffee shop (Radio Komedia Suginami).

By the late 1980s more than a thousand mini-fm stations were on air. The sterility of the Japanese airwaves (two radio stations in total in the 1980s) and abhorrence for the idea that the mainstream media would absorb and commodify the underground culture, prepared the ground for such a large-scale outburst of mini-stations. 'Mini FM' responded to the need to express oneself freely and to be given the option to share ideas, experiment artistically and connect to a group of listeners. It provided new and creative ways of communication and distanced itself from the role of radio as global mediator of information. Testuo Kogawa in his account (Kogawa 1990) of the 'Mini-FM' revolution adds that, in many cases unconsciously, the mini-station functioned as a form of psychotherapy between people who, for example, never confronted an audience or couples who wanted to bridge their communication gap. Kogawa (Chandler & Neumark, 2005) expanded the use of Mini-FM in the context of sound installation (multiple transmitter/receiver set-ups in gardens and houses), dance performances (dancers interacting with portable transmitters and creating sounds by the movements of their bodies) or performance art events like *Radio Party* (an event where the audience builds a transmitter and then uses it as an entertainment station for the party).

In the US, DeWayne Readus, also known as Mbanna Kantako, founded WTRA, a low-powered mini-station that voiced the issues and concerns of the tenants of his project building in Springfield, Illinois, in 1986. Since its launch, WTRA has fought for the emancipation of marginalized black communities and their protection from racist assaults and other criminal acts. Kantako was prosecuted many times by the Federal Communications Committee (FCC) for unlicensed broadcasting. In 1990 he received a fine of $750 that Kantako continues to challenge. Kantako took advantage of the portability of his transmission station and relocated every time the FCC knocked on his door. He kept changing the name of his station from WTRA to Black Liberation Radio and finally to Human Rights Radio (Dunifer & Sakolsky 1998). Similar to Radio Alice or the Japanese model of mini-radio, Kantako's project was a system of survival with an open member base that creatively contributed to the community dialogue. It also significantly and positively impacted upon local violence by giving the victims the ability to speak out about police brutality against African Americans. WTRA introduced the members of the community to the art of radio-making and the empowerment of free expression.

Stephen Dunnifer's Free Radio Berkeley in San Fransisco in 1993, stemmed from his long engagement with activist media and pirate radio. Dunifer had initiated a portable station that was prosecuted by the FCC, and he was fined $20,000. Nonetheless, Free Radio Berkeley managed to legally reclaim its right to free speech and free-form expression.[1] Broadcasting from all kinds of spaces (run down buildings, cars and hills), Free Radio Berkeley became a tool that nurtured freedom of expression and artistic creativity. People from all over the Bay area were producing programmes about politics, comedy, activism, community, free speech, local music and activities that assisted in shaping the character and the identity of their city and community. To this day, Free Radio Berkeley is acknowledged as an influential and successful example of the Micro-radio movement in the US.

A few years later in 1997, on the other side of the country, New York-based artists Tom Roe, Greg Anderson and Violet Hopkins launched their own micro-radio station under the name free103point9 in Brooklyn. With a portable narrowcasting kit, free103point9 amplified the under-recognized activities and voices of New York communities. The activities of free103point9 contributed to and were the catalyst for the formation of a growing artist community who mainly experimented with the creative use of radio and transmission in the framework of performances, installations and sound art. In order to best serve this emerging community, free103point9 evolved from a micro-radio collective to a non-profit arts organization in 2002, with the mission to assist emerging artists and communities who work or wish to work in the field of transmission art. All the works featured in this section affirm McLuhan's (1964) belief that 'the mark of our times is its revulsion against imposed patterns'. In that sense, free radio offered a new interpretation of radio where the medium itself mattered more than the content, and where locality, plurality and creativity outgunned the model of global mainstream radio stations.

## Rediscovering the environment

Radio asserts a sense of intimacy with its listeners. It assumes the role of mesmerizing the soul and leading a listener into a state of somnambulance and disembodiment. Or at least that was the idea many people had about radio until early in the twentieth century when the Weimar Era Radio and the futurist radio manifesto *La Radia* emerged. Marinetti's and Masnatta's *La Radia* (1933) proclaimed a new fashion of radio-making that is aware of its surrounding environment and matter; it absorbs the commodities of everyday life and transforms them into a study through sound. The sounds of the city, the forest, the sea, the body, the sound of cooking and the normally inaudible noises of food digestion are foregrounded. *La Radia* sought to exclude the dramatic clichés of the past and challenged the audience's sensations with a radical change in content.

The radio of the Golden Weimar period in Germany (1923–30) arguably followed a similar pattern. Hans Flesch, director of the Berlin Radio Hour, pioneered a new genre of radio work based on the sounds of the environment, the city and everyday life. Acoustical Films (audio recordings made on the soundstrip of the film) were the first phonographic sound collages to be broadcast on the German airwaves. The film director Walter Ruttman was commissioned to construct *Weekend* in 1930, based on the sounds of the city of Berlin. Flesch's rendition of radio art channelled the sound of life inside the broadcast studio just to rebroadcast it back out again.

Flesch suggested a system of mirroring the outside that recalls Radio Alice's mission and is aligned to a more contemporary set of artists who dealt with the same issues. During the mid-seventies Hildegard Westerkamp's *Soundwalking* radio shows reappraised the 'Fleschian' model and suggested to the audience of Vancouver Cooperative Radio different ways of experiencing and re-evaluating their surrounding soundscape. Westerkamp used the microphone as a magnifying lens to record and amplify aural details, ignoring sounds from Vancouver's locale and commenting on the impact of these soundscapes on the composition, identity and sound-ecology of the place. Sometimes combined with book excerpts read on air, the soundwalks formed an act of creative criticism and deep reflection on the issues of sound and the environment.

Bill Fontana's *Landscape Soundings* was a large-scale sound and radio installation for the Vienna Festival in 1990. Fontana used various types of transmitters to broadcast the sounds of nature and the river near Stopfenreuther Au (Danube) back to Vienna, mixed them with local sounds, and fed them to an array of speakers strategically placed to bridge the sound space between the Museum of Art History and the Museum of Natural History in Vienna. The transforming power of sound refreshed the listener's memories of the places they have visited or have lived in, by triggering their aural sensibility. The soundscapes were also broadcast on conventional radio and soon gained great popularity. Like Westerkamp, Fontana raised issues of acoustic ecology and perception by sculpturally intervening in the obtrusive city sounds surrounding the two museums.

New York-based transmission art duo Angel Nevarez and Valerie Tevere (neuroTransmitter) offer another example of radio-architectural intervention in a set environment with their project *Branching to Broadcast* (in collaboration with Daniela Fabricius). Installed in Colonels Row (Governors Island, New York), *Branching to Broadcast* consisted of a small house built on a tree that hosted a micro-radio station. The radio assimilated the local soundscape and fed it back to a set of receivers placed in a variety of spots around the island. On a first level of interpretation the 'micro-radio tree house' makes up an unusual type of architectural intervention. Additionally, *Branching to Broadcast* highlights the value of locality and low-powered transmission and the importance of mediating the hidden sounds of the airwaves as well as the activities of the surrounding environment to its native listeners.

Similarly, the UK-based artist Simon Elvins explores the inaudible environments that surround us with his series of site-specific radio installations titled *Public Radio*. Exhibited at Deptford Design Market Challenge, at the Royal Festival Hall in London, *Public Radio* used AM transmitters made out of discarded and everyday objects. With their earth connection attached literally to the ground and their aerial clamped on top of trees, poles and other objects high enough to access the airwaves, the transmitters were powered solely by the energy of radio waves. In *Public Radio*, Elvins' background in design merges with his engagement with sound as a form of translating and understanding the everyday environments. In the case of *Public Radio* the listeners interact closely with the invisible and otherwise inaudible radio waves that surround them.

## Performing the airwaves

In all the aforementioned cases, radio transmission becomes an extension of the environment and assists in its magnification, re-interpretation and re-evaluation. In this section we examine artists who put radio in the context of performance. By performance we allude to projects that either require radio as an 'instrument' or apply innovative methods in the process of radio-making. According to Walter Benjamin (Benjamin et al. 2005) radio should become a medium through which listeners cultivate a sound awareness of what they hear. Hence radio should reflect the audience and its interests. Radio should also provide its listeners with interactive engagement as part of a process of defining its content. The American sound art pioneer Max Neuhaus experimented with this concept in *Drive In Music* between 1967 and 1968. Neuhaus's initial idea was to create a site-specific sound installation where the drivers on Lincoln Parkway Avenue (Buffalo, New York) could trigger the perception of a set of custom sounds with the movement of their car. To realize this, he attached twenty low-powered transmitters on the tree-lines along a six-hundred-metre distance. Each transmitter produced a specific continuous sound that overlapped with the others at specific points of the trajectory. By having all the transmitters set to the same frequency, Neuhaus created an immersive soundscape whose content was primarily defined by the drivers' tempo, directionality and taste over tonality. Hence, *Drive In Music* permitted an endless set of possible incarnations. Last, but not the least, *Drive In Music* demonstrated to the drivers/performers with clarity how one can experience a space by interacting with it through sound.

The Canadian radio artist Anna Friz uses multiple radio transmitters and receivers to perform in public spaces, galleries and other unusual locations. Friz describes her radio art projects as self-reflective. In that sense she extends Benjamin's idea of 'conscious participation in the making' to the level of conceptual engagement. *You are far from us* was performed at the Radio Revolten festival in Halle, Germany, in 2006. Designed to be a solo performance for four transmitters and fifty receivers, the piece balanced the notion that even though radio creates a physical distance with its receivers, it opens up the possibilities of conscious and attentive listening. *You are far from us* explores the hidden poetry found between static radio signals, air and the space that contains them.

The New York-based non-profit arts organization free103point9 has been the driving-force behind many radio and transmission art projects and events in New York. In 2004

Tune (In))) at The Kitchen in New York invited over thirty emerging and established sound artists to perform on four separate but simultaneous stages. Four transmitters, (one for each stage,) broadcast their signals inside the Kitchen Gallery where the audience was seated in a seemingly silent space. A fifth frequency transmitted the soundtrack to a video programme of works connected to the concept of transmission. Equipped with radio headsets, the listeners explored the variety of stations hosted in the FM spectrum while tuning in to the five Tune (In))) radio stations. Among the performers were artists like Ikue Mori, Zeena Parkins, Thurston Moore, Scanner, Tom Roe and Espers. Tune (In))) successfully and courageously affirmed the possibility of turning the radio spectrum into a venue, in and of itself, where the audience develops a cerebral affinity with performers via the FM dial.

Alternatively, free103point9's *Radio 4x4* merges the physical and ethereal space in the process of creating a hybrid performance. Staged in more than twenty international events and venues, *Radio 4x4* involves four performers whose sound is amplified by using four low-powered transmitters. The four signals are transmitted separately in four frequencies picked up and amplified by a series of boombox radios distributed within the space. The audience becomes part of the performance by moving around the space and mixing the different signals as determined by their movements and hence defining the final form and content of the work. Most importantly, *Radio 4x4* is open to as many different interpretations and unique approaches as its audience can conceive.

## The digital age

Creative practice has always been stimulated by emergent technologies. In fact, art functions like an agent of convergence between experience and technology by extending our relation with and our understanding of them. Since its birth, radio has anticipated a cross-breeding with other media, forms of expression, and notions of perceiving public life and the environment. In many of the cases examined in this paper, radio intersects with activism, architecture, music performance, film, site specificity, interactivity, locality, reviving the Brechtian (1964) 'network of pipes'; an ethereal place were the audience not only receives but also transmits, and a medium that aides public communication. Nonetheless in the digital age, the notions of locality and interactivity face a significant shift in scale and directionality. From the early 1990s, the World Wide Web fostered the first experiments with webradio and telematic performances. Austria has presented a few exceptional paradigms of telematic performances with projects like Mia Zibelka's *Space Bodies* (Chandler & Neumark 2005) where a violin performance was augmented with the use of violin midi data streamed via the Web and triggered with the use of telerobotic interfaces. Additionally, in 1992, a non-profit organization TRANSIT (a spinoff of KUNSTRADIO) staged *Chip-Radio* – a polyphonic telematic radio concert where four different performers (Andres Bosshard, Seppo Gruendler, Gerfried Stocker and Mia Zabelka) streamed their sounds simultaneously from four different cities in Austria, while interacting with each other. The locality of a performance expands from a room to a group of neighbouring cities and the network covers up the distance in-between.

The Internet has dilated the radius of transmission by diminishing the distance between the performers; a permutation of locality that Kogawa (1990) termed as translocality. The physical space that contains the action of transmitting (i.e. a radio station studio, a concert stage) is superseded by the personal space of the 'transmitter' and in that sense it echoes the portability and adjustability of the micro-radio formulae. In my site-specific telematic performance Trajectory (2008), an outdoor roamer jammed with an audience inside a gallery via audiostreaming and mobile messaging aiming to unfold the sonic activities and environments behind the walls.

## Conclusion

The aforementioned projects exemplify in different ways the idea that the immediacy of telematic presence does not liquidate but enhances the notions of locality, community and interactivity. Digital radio-art has a strong reference to its analogue predecessor, but it is bigger and faster in scale. Nonetheless, that does not mean that the unique properties of the old must die away. On the contrary, both the old and the new, share the same conceptual underpinning of locality, community, creative exploration and experimentation; opposing the model of mass communication and centralized media. As long as new communication technologies emerge, new environments are created that stretch the equilibrium of polyphony versus uniformity towards new lengths. In such a spectrum of possibilities the artist is found on the frontline, experimenting with the evolving structures and assuming the solemn role to enhance in an inventive and creative manner the public's awareness and knowledge of the new media taxonomy (McLuhan 1964).

## Note

1. In 1978, the FCC put into effect legislation that banned any type of transmitter under 100 Watts. Free Radio Berkley's struggle against the FCC's lawsuit culminated in Stephen Dunifer's court victory in 1997.

## References and further reading

Dunifer, S. & Sakolsky, R. (eds), *Seizing the airwaves: A free-radio andbook*. San Fransisco: AK Press, 1998.

McLuhan, M. *Understanding the media: The extensions of man*. Toronto: McGraw-Hill, 1964.

Walker, J. *Rebels on the air: An alternative history of radio in America*. New York: New York University Press, 2001.

Chandler, A. & Neumark, N. *At a distance: Precursors to art and activism on the internet.* Cambridge: The MIT Press, 2005.

Augaitis, D. & Lander, D. (eds), *Radio rethink: Art, sound and transmission.* Banff: Walter Phillips Gallery, 1994.

Brecht, B. & Willett, J. (ed.), *Brecht on theater: The development of an aesthetic, Translated.* Translated by J. Willett. London: Methuen, 1964.

Benjamin, W., Livingstone, R., Jennings, W., M., Eiland, H., Smith, H. (eds), *Walter Benjamin: Selected writings volume 2, 1927–1934.* Cambridge: Harvard University Press, 2005.

Anarchy Translocal: Tetsuo Kogawa's Website. *Towards polymorphous radio.* [Online], http://anarchy. translocal.jp/non-japanese/radiorethink.html 1990. Accessed 12 July 2009.

Max Neuhaus' Website. *Drive In Music.* [Online], http://www.max-neuhaus.info/soundworks/ vectors/passage/ 1967. Accessed 19 July 2009.

KUNSTRADIO *La Radia.* [Online], http://www.kunstradio.at/THEORIE/theorymain.html 1933. Accessed 25 July 2009.

free103point9.*Transmission Projects.* [Online], http://www.free103point9.org/transmissionprojects/. Accessed 29 July 2009.

Simon Elvins' Website. *Public Radio.* [Online], http://www.simonelvins.com/public_radio.html. Accessed 27 July 2009.

neuroTransmitter's Website. *Branching to Broadcast* [Online], http://www.neurotransmitter.fm/ projects/branching.html. Accessed 25 July 2009.

# Part II

Content

# Chapter 6

Blurring Fiction with Reality: The Strange Case of *Amnésia*, an Italian 'Mockumentary'

Tiziano Bonini

This research does not aim to cover the history of media on the basis of a dialectic between fiction and reality. The chapter's main objective is to analyse the case of an Italian radio programme which was very successful during the 2008/09 radio season. We have chosen to analyse the format and language of this programme as we believe that it represents a fitting example of innovation with regard to a traditional radio genre such as fiction. *Amnésia*, contaminating a traditional genre with the use of new media, is in our opinion a valid answer to the question, 'What should radio content be like in the digital age?' Moreover, *Amnésia* is an interesting case study for another reason: the programme's initial idea (its format) was in itself a further attempt to question the boundary between fiction and reality and had many similarities with the first case in which this boundary was crossed: the *War of the Worlds* by Orson Welles. However, before we deal with the object of our study we must first return briefly to the history of the radio programme that for the first time breached the thin line that separates fiction and reality.

### When fiction crossed over into reality: the War of the Worlds of 1938

> "It was the night before Halloween…
> the only trouble was that an
> impressive number of listeners
> forgot what day it was".[1]

On the night of Sunday, 30 October 1938, at 8pm, CBS broadcast live *The War of the Worlds*, a radio drama based on a novel by H. G. Wells and directed by a young Orson Welles. The programme was part of the series of radio adaptations *Mercury Theatre on Air*, which had already been aired for sixteen weeks without being particularly successful. On Sunday night, at the same time, NBC broadcast the more popular *Charlie McCarthy Show*, and CBS had not yet found a commercial company who would sponsor Orson Welles' programme. The series was in risk of being cancelled. Welles himself was rather sceptical of the British novel's potential to capture the attention of American listeners. On the Thursday prior to the broadcast, Mercury Theatre's board (which included Welles) met to listen to recordings of the rehearsals. "We have only one way of keeping this program running", said Houseman, Mercury's co-director, "By playing up the realism as far as possible. We have to make it more real, more believable, using the radio newscast format".[2] The script was changed according to this suggestion and in some parts entirely re-written. It was decided that the story of the Martians landing was to be told as a radio newscast. Even so, Welles was not convinced. Then came the night of the live broadcast. The theme song played. The story's introduction, read by Orson Welles' slow and deep voice, began: "We know now that in the early years of the 20th century this world was being watched closely by intelligences greater than man's and yet as mortal as his own…". The Crosley agency calculated that on that night 32 million people were listening to the radio.

Then the anonymous voice of a presenter, followed on after Welles, reading a normal weather report and announcing that programmes would continue with a live broadcast from a ballroom in a New York restaurant. After a couple of minutes of music, there was a sudden interruption: "Ladies and gentlemen, we interrupt our program…". It was 1938, shortly after the Munich crisis, and the world was on the brink of war. The first news flash of the radio newscast, which stated that strange phenomena had been sighted on planet Mars, was followed by others, until finally it was announced that mysterious flying machines had landed in New Jersey. The voice of an on-the-spot correspondent broke into the houses of Americans: "Good heavens, something's wriggling out of the shadow like a grey snake… the crowd falls back… Well, I'll pull this microphone with me as I talk. I'll have to stop the description until I can take a new position. Hold on, will you please, I'll be right back in a minute". Then it was the turn of the 'Secretary of the Interior' who, speaking in a flat, official tone, said: "Citizens of the nation: I shall not try to conceal the gravity of the situation that confronts the country […] Placing our faith in God we must continue the performance of our duties each and every one of us, so that we may confront this destructive adversary with a nation united, courageous, and consecrated to the preservation of human supremacy on this earth". This message contributed significantly towards spreading panic. Thousands of families abandoned their homes and took refuge in the woods. Many National Guard stations were stormed by people trying to obtain gas masks from the army. In some towns in the South the entire population poured onto the streets to pray and sing religious hymns. In the meantime, the broadcast was coming to an end: "I'm speaking from the roof of the Broadcasting Building, New York City… The Martians [are] approach[ing]. Estimated in the last two hours, three million people have moved out along the roads to the north […] Avoid bridges to Long Island – hopelessly jammed. All communication with Jersey shore closed ten minutes ago. No more defenses. Our army wiped out […] This may be the last broadcast. We'll stay here to the end. […] Martian cylinders are falling all over the country […] [Everybody is] running towards the East River, thousands of them, dropping in like rats. Now the smoke […] [has] reached Times Square. [It's] a hundred yards away[…] it's – it's fifty feet […]". A sigh, a moan, the muffled sound of a body falling down and of the microphone rolling on the concrete: death of a reporter, live on the radio.

The next day newspaper titles read: 'Orson Welles's radio war terrorizes the US'. Six weeks after the broadcast people were still found camping in the woods for fear of the Martians. The Hooper Rating Company calculated that on that night the most popular radio programme had been the *Charlie McCarthy Show* with a share of 34.7%. However, when the show ended,

12% of that audience moved to CBS and *Mercury Theatre on Air*'s share went from a normal 3.6% to 15% in the first twenty minutes of the broadcast.[3] Listeners' word of mouth and phone calls to friends and family telling them to turn on the radio (something similar to what happened on September 11, 2001 with text messaging) contributed to further increase the number of listeners, taking it to six million.

According to the classic psychological study by Cantril on audience reactions to Welles' radio drama,[4] of those six million about one million and seven hundred thousand believed that Martians were invading the Earth, and of these one million two hundred thousand not only took the broadcast seriously, but experienced feelings of fear and panic. Cantril's study on audience reactions, conducted by analysing letters to the programme and a series of interviews, led him to conclude that the percentage of people who, that Halloween, believed that Martians were landing did so for a number of reasons, which can be summed up as follows:

- The nature of the public's trust in the radio itself. *The War of the Worlds* was aired at a time when the radio had replaced newspapers as the primary source of information.
- The degree of instability of that period. The United States was emerging from the Great Depression and the crisis of European politics was extremely topical in those days. American society was living in a period of uncertainty. Only one month before (30 September) programmes were interrupted to announce the Munich agreement.[5] It was a time of crisis: an economic slump was in full swing, a world war was around the corner and now the Martians were landing. Another external event, explains Cantril, which was beyond the control and comprehension of individuals.
- The listening mode: many tuned in after the show began or "by contagion", urged to listen to the programme by people they knew and fuelling each other.
- The audience's psychological and social profile: Cantril noted that the personality of some listeners led them to be much more inclined than others to believe unconditionally, unable to exercise their critical judgement. In particular, a lack of critical judgement was especially found, in Cantril's interviews, in those listeners with a lower literacy level and limited cultural consumption.
- The broadcast's high degree of realism: "It didn't sound like a radio drama", said one of the listeners to the American sociologist.

## Why Martians were believable

Cantril's analysis and conclusions are certainly important, as they represent the first and most detailed study on the psychology of radio listening, and they were able to grasp the complexity of the radio audience's reactions.

However, the fact that one out of three American listeners that night believed that the Martians had landed does not depend only on the psychology of listeners and on the USA's specific historical and political context at the time. Another decisive factor, which Cantril's analysis does not really shed light on, was the particular way in which Orson Welles used radio language.[6] The choice to translate Wells' text into a breaking news story contributed significantly to the false event's credibility.

A regular listener of CBS who tuned into Welles' radio drama from the beginning and listened carefully for the whole time would have had plenty of occasions to realize that he was listening to a radio fiction.[7] The programme was interspersed with a host of linguistic and narrative signs that could easily lead the audience to interpret it as fictional: the programme's jingle specifying that *Mercury Theatre on Air* was presenting *The War of the Worlds* by H. G. Wells was repeated as many as four times during the broadcast. Moreover, it was rather implausible, with the technical means available at the time, that a radio studio could hook up to a jet pilot and broadcast his voice. In addition, many of the names in the story were changed. The CBS executive Davidson Taylor and the network's team of lawyers forced the authors to modify the script, changing as many as 28 names, fearing that the programme would otherwise be too realistic. However, the new names were quite similar to the original ones, especially when heard and not read. Langley Field became Langham Field. Princeton University Observatory became Princeton Observatory and New Jersey's National Guard became the State Militia.[8]

Furthermore, listeners doubting the broadcast's truthfulness could have attempted to verify its plausibility by looking for other sources: they could have switched to another radio station to check whether anyone else was talking about the event, or called an acquaintance in New Jersey or in one of the 'landing' spots. In fact, the majority of listeners that night came to the conclusion that the landing was actually fictional. Everyone, however, even the 'non-believers', asked themselves for a second if it was all really happening. And if some people kept believing the story until the end of the programme, it was also due to the fact that Welles had recreated an almost exact copy of a radio newscast of the time. Despite inconsistencies (the pilot connected via radio) and signifiers (the programme's jingle), a few highly plausible elements were sufficient to make the story sound real to listeners. The first realistic element that contributed to question the programme's fictional status was the interruption of the music by the news bulletin. At the time, these interruptions were quite frequent: the European crisis and Nazism's advance were topical news and American networks often interrupted music and soap operas in order to update the audience on new developments. The second element was the use of an expert authority (the astronomer from Princeton Observatory). Another crucial element was the inclusion of the voice of the Minister of the Interior, whose tone and rhythm were perfectly imitated by an actor. Radio at the time was the most important news medium and people habitually used it to gain information. The trustworthiness of news items broadcast by the radio was not usually questioned. All these elements, and more generally the choice of the radio commentary as the linguistic register used to adapt H. G. Wells's novel for the radio, played an important role in convincing listeners that the programme's story was real.

## Attention! *La radio ment!*[9]

The case of *The War of the Worlds* is important because for the first time fiction disguised itself as reality. Welles was the first to cross the line between fiction and reality within electronic media, to shatter the sacredness of the real, to show that the emperor was not wearing any clothes. Whether he was conscious of it or not, he demonstrated that the media could lie and showed the whole world how dangerous it was to believe them unconditionally. Welles was also the first to betray the implicit pact between the author of a story and its reader/listener, that is that 'suspension of disbelief' that allows those who listen to or read a story to make-believe, to pretend that it is all true in order to derive an aesthetic pleasure from the story. The suspension of disbelief[10] is a conscious act on the part of readers, who recognize the fictional status of the story but decide to believe it, so that they can enjoy it fully and feel the emotions that the story conveys. Those listeners who on that Halloween believed that Martians had landed were not capable of recognizing the broadcast's fictional elements; they only recognized elements of reality and they panicked because for them that broadcast was not a game ("Let's pretend that we believe in Martians landing on the Earth"). We could say that they did not recognize the rules of the game, that they did not play along. In their defence it must be noted that it was a game with new rules: they could not believe that someone could imitate the Minister of the Interior's voice; they could not believe that a journalist could announce false events. They could not believe that the radio could lie. Until that night in 1938 the boundary between fiction and reality was clear: listeners thought that they could recognize an account of reality (news, newscasts) from fictional accounts (radio dramas, soap operas). Welles mixed the languages of the two genres and paved the way to the long process of redefinition of the boundary between fiction and reality, which to this day is still taking place. From that night on, that boundary started to increasingly look like frontier land. Television and, later, new digital media, have contributed to making that line thinner and thinner.

If it is true that the audience is not as naive as it was in Welles' time, and that media literacy on the whole has increased, it is also true that the techniques used to contaminate reality are becoming increasingly more sophisticated, so that to this day it may be that even the savviest members of the public may not immediately recognize the boundary between fiction and reality. The definition of this boundary is constantly evolving and depends on a continuous negotiation between the author and the reader. Each time the two parties reach an implicit agreement on which to base the suspension of disbelief, somebody questions the boundary, crosses it, makes it a frontier once again. Authors are not the only ones to blame (if indeed we wish to blame someone). Both sides are pushing at this boundary. For the author, the challenge is to invent new ways to entertain the public, to test the limits of media language. For the public – at least for its most 'expert' and media-literate members – the urge to question the boundary derives from an aesthetic need to keep feeling emotions, to play at the ancient game of 'Let's pretend'. This 'expert' public, which is fully aware of the mechanism governing the suspension of disbelief, has learnt the rules of the game and knows that the media can lie. To maintain the same level of aesthetic and emotional 'immersion' in a story, this public needs new linguistic stimuli, new games with more complex rules. Even today, however, exactly as in 1938, there is a public which believes the media unconditionally ('lacking critical judgement', as Cantril would say) and does not recognize the boundary between fiction and reality. Media content that questions this boundary, in addition to its main role as provider of good entertainment, has the secondary role of educating (training) a 'naïve' public to recognize the traps of media language.

### Amnésia: radio serial? Fiction? Mockumentary?

*Amnésia* is a radio programme that was aired from 12.10 am to 12.25 am on Rai's Radio2[11] from 8 September 2008 to 31 July 2009 for a total of 235 episodes. The slot in which it was scheduled belonged traditionally to fiction. However, *Amnésia* is not fiction, or rather: it is fictional but it is presented as the narration/diary of a true story:

> "My name is Matteo Caccia. I was born on 8 September 1975. I am thirty-three-years-old. I live in Milan. I don't know if anybody remembers me. I don't. Exactly one year ago I suffered from a global retrograde Amnésia. Basically all my memories were cancelled. Completely. All of a sudden I didn't know who I was, where I was and why I was there. During the course of this year I was able to reconstruct many things, but to all intents and purposes it is as if my life began one year ago. I have worked for Radio2, over the past years. I hosted a summer programme. This is why I said before that maybe somebody remembers me. When the director heard about my story, he asked me to tell the listeners about it. To tell my story live, day by day. Every day I will tell you a little piece of it. It's an incredible story, it's mine, and it's true. I swear it's true. It started on 8 September, one year ago. Since that day, every time for me is the first time".

This was the beginning of the programme. The speaker, Matteo Caccia, began every episode, each one of them, repeating the same words, the same ritual formula.[12]

*Amnésia* could be defined as a radio mockumentary,[13] although this definition would not be entirely correct, due to the fact that the story told by *Amnésia* maintained some elements of truth, as we will see later in the chapter. The programme was structured as a diary, as a first person narration. During the fifteen minutes that the programme was on air the speaker told the story of his personal rediscovery of the world, commented on the day's news, interacted with listeners via text message or e-mail (and less frequently live on the telephone), played music that he was discovering or re-discovering (the music he claimed to have found on his i-pod when he recovered from his Amnésia and which he did not remember). The programme's format was apparently very simple: the only voice listeners would hear was that of the speaker, who took on two different linguistic registers: that of a radio speaker who improvises without a written script, and that of an actor, who interprets a written script – a diary written by the speaker himself – in which he recalled the events (love affairs, travels, discoveries, disappointments) that he went through during the past year of his new life.

## Reality versus fiction in *Amnésia*: the first radio autofiction

As with *The War of the Worlds*, the choice of including extremely realistic elements within a format traditionally labelled as 'fiction' led many listeners to believe unconditionally in the speaker's memory loss, without having to resort to 'suspension of disbelief' as a cognitive resource necessary to enjoy the story. Listening to the first episodes, the more dramatic and enigmatic ones, many members of the audience (as we will see when analysing e-mails sent to the programme), instead of suspending disbelief and enjoying the show, immediately thought that this story just had to be true.

The less 'naïve' public, on the other hand, immediately recognized the artifice, and felt that this was a reason to enjoy the programme:

'The doubt that never leaves listeners and forces them to suspend their judgement on the truthfulness of the story is the programme's main value. […] That's it. We are hooked by the Amnésiac from Corso Sempione[14] and we cannot tear ourselves away'.[15]

In any case, the reality effect given by *Amnésia*'s specific radio language (and, as we shall see below, by its specific use of the internet) is the key element that attracted a cross-section of the public (the 'naive' members of the audience who listened to the programme because they believed it was a true story and the 'expert' listeners who recognized the novelty and experimental nature of the language used and decided to play along). The following linguistic elements contributed to generate the effect of reality:

- the identity of the speaker was the same as that of the main character (as in autofictional literature);
- the programme was broadcast live: it rang true. The speaker/actor made some mistakes;
- not only did the speaker repeat every day that his story was true, but he also swore it was;
- some national newspapers published his story taking for granted that it was true;
- some details of his biography published on the website and on Wikipedia were true (as in autofictional literature);
- some characters were real (i.e.: the voice of his grandmother);
- some sound effects and sound recordings were real;
- there was a kind of ambiguity on what was true and what was false.

Despite the fact that some of these realistic elements were sufficient, so it seems, to make the story believable to the eyes (and especially the ears) of the audience, the programme maintained many fictional elements that should have functioned as signifiers, warning the listener that this programme –no matter how far it had crossed the line into reality – was to all intents and purposes fiction. These were:

- memories being based on written texts and were traditionally dramatized using sound and music effects;
- narrative 'bugs' throughout the plot: a patient and careful listener could easily deduce that the story was false (but radio listening is episodic, it continuously shifts from foreground to background and the attention span of the listener is usually short),[16]
- some details of the speaker's biography being false;
- most of the characters being fictional (however most of them were not actors, but rather 'ordinary' people).

The difference between a TV or cinema mockumentary (a false story told in the form of a documentary) and the innovative elements with reference to this genre, lies in the choice of telling a story which is not entirely true, but also not entirely false. Some memories, some data, some events were authentic, some were not. The boundary between what was real and what was not was hidden to listeners, not to trick them but to further get them involved in the narrative game. The authors of *Amnésia* deliberately chose to create a character with a hybrid biography, partly true and partly false, partly linked to references from the real world and partly without any references to the physical world. The character's name is real (he exists in reality), his date of birth is real, his past as a presenter is real, the places where he was born and raised are real, the voice of his grandmother who occasionally appears on the programme is real. Matteo Caccia exists in the real world and in the world of *Amnésia*: the audience believes it is the same person, but the 'truth' is that they are two different people with many elements in common.

In literature, this narrative strategy has a name: autofiction,[17] a genre of autobiographical account in which the character's life also includes some fictional elements.

The hybridization of reality and fiction turns Matteo Caccia's biographical story into a form of radio autofiction, the first of its kind.

### Attention! *Internet ment*! The continuation of fiction by other means (the web)

A further element of novelty in *Amnésia* was introduced by using new media, and not only radio, to tell the story of Matteo Caccia.

*Amnésia* is a multimedia format in which radio is only the initial medium, the main channel through which the story of the amnesiac is told. From the radio platform, the story lands on the web and its existence continues in other linguistic forms (text blog, photos, videos, comics). The web is a place where the story of *Amnésia* continues beyond the fifteen minutes of live broadcast. The website (www.Amnésia.rai.it) has four main functions. It is:

- a continuation of the radio programme by other means
- an archive for revealing additional information on the identity of the character and his story;
- a living body (the site changes as months go by);
- a 'metamedium', that is, a medium able to *remediate* different media languages. Remediation entails 'the representation of one medium in another', and is 'a defining characteristic of the new digital media.'[18]

The programme's online version, with these characteristics, contributed to reinforce the suspension of disbelief on the part of the listener. The website's homepage is structured as a Polaroid photo album. Each Polaroid links to a section of the website (blog, videos, photos, playlists, biography, illustrations, press review, podcasts, live streaming, webcam). The homepage's aesthetic feel is consistent with the intimacy code chosen as the programme's dominant language, both on air and online. The aesthetics of the Polaroid immediately reference (at least for those who grew up in the years of the mass distribution of the Super8 and Polaroid technologies) the world of memories and of private relations.[19] Images inserted in the Polaroid's white frame take on a higher degree of realism. Once again McLuhan was right: the medium (in this case, the Polaroid) is the message: the Polaroid picture represents a trace of reality, a document that seems to be testifying to the project's truthfulness.

The reality effect in *Amnésia* is the result of a combination of radio realism (obtained by 'contaminating' fiction with real elements such as those outlined above) with the realism of online content.[20] Everyday (or almost every day) the real Matteo Caccia updated the programme's blog, telling another fragment of his new life and of his discoveries, published pictures relating to the stories just told on the radio (creating a sort of serialized photostory), published the videos he shot himself in an amateur style, published the songs he re-discovered on his MP3 player and that belonged to his previous life. The dominant aesthetic code of this content, from photos to videos, is that of the *tranche de vie*: images (photos and videos) are rough, shot in low quality, with equipment that everyone can access (mobile phones), they are not edited, they are short and fragmented, they focus on very small details, their framing is unconventional and 'wrong'. Fragments of 'real' life, lived by the 'real' Matteo, shot from a subjective point of view, in the same way as the narration on the radio is in the first person. The 'grain' of this content mirrors that of family movies, of backstage images, of 'off-air' audio recordings. This 'low-fi' and 'realistic' aesthetic, so far removed from the qualitative standards of content produced by media professionals, is in actual fact an aesthetic which was affected and especially designed to conform to the language of intimacy that was the format's fundamental framework.

## Letters to *Amnésia*

Over the course of *Amnésia*'s 235 episodes, from September 2008 to July 2009, the editorial staff received approximately 2600 e-mails (on average, eleven per episode). Excluding those who wrote more than once and e-mail exchanges between the presenter and listeners, there were approximately 1200 individuals who wrote at least once to the programme (that represents 0.35% of the programme's average audience). The series of emails considered for this study consists of 176 messages sent by single listeners.

The choice of which emails to analyse was made on the basis of one criterion: the only e-mails taken into consideration were those that dealt, explicitly or implicitly, with the dialectics 'true/false' or more colloquially, 'I believe in it' / 'I do not believe in it' / 'It does not matter'. The 176 e-mails analysed all share one other feature: they were all written spontaneously by listeners. Each one of these e-mails shows the desire, on the part of listeners, to introduce themselves and tell the speaker how much they admire and respect him, their feelings of empathy, and nothing else. The rest of the e-mails, the majority of which were left out of this study, on the other hand include various types of messages, differing greatly from each other: letters simply saying how much they enjoy the show, letters expressing critical views, requests for technical information (names of songs being aired, ways to download podcasts, reports of errors on the website) and comments on themes launched by the presenter during the episodes.

An initial quantitative analysis shows that of the 176 e-mails examined, 102 (58% of the total, of whom 42% were men and 58% women) were written by people who believed that the story being told by Matteo was true; 9 (5% of the total, of whom 33% men and 67% women) by people who claimed that they did not believe in it; 12 by people who were not able to tell if it was true or not (7% of the total, divided into 44% men and 56% cent women); and finally 53 (30% of the total, of whom 35% per cent were men and 64% women) were written by people arguing that it did not matter if the story were true or false.

Although from February 2009 onwards the number of listeners claiming that it was no longer important to assess the story's truthfulness grew, while the number of e-mails by listeners asking the speaker whether his story was true decreased, the fact remains that 58% of emails analysed came from people who believed in Matteo's story and were not aware that the programme was fictional.[21]

## 'I believe in it'

Among the e-mails that express belief in the speaker's amnesia, a large percentage (57 out of 102, that is 54%) was sent by people who felt the urge to write simply because Matteo's story generated a feeling of empathy in them: these listeners wished to tell Matteo that they felt close to him in terms of age, culture or sensitivity, and that they were deeply sorry that someone who was so 'similar' to them could have forgotten everything:

> "[t]he music, the intonation of your voice, your words, your story: I totally identify with you, even though I have never experienced anything similar. Vale." (19 September 2008)

"[m]y name is Denis Gheller, I live in the province of Reggio Emilia. At the end of April 2008 I lost my memory. After a couple of months I recovered it. When you tell us about your experience I see many similarities with my own. Many things have changed now. I have a different outlook on the things that happen to me. [...] Well done. Yours sincerely, Denis." (11 September 2008)

Thirty-seven e-mails, on the other hand, were written in response to a need, on the part of listeners, to express their respect/admiration for the way in which Matteo was reacting to his memory loss:

"My name is Fabio and I live in a small town called Adria [...]. You have all my respect and I wish you all the best in rebuilding your life. If I could, I would help you with pleasure. [...] You experienced important emotions in the past. Don't give up! You will experience new and equally important ones [in the future]. Yours affectionately, Fabio." (12 September 2008)

"My name is Elena and I am 27 [...]. I admire your courage and your strength. I will keep on listening and learning. You can always learn something from the strength of others." (25 September 2008)

"I am an occasional listener. Sometimes I happen to listen to your programme and I am moved. For a reason that is different from yours (mine is called bipolar syndrome) I also had to reconsider my entire life. I understand you. I believe that your programme, aside from being "awesome" is also therapeutic, not only for you but also for those who have to come to terms with themselves." (25 February 2009)

About a dozen emails express the listeners' curiosity about memory loss:

"I would like to ask you a thousand questions. Do you remember how to drive a car? Who Valentino Rossi is? How to tie your laces? How to make love? Yours, Marco." (23 September 2008)

Six e-mails were written by listeners who would somehow like to help Matteo, such as the message by this woman:

"I am almost sixty and I am touched by the thought of the difficulties you had to go through, and by the thought of your mother. I could be your mother. On Friday I am going on a pilgrimage to Santiago de Compostela. Please allow me to pray for you, and all the best in recovering everything that you care about. Alessandra." (10 September 2008)

## 'I do not believe in it'

'Non-believers' can be divided into those who immediately understood that the programme was fictional and appreciated the idea (the minority):

> "You are making a great programme: a modern day Candide. Anyway, I think that your story is as true as the fact that Manzoni found the original Sixteenth Century manuscript of the *Promessi Sposi*. A great idea, in any case. Andrea." (22 October 2008)

There were many (more) who initially believed in the story and later found out from other sources that it was not true. They were not responsible for this discovery, so they felt cheated. The interesting thing is that these listeners accepted fiction on other media, but not on the radio:

> "I might be naive, but I believed you. Now I read on Vanity Fair that you leave room for doubt. For us it wasn't like going to the theatre. We didn't know that it was fiction. I believed in it and now I feel cheated. Have I been listening to a radio drama for all these months? Well done. Angela." (17 April 2009)

> "Dear Matteo, I just read on Repubblica's Venerdì that the story you've been telling could be fictional. I am really astonished. I had been discussing this with my husband. According to him, it was increasingly clear that the story was fake. From my experience, I could see some fictional elements, but I believed you. I can tolerate artistic fiction in various areas: literature, theatre, comics, but it should always be openly stated, never denied. This discovery disappoints me and makes me question the programme's quality. Well done, *actor*. Maria." (4 May 2009)

## 'I can't tell'

In this category we find those listeners who are still in doubt, but have started to appreciate the programme beyond the true/not true question:

> "Now, I don't know if all this is real or fictional. If it's real [...] I understand what you feel, but look on the bright side: you can get rid of all the baggage we carry around due to apathy, boredom, laziness. If it's not: you're a genius, not for what you're telling us, but because you leave it to us to decide [whether or not it's true]. Regards and [...] re-live your new life! Maurizio." (8 October 2008)

"I don't know if your story is real or not. All I know is that I would also like to lose my memory so that I can forget all the pain and disappointments. Francesco." (12 January 2009)

"I can't tell if your Amnésia is real or just a great idea for a great radio programme. [...] In any case I appreciate the fact that the public service broadcasting offers us ideas that promote unconventional thought. Dina." (25 September 2008)

## 'It doesn't matter'

Listeners belonging to this category understood that the programme was fictional, but they grew attached to the story in itself and took pleasure in listening to it: they went beyond the phase in which it was important to know if the story was true or not to enjoy it fully. These are the 'model' listeners, those who have understood the game and its rules, and have decided to play along:

"Congratulations for the new Radio2 radio drama. The radio diary idea is brilliant, and the context really innovative: the live broadcast, the main actor hosting the show as if it were a live programme, the playlist. I am sure this is just a radio drama, but after all it doesn't matter. Well done for now. A faithful listener." (9 September 2008)

"Hi Matteo. When you start telling your story, I am finishing my piano lessons. [...] Thank you for this programme. I don't ask myself if your Amnésia is real or not, because it's none of my business, I just listen to your story and I am happy to do so. Patrizia." (4 November 2008)

"I don't know if what you're telling us really happened, but even if it is all made up I am moved by the mere sound of your voice. Thank you. Love, Chicca." (2 March 2009)

"You gave me the chills! Today's episode was strange, bizarre, original. Mind-blowing! [...] It doesn't matter how true what you're saying is: you describe it well and for a few minutes you make us feel real emotions. That is already a lot! Have a nice day, Elena." (11 March 2009)

"I wanted to thank you, because by describing your experience the way you do, whether it is all true or false, you are teaching those who listen to you to live fully, with curiosity and with a real love for life. You teach people to see life with hungry eyes, in a world where it's easy to close your eyes and accept what you are given. Dario." (7 April 2009)

## The last episode

On 31 July 2009, the 235th and final episode of *Amnésia* went on air. In the last 15 of the programme's total 3525 minutes, the identity of Matteo Caccia the radio presenter was separated forever from the identity of the Matteo Caccia who lost his memory. The game that saw the overlapping of two identities – one real and one fictional – was finally revealed:

> "Is this story true? No. It's not true. I never lost my memory. I never suffered from Amnésia, but yes, I am Matteo Caccia and I am not that different from the person I've been telling you about."

These were the words the programme's authors used to shatter the illusion that allowed some listeners to suspend their disbelief and admit the show's fictional nature. Listeners reacted immediately: during the last 15 minutes of the programme, about sixty text messages (80% of which were congratulating and thanking the authors for the show's ingenuity) were sent; within two hours, the blog received around twenty posts (in this case too, 80% were in favour of the idea, even though the confession came as a surprise). Over the next two days the programme received approximately fifty e-mails. Only four of them openly condemned the programme for being false. The following example is the angriest one (its subject line read: 'SHAME ON YOU!'). It continued:

> "[…] And instead I let myself be duped by your lie, by your well-constructed, well-written and well-interpreted super-story, which in the end turned out to be, as usual, a SUPER-SPOOF!! What a fool I was. A real fool. However this fool, together with many others I think, in future will beware of people like you and probably of others who are not nearly as dishonest (I mean from a radio production, as well as intellectual and human point of view, of course) as you are." (Paolo, 31 July 2009)

These listeners (less conversant with media grammar) were compelled to follow the show only by their curiosity for the story's truthfulness. Their interest was of a morbid nature. They experienced real emotions while listening and the discovery of the story's falseness disappointed and hurt them because they felt tricked.

Although initially many listeners were driven to follow the show by their interest for a true story, it is also true that during the course of the programme many of these listeners started to be less concerned with the question of the story's truthfulness and began to simply enjoy the story and the quality of the radio show.

With the exclusion of this minority, the majority of letters can be divided into two categories:

(1) Those from listeners who had already sensed that the story was not true, but had decided to play along anyway, to suspend their disbelief, in order to enjoy the story:

"even though I had begun to see through your story, I was a bit sorry to hear you say that it was all false [...] but anyway, did it really matter? it was a pretext, a good story that after all contained more truth than many other "admissions"[...] thanks again, it has been wonderful! Have a nice summer, especially Matteo (both of them)! Laura."

"True or false, it doesn't really matter. A good story for grown ups, and I really needed it [...] Thanks also for the great playlists [...] Roberto Vaccari, 44-years-old, Modena. I swear it's true!"

These listeners made up the audience's more media-literate section, the programme's 'ideal' public, who were able to enjoy the game of seeing the world as if it was the first time, through Matteo Caccia's character and radio style, as well as the show's sound track.

(2) Those by listeners who believed the story until the end and were surprised by the final revelation. The majority of them, however, appreciated the game and admitted that this revelation did not spoil their enjoyment of the show:

"Dear Matteo,
We finally got to the end and I must confess to you that I even cried, although it's not that hard to make me cry because I cry easily. I was convinced that the memory loss was real, but unlike my husband, who was a bit upset, and my sister, who was also a bit upset, after all I don't care that much. In fact, I think that it must have been quite hard to identify with the character, and that you must have had to do lots of research on this topic. My daughter had some doubts actually. Anyway, the programme was great and the music wonderful. So who cares if it was true or false?" (Betta)

"Today you sent a shiver down our spines [...] when you said "no, it's not true" we thought: "BASTARD!! He tricked us!!!". But then we thought about it and we decided that you are a genius. No, a master [...] Regards, Cecilia and Claudio."

"Well Matteo, your illusion worked really well.
    We listeners had doubts, but we let ourselves be carried away by this new and original journey. Initially I said to myself: "if I find out that it's all false I'll go and find him and punch his face"; today however, after a few seconds of disappointment, I am realising how excellent this programme was and I am still appreciating its sheer genius. Davide."

## Conclusion

Seventy years have gone by since Orson Welles' experiment. The world has changed. The world of media has changed. Radio, the twentieth century's oldest medium, is making way for new media. Those who live in technologically advanced societies have to come to terms with a media-saturated world, with a prismatic reality. The real world is often experienced as being mediated by different forms of communication and languages. Never before have we had so many opportunities to access distant realities: satellite channels that bring the world to our homes, websites in which we can read the *New Yorker*'s latest edition, blogs that update us on the situation in Iran, thousands of amateur videos and a host of information by private citizens. In a world in which tales of reality are so plentiful, reality, the un-mediated one, paradoxically risks extinction: we run the risk of finding ourselves in a de-realized world, a world from which reality has been subtracted, only to be re-channelled on the screens that, to varying degrees, have conquered our habitat. 'What mass communications offer us is not reality, but the *dizziness* of reality'.[22] Baudrillard's intuition is even truer today, in the age of electronic reproduction. The life of 'seclusion' lived by postmodernity's inhabitants, trapped by the limited horizons of their private lives, is only apparently 'freed' by the 'window on the world' offered by the media.[23] The greatest risk is that this window – this electronic simulacrum of the world (full of 'reality effects') – ends up by being considered truer than the truth, more real than reality. This risk has always existed, since media were first invented. It existed in Welles' time, when one American out of six believed what they were hearing on the radio rather than what they were seeing out of their (non-electronic) window, and it is even more relevant today, in a world in which media content increasingly enhances daily life experiences, in which media are multiplying and are being contaminated with each other and in which media languages have become more sophisticated. *Amnésia*'s example teaches us that not much has changed since Welles' time: media still play a fundamental role in shaping and influencing the public's beliefs. In the case of *Amnésia*, an analysis of e-mails – although conclusions cannot be generalized to the programme's entire public – reveals that more than half the people who wrote to the programme had believed in the story's truthfulness. At the same time, as Mauro Wolf stressed in relation to the case of *The War of the Worlds*,[24] the public is not a shapeless mass that responds in a mechanical way to media stimuli.

As with *The War of the Worlds*, in this case, too, differences in character, psychology and culture have been crucial in the interpretation, decoding and enjoyment of *Amnésia*. The final confession of the story's falseness was an act of honesty on the part of the authors towards 'naive' listeners who, if they had lived in New York in 1938, would have believed that aliens were really landing. The admission of the fictional nature of Matteo Caccia's story takes on, indirectly, an educational value for that section of the public which is by now accustomed to (and McLuhan would say 'narcotized by') the media's reality: no, electronic media, by their very nature, can be tampered with, modified, reproduced and falsified. The objective of Welles and *Amnésia* was merely to entertain in an intelligent, new and surprising manner, to put on a good show, to produce good fiction. *Amnésia*, in particular, demonstrated that it was possible to update the traditional language of radio serials, adapting it to a new media context. Both did so by using the means they had at their disposal in an innovative fashion. The majority of their listeners, luckily, enjoyed the programmes for what they were – a fictional product. Others, with lower 'defence' mechanisms in terms of media grammar, took them incredibly seriously. The unforeseen effect of these two experiments, in a world teeming with 'media truths' and 'media illiterates', was to teach that media, all media, can lie. Parisian students already understood this in May 1968. However, every period probably needs its own May 1968.

## Notes

1. Orson Welles in P. Mereghetti, *Il cinema secondo Orson Welles*, SNCCI 1977.
2. P. Noble, 'I Marziani sono tra noi!', in *L'Europeo*, 1959, n. 23.
3. T. Crook T., *Radio drama: Theory and practice*, London and NY: Routledge, 1999, pp. 111–12.
4. See H. Cantril, *The invasion from Mars: A study in the psychology of panic*. Princeton, NJ: Princeton University Press, 1940. Cantril analysed the 1400 letters mailed to CBS in the days after the radio drama was broadcast, establishing that only 9% of them openly condemned the network.
5. The Munich conference was held on 29 and 30 September 1938 among the heads of the government of Great Britain, France, Germany and Italy. The conference's objective was to discuss, shortly before the Second World War, Germany's claims over a portion of Czechoslovakia inhabited by the Sudeten Germans and culminated in the Munich agreement, which lead to a de facto annexation of Czechoslovakia to Germany.
6. The theory according to which the realistic register chosen by Welles had an important role in 'tricking' the audience beyond the historical, social and political context of the time is confirmed by the fact that *The War of the Worlds* was aired by other national broadcasters, in different cultural contexts and historical periods, generating similar effects among the public: 'In the rare 1970 publication *The Panic Broadcast: the whole story of Orson Welles' legendary radio show*, Howard Koch [the scriptwriter who worked on the radio drama's adaptation together with Welles], describes the story of a radio production group in Quito, Ecuador, who appropriated the play, translated it into Spanish and broadcasted it on 12 February 1949. Thousands of listeners in Quito fled into the streets to escape Martians. The *New York Times* (14 February 1949) claimed that a mob burned down the radio station, killing fifteen people inside. A broadcast of the *War of the Worlds* script in Santiago, Chile, on 12 November 1944 is alleged to have caused many listeners to run into the streets' (T. Crook, op. cit., pp. 113–14).
7. The image of a radio listener who is engrossed in a programme from the beginning to the end is an ideal one, a utopia created by radio authors. In fact, radio is a medium that is listened to in a distracted, discontinuous, temporary manner, frequently while carrying out other activities.
8. Crook, op. cit., p. 109.
9. This writing appeared for the first time on the walls of Paris in May 1968. For an analysis of the role of radio during uprisings in Paris in May 1968, see T. Bonini, 'Revolution will not be televised: la rivoluzione raccontata via radio, da Parigi a Città del Messico' in S. Casilio and L. Guerrieri (eds) *Il '68 diffuso*, Bologna: Clueb, 2009.

10. The suspension of disbelief is a voluntary suspension, on the part of the reader/viewer/listener, of critical judgement in order to enjoy a work of fiction. It was Samuel Taylor Coleridge who formulated this concept for the first time: '... it was agreed, that my endeavours should be directed to persons and characters supernatural, or at least romantic; yet so far as to transfer from our inward nature a human interest and a semblance of truth sufficient to procure for these shadows of imagination that willing suspicion or disbelief for the moment, which constitutes poetic faith'. In S. T. Coleridge, *Biographia literaria* (1817), Princeton University Press, 1985, vol. 2, p. 6.

11. Radio2 Rai is the second Italian public radio station. While the first channel offers mainly news programmes and the third broadcasts cultural programmes and debate, Radio2 focuses on entertainment and is more openly in competition with private commercial networks. Its average audience is 3.9 million listeners a day and it is the sixth most popular channel in Italy (Audiradio, first two months of 2009). In particular *Amnésia*, according to Audiradio data, during the time in which it was broadcast had on average an audience of 380,000 listeners everyday and an average share of around 6% (Audiradio, first two months of 2009), almost doubling its audience compared to the previous season.

12. Over time, the introduction was increasingly cut to include only the essential information.

13. A *mockumentary* is a film and television genre. The mockumentary is presented as a documentary recording real life, but it is actually fictional. The term 'mockumentary' is thought to have first appeared in the mid-1980s when *This Is Spinal Tap* director Rob Reiner used it in interviews to describe his film.

14. Corso Sempione is where the Italian public radio's building is located in Milan. This is where *Amnésia* was broadcast from.

15. B. Gambarotta, 'Lo smemorato di Corso Sempione', in *La Stampa*, 10 September 2008, p. 36.

16. Some listeners actually noticed the 'bugs' in the story: "I was in New York almost exactly a year ago, and there was no snow whatsoever. Damn, I was so moved by your story, and it also made me think of my son who is your age and has been living in NY for some years. It is no doubt a good story, but you can tell me that it is not really true. Cristina" (30 December 2008). In this case, the listener is referring to Matteo's account of his life in New York: the speaker had said that a year before (December 2007) there was snow in New York; however, this was not true.

17. Coined by Serge Doubrovsky in 1977 with reference to his novel *Fils*, the term 'autofiction' refers to a form of fictionalized autobiography. Autofiction combines two paradoxically contradictory styles: that of autobiography and fiction. An author may decide to recount his/her life in the third person, to modify significant details or 'characters', using fiction as a way to search for Self. It has parallels with *faction*, a genre devised by Truman Capote to describe his novel *In Cold Blood*. Autofiction is primarily a genre associated with contemporary French authors such as Guillaume Dustan, Alice Ferney, Annie Ernaux, Olivia Rosenthal, Anne Wiazemsky and Vassilis Alexakis. Catherine Millet's 2002 memoir *The Sexual Life of Catherine M.* famously used autofiction to explore the author's sexual experiences http://en.wikipedia.org/wiki/Autofiction, accessed 18 July 2009). See also G. Bouillier, *Rapporto su me stesso: Racconto di un'infanzia felice*, Roma, ISBN Ed., 2009.

18. J. D. Bolter and R. Grusin, *Remediation*, Cambridge, MA: MIT Press 1999, p. 45.

19. Those who, like Matteo Caccia, were children at the end of the 1970s share with him a 'mediatized' past made of Super8 films and Polaroid pictures depicting their childhood. In this respect, then, *Amnésia* is a generational programme that captures the life of a man (and of a generation) born in the 1970s.

20. Separate reference should be made to the Wikipedia page devoted to the entry 'Matteo Caccia'. A false biography for 'Matteo Caccia' was deliberately added by the authors to the online encyclopaedia the day the programme started. Listeners who were in doubt regarding the story's authenticity and

wanted to check its truthfulness on the Web would have found a real Wikipedia page devoted to Matteo Caccia, former Radio2 speaker who suffered from a form of global retrograde Amnésia. The fact that Wikipedia confirmed the story told by Matteo Caccia on the radio was sufficient proof of its authenticity for many listeners: "I didn't know whether to believe your story or not, but then I found out that Wikipedia confirmed everything and from then on I no longer had any doubts" (e-mail by Francesco, 11 September 2008). Wikipedia, despite its status as a medium that can be easily manipulated, contributed significantly to the suspension of judgement on the part of the listeners. In the same way as the more critical listeners of Welles' radio drama had attempted to check other sources (other radio stations or the opinion of friends and family) before they put aside their doubts regarding the authenticity of the Martian landing, the more 'expert' and critical listeners of *Amnésia* used the Web, before newspapers or other sources, to check the programme's truthfulness. Few among these, once the story was confirmed, dared to question even the Web. However, Wikipedia's open source nature prevailed: a few days after the beginning of the programme some of the more sceptical listeners had already modified Wikipedia's page on Matteo Caccia adding that 'alternative sources claim that this story is not real'. The authors, aware of the game being played with listeners, allowed the page to be modified without further interventions.

21. This figure cannot be applied generally to the programme's entire audience. From it we can only deduce that 10% of the listeners who wrote to *Amnésia* over time (and thus 0.35% of its average public) maintained or showed that they believed in the story's truthfulness.

22. J. Baudrillard, *La società dei consumi* (*The Consumer Society*) (1970), Bologna, Il Mulino, 2008, p. 15. On this theme see also J. Baudrillard, *Il delitto perfetto: La televisione ha ucciso la realtà?* (*The Perfect Crime*), Milano: Cortina, 1996.

23. 'Living a cloistered everyday life would be unbearable without a simulacrum of the world, without the alibi of participating in the world' (Baudrillard, op. cit., p. 16).

24. M. Wolf, postscript to O. Welles, *La Guerra dei mondi*, Bologna: Baskerville, 1990, p. 169.

## References and further reading

Baudrillard J., *La società dei consumi* (1970), Bologna: Il Mulino, 2008.

Bolter J. D. & Grusin R., *Remediation*. Cambridge, MA: MIT Press, 1999.

Bonini T., 'Revolution will not be televised: la rivoluzione raccontata via radio, da Parigi a Città del Messico", in S. Casilio and L. Guerrieri (a cura di), *Il '68 diffuso*, Bologna: Clueb, 2009.

Cantril H., *The invasion from Mars: A study in the psychology of panic*. Princeton, NJ: Princeton University Press, 1940.

Coleridge S. T., *Biographia literaria* (1817), Princeton University Press, 1985, vol. 2.

Crook T., *Radiodrama: Theory and practice*. Londra e NY: Routledge, 1999.

Gambarotta B., 'Lo smemorato di Corso Sempione', in *La Stampa*, 10 September 2008.

Koch H., *The panic broadcast: The whole story of Orson Welles' legendary radio show*, Avon (ed.), 1970.

Noble, Peter, 'I Marziani sono tra noi!', in 'L'Europeo', 1959, n. 23.

Welles O., in P. Mereghetti (a cura di), *Il cinema secondo Orson Welles*, Roma, SNCCI 1977.

Welles O., *La Guerra dei mondi*, Bologna: Baskerville, 1990.

http://en.wikipedia.org/wiki/Autofiction.
http://www.audiradio.it.
http://www.Amnésia.rai.it.
http://it.wikipedia.org/wiki/Matteo_Caccia.

**Chapter 7**

Radio and the Web: Analysis of the News Strategies of the Spanish Talk Radio Networks, 2008-9

Elsa Moreno, Maria del Pilar Martinez-Costa and Avelino Amoedo

The development of online radio has given rise to innovative news tendencies, proposals and uses. The news continuity of traditional broadcasting – an essential part of generalist talk radio – can be enhanced and updated with the news found on a radio station's website, that is, through the communication strategy conceived and produced on the internet, while simultaneously growing in social penetration and becoming a clear reference point for current affairs in most societies. However, talk radio networks in Spain have different online news tactics. In some cases indeed, the news presence is created on a very limited basis in spite of the fact that Spanish radio is showing growing interest in the internet. The aim of this study is to carry out a quantitative and qualitative analysis of the communication strategies of the Spanish talk radio channels – SER, COPE, Onda Cero, Punto Radio and Radio Nacional – on the web, in order to give a precise description and clearly identify how they are presented.

To do so, during the 2008–09 radio period, we carried out a comparative tracking of the main pages of the websites www.cadenaser.com, www.cope.es, www.ondacero.es, www.puntoradio.com and www.rtve.es, between 12 noon and 2 p.m. on 12 December 2008, 24 April 2009 and 4 June 2009. This time-slot was chosen as it is the moment of transition and evaluation of the news produced during the morning which, therefore, all talk radio stations must undertake. In all, forty-five samples – nine per station – were evaluated, at the times of the news bulletins and the 12 noon news programme.

For each of these forty-five captures, a content analysis form was used that included, among others, the evolution of the four elements in the study. They are as follows:

- the *number of news items* that each radio station offered to the listener on the homepage of its website;
- the *type of story or the news issue* to which it corresponded;
- the *multimedia and narrative handling* of the three main news items on the homepage, that is, the sources used, the number of words used in the headline and the text; whether sound, photographs, videos, other graphic elements, links or associated documents were used;
- the *interactive web techniques* which were available to the user, such as the possibility of adding comments on a news story or of sharing it, of showing personal interest in the news content or of consulting its popularity among the channel's listeners.

Also, in order to verify if there is a synergy in the communication strategies of the Spanish talk radio stations online and in traditional broadcasting, this study considered the main stories on the news bulletins at 12 noon and 1 p.m., and the headlines of the noon news programmes on the radio stations SER – *Hora 14*, COPE – *La palestra*, Onda Cero – *Noticias mediodía*, Punto Radio – *Primera plana* and Radio Nacional – *14 Horas*. That is to say, we have also evaluated forty-five sound samples from traditional broadcasting. A wider analysis of the news programmes on this platform at the times chosen will allow us to identify the channels which use convergent news tactics on both platforms.[1] This paper gives further information on the line of research the authors have worked on over the last three years, and deals with the communication strategies of the talk and music radios on the web. In addition, it examines similar lines of research by other authors from a Spanish perspective.[2]

At present, the quality and innovation of the news offer on Spanish radio is a relevant issue in our multimedia society, where the medium of radio has lost its exclusive characteristic of news immediacy when compared with the web. The conclusions of this study will show just how important the channels SER, COPE, Onda Cero, Punto Radio and Radio Nacional consider the internet to be the platform which will permit them to find a new niche and improve their news coverage, and to increase their dialogue with the listener with the intention of offering an ever better service. The following are the results of the analysis, which show the challenges faced by Spanish talk radio on the web, among which is the need to improve their news strategies and work dynamics – the production, editing, and up-dating of online news, and its convergence with the programmes and tasks of traditional news services.

### The number of news items on the online homepage

The comparative analysis of the news content of these broadcasters online confirms the different strategies each broadcaster has adopted on this platform; this evolution has been studied previously.[3] The news option is reflected in the number of news items and special reports –the two main news formats– which each of the channels offers to its online public. This even includes direct coverage of exceptional events, such as, for example, the speech given by the US President Barack Obama at Cairo University on 4 June 2009.

SER provided a consistent news follow-up on the internet and presented approximately thirty news items on its homepage at the times the samples were taken. The main news stories were more developed in the second and third samples, including special reports and coverage. The permanent sections – Politics, International, Economy, Culture and Society, Technology and Sport – always include three headlines which are later developed on the corresponding pages. Meanwhile, COPE has increased the number of news items on its homepage – from twenty items in December 2008 to twenty-two items in April and June 2009 – and gives greater depth to its news presence by incorporating and emphasizing regional and local news, and also sports, on its homepage. This online news edition still uses the layout of two main items and three headlines on national and international news on the top of the homepage, three local items and four sports items in the central section, and ten highlighted headlines in 'The Latest/Most Watched/Most Listened/Most Commented/Most Shared'. However, there were fewer special reports in April and June 2009 than in December 2008.

The main website of Radiotelevisión Española, on the other hand, has presented approximately twelve news stories per sampled day in the 2008–09 season. The subject matter is divided into two main sections: 'News' and 'Sports'. This content is shown together with others that advertise the national public TV and radio channel programmes. By contrast, www.ondacero.es offers a small number of news items on its homepage: an average of four or five news items of a total ten or twelve main stories. Despite the fact that the title 'In the News' is above the main news items, it is placed about halfway down the page, and the mishmash with suggestions for other productions from its radio programmes makes it difficult to identify the most relevant news contents. Promos of programmes and the channel brand are very noticeable, and these items are structured and presented on the page layout jumbled with the news headlines. Finally, the news strategy on Punto Radio online is very limited. This channel only puts two news headlines on its homepage and it gives more importance to its main programme content.

If we compare the number of news items that each channel offers on the internet in the samples at the time of the main news programme (2 p.m.), we find that the quantity has remained unchanged between December 2008 and June 2009.

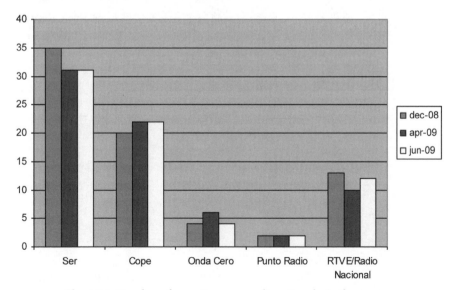

**14:00 hours**

**Chart 7.1:** Number of news items per radio network. Authors own

So we can conclude that this offer responds to a news strategy which was adopted earlier in relation to the design of each website and of the remaining permanent contents. Thus the news criterion does not determine the number of news items to be included on the homepages.

**Subject matter**

The news content offer of the talk radio networks on the internet gives great importance to news on politics, economy and society/culture; and COPE, SER and Radiotelevisión Española also value Sports news. In addition, the Punto Radio website emphasizes news on the economy, as can be seen in Charts 7.2, 7.3 and 7.4.

### 14:00 hours - 12 December 2008

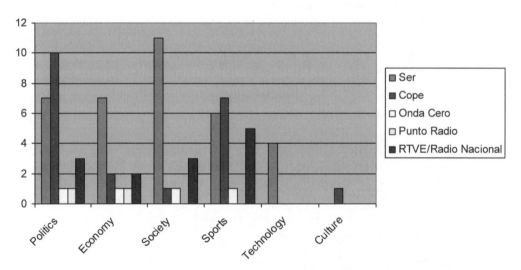

**Chart 7.2:** News content offer per radio network. Authors own

**14:00 hours - 24 April 2009**

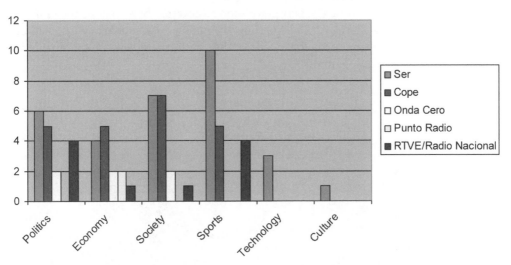

**Chart 7.3:** News content offer per radio network. Authors own

**14:00 hours - 4 Jun 2009**

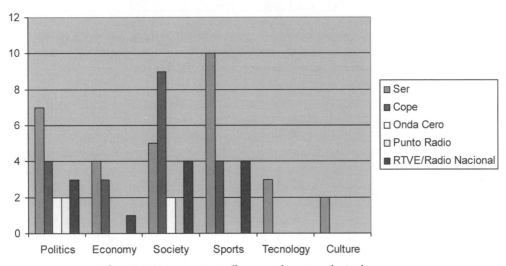

**Chart 7.4:** News content offer per radio network. Authors own

The increased interest in international news is greater when covering exceptional news events, such as the above-mentioned speech by the US President Barack Obama at Cairo University on 4 June 2009, which was given widespread coverage by all the channels on their websites. The following charts, 7.5 and 7.6, show the number of national and international news per radio networks at 2 p.m., the broadcast time of the main news programme in the Spanish talk radio schedule at midday.

**14:00 hours**

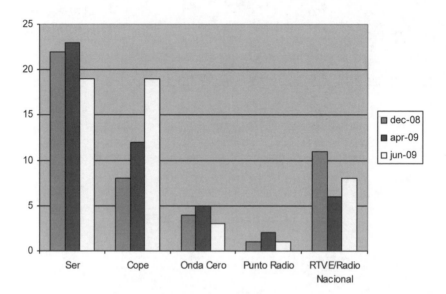

**Chart 7.5:** National news per network. Authors own

**14:00 hours**

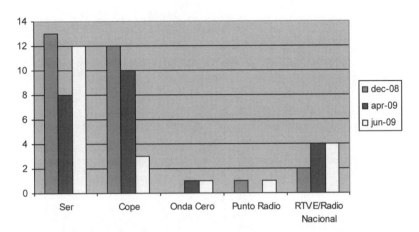

**Chart 7.6:** International news per network. Authors own

The subject matter tactics of the radio networks have changed over the course of the 2008–09 period, as shown in charts 7.7, 7.8 and 7.9. The particular news editorial strategies on the different networks have left their mark on certain topics. SER has increased its Sports coverage, to the detriment of news on society and the economy (chart 7.7).

**Cadena SER - 14:00 hours**

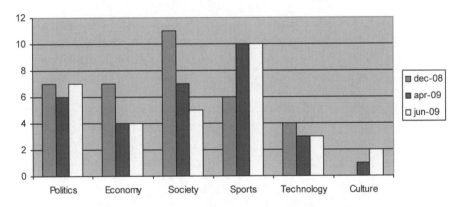

**Chart 7.7:** News topics evolution. Authors own

COPE, however, has boosted the number of society stories, and reduced its political coverage (chart 7.8).

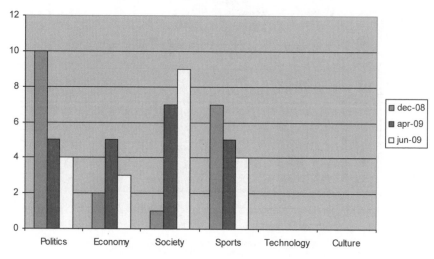

**Chart 7.8:** News topics evolution. Authors own

Finally, for www.rtve.es, there is also a significant rise in 'society' items while the amounts of coverage of sport and the economy has remained constant (chart 7.9).

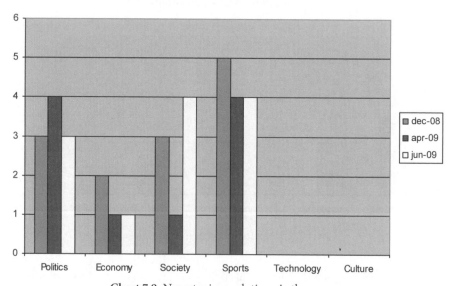

**Chart 7.9:** News topics evolution. Authors own

In addition to the subject matter observed, the analysis reveals that the SER and COPE homepages present a series of news items from their own sources, and pay more attention to these than to other news. And on SER, there is special coverage for the web. An example of this is the 12 December 2008 headline: 'Iberia Pilots, Work-to-rule Causes Cancellations' on www.cadenaser.com. COPE also uses its own productions on the web. For example, the headline 'Defense tried to break up soldiers' rally against Law on Careers' (4 June 2009).

## Updating of news contents

In general we have found that there is little news updating considering the means available online, both for the addition of breaking news and the renewal of the news articles. This means that the Spanish talk radio news strategy does not make the most of the updating opportunities offered by the internet. And the renewal of texts and other news content online is decided by the pace of work in each newsroom. On this point, we have seen the specific web-news broadcasting strategies for each channel.

For SER, the changes in news content are fewer online than on the airwaves. The topics on the homepage were unchanged during the three hours analysed with some rotation in the order of presentation, and there is an appreciable development of the news as the morning goes by. Naturally, breaking news alerts are an exception, as they have their own space when published and do not affect the other web content. At COPE, the updating of web news content also depends on what is broadcast on the air. The www.cope.es homepage quite frequently renewed the three main items during the period analysed. However, in general, the writing of the homepage headlines does not vary, even when there is new data on the topics dealt with. On www.rtve.es we also find an effort to update the news, although this is after the traditional broadcast. The public corporation puts out quite a few pieces referring to the main news item, and uploads the videos and audiocuts produced by its TV and radio channels, particularly from Radio Nacional. As for Onda Cero and Punto Radio, their news updating is much slower and there was very little change during the observation period.

## Synergy with traditional radio

The channels studied are evolving towards news coverage that is coherent and simultaneous on the traditional platform and online. The comparative analysis reveals a growing synergy between the criteria for selection and evaluation of the news offered to the listener on both platforms. The radio continues to be a clear reference point for news for this kind of broadcasting, which sees the web as a secondary platform that depends on the changes on the noon news bulletins and news programmes. As the morning goes by, the news offered on the airwaves and online by Cadena SER is more alike. At noon, urgency and breaking news are given precedence on the radio, and only a few of the topics, in a different order, coincide with the web offer. However, at 1 p.m., the news bulletin reflects the editorial criterion of the Cadena SER newsroom and leads the main news service called 'Hora 14.00' at 2 p.m. At this time, the main topic is frequently the same on the radio and on the internet, but is dealt with in a very different way, consistent with the narrative style of each platform.

The main news items on the COPE website at noon, 1 p.m. and 2 p.m. do not coincide with the main items on the radio news bulletins. Nevertheless, this channel is advancing towards greater news convergence between the radio and the web as can be seen in the 2009 samples in comparison with those of 12 December 2008. The selection and evaluation criteria for news items tend to be less divergent, although the radio is considered of greater importance. In general, the news edition on the COPE website stems from its traditional broadcasting content. So, after the corresponding news bulletin, some of the main online items are updated.

As for the Radiotelevisión Española/Radio Nacional website, there is a noticeable similarity between the three main topics on its homepage and the Radio Nacional news bulletins. For example, on 24 April, both the web and the radio treatment of the data on unemployment in the first three months of the year coincide. On other occasions, such as the sample for 4 June 2009, the web was ahead of the radio in its approach to the day's main stories: before noon, the web gave advance news on Barack Obama's speech in Cairo, and the speech itself was available live on www.rtve.es, and could be listened to on Radiotelevisión Española's *Canal 24 Horas*. Later, this was the first item on the 1 p.m. news bulletin and the 2 p.m. news programme began with this topic.

As for the headlines on the homepage of Punto Radio, there is also a certain harmony between the online edition of the news and its noon news programme, *Primera plana*. Normally, the online headlines are the main news items on the radio, although occasionally they do not coincide in the opening item. On Onda Cero, however, we find less synergy between the web news content and that of the radio, and the radio broadcasts are more up to date. Certain radio programmes – particularly the morning magazine *Herrera en la Onda* – are hung on the web after being broadcast. This is the case for the sample taken on 4 June where only the first three news items coincide on the web homepage and the radio news bulletins: the Obama speech in Cairo. The remaining items are different. Table 7.1 shows a comparison of the first three news items online and on the radio channels at 2 p.m. on 4 June 2009.

Table 7.1: The three main news items on the web and on traditional radio at 12 noon, 1 p.m. and 2 p.m.

*June 4 2009*

| | SER | | COPE | | Onda Cero | | Punto Radio | | Radio Nacional | |
|---|---|---|---|---|---|---|---|---|---|---|
| | *Web* | *Traditional Radio* | *Web* | *Traditional Radio* | *Web* | *Traditional Radio* | *Web* | *Traditional Radio* | *Web* | *Traditional Radio* |
| **At noon** | Odyssey must return treasure found in Portugal to Spain. Gaza will hear Obama speech with no hope. Obama will speak to Muslims. | 24 immigrants rescued in Tarifa. 11.38% rise in birthrate in Spain. Real estate sales falling more slowly. | Defence tried to break up soldiers rally against Law on Careers. Error in central computer may have caused Airbus tragedy. Mayor Oreja on COPE: 'My only rival in elections is Zapatero.' | Justice Minister asks Constitutional Court to decide on Catalonian Statute. Mariano Rajoy criticizes José Blanco for revealing sensitive data. COPE news: Zapatero campaign surveillance complicated rescue in Picos de Europa. | David Attenborough, Prince of Asturias award for Social Sciences. French experts do not rule out explosion on Airbus in the air. Rosa Díez: 'Pajín behavior was loutish.' | 24 immigrants rescued in Tarifa. Confrontations between metal workers and police in Vigo. Aragonese government happy with new Opel model. | Cándido Méndez, relatively optimistic on unemployment drop in May. UK and Netherlands hold EU elections. | Expectation at Obama speech. False bomb threat in Baracaldo. Marcos Peña, President of Economic and Social Council: ECB decision late and inadequate. | Obama to promote Middle East peace process. David Attenborough, Prince of Asturias award for Social Sciences. French press: Air France plane flying at 'incorrect' speed. | David Attenborough, Prince of Asturias award for Social Sciences. 24 immigrants rescued in Tarifa. Confrontations between metal workers and police in Vigo. |

| SER | | COPE | | Onda Cero | | Punto Radio | | Radio Nacional | |
|---|---|---|---|---|---|---|---|---|---|
| *Web* | *Traditional Radio* | *Web* | *Traditional Radio* | *Web* | *Traditional Radio* | *Web* | *Traditional Radio* | *Web* | *Traditional Radio* |
| **At 1 p.m.** | | | | | | | | | |
| Obama: Islam is part of the USA. Gaza will hear Obama speech with no hope. Odyssey must return treasure found in Portugal to Spain. | Obama chooses dialogue with Arab world. Agreement with USA to accept Guantanamo prisoners Spanish Police make formal accusation against Franco grandson. | Obama: 'This cycle of suspicion and discord (between US and Muslim world) must end'. Caamaño gives warning to Constitutional Court on Catalonian Statute. Defense tried to break up soldiers… | María San Gil begins campaign. PP headquarters in Tarragona attacked. Obama ask for new start in relations with Muslims. | Obama: 'I will relentlessly confront extremists that pose a threat'. David Attenborough, Prince of Asturias award for Social Sciences. Prince and Princess of Asturias help woman in Las Ventas. | Obama speech to Islam world. Rosa Díez evaluates Leire Pajín statements. Community of Madrid to abolish tax on documented judicial acts. | Obama wants new start in US/Muslim relations. Cándido Méndez, relatively optimistic on unemployment drop in May. | Obama offers his hand to Muslim world. 24 immigrants rescued in Tarifa. Associations for recovery of Historical Memory present 113 writs to Supreme Court. | Direct: Obama speech to Muslim world. David Attenborough, Prince of Asturias award for Social Sciences. French press: Air France plane flying at 'incorrect' speed. | Obama speech in Cairo. EU ministers negotiate on Guantanamo prisoners. EU election day in UK. |

| | | | | | | | | | |
|---|---|---|---|---|---|---|---|---|---|
| Obama: 'Islam is part of the USA.' Bin Laden response and treat. Gaza will hear Obama speech with no hope. | Obama: Israel and Palestine must be recognized to achieve peace. Hamas number 2 wary. Esperanza Aguirre and Juan José Güemes evaluate Leire Pajín statements. | Obama: 'This cycle of suspicion and discord (between US and Muslim world) must end.' María San Gil reappears. Defense tried to break up… | María San Gil begins campaign. Rajoy says Blanco inopportune in revealing ex – President Aznar security. Mayor Oreja on COPE: … | Obama: 'I will relentlessly confront extremists that pose a threat.' David Attenborough, Prince of Asturias award for Social Sciences. Prince and Princess of Asturias help … | Obama speech in Cairo. Spanish President explains his sustainable economic model. EU elections in Netherlands and UK. | Obama wants new start in US/Muslim relations. Cándido Méndez, relatively optimistic on unemployment drop in May. | Historic speech by Obama. EU elections begin and campaign ends in Spain. Cándido Méndez, controversy on presidential and ex – presidential security deplorable. | USA will not turn back on Palestinian state. David Attenborough, Prince of Asturias award for Social Sciences. ECB holds interest rate at 1%. | Obama speech. EU elections in UK and Netherlands. Differing hypotheses on Air France accident. |

*Source:* Original.

## Use of multimedia resources

The Spanish talk radio network screens analysed show an evolution in the use of multimedia resources. However, here improvement could still be made in their use of hypertext, multimedia – as per Salaverría (2005), text integration, image, video and sound to create a coherent communicative unit – and interactivity, in addition to simultaneity and the updating of online news. Among the samples taken between December and June, SER makes the most use of multimedia resources: it increased the audiocuts available and included photographs and videos for the main news items, but text still dominates in its online offer. In its own coverage, there is greater planning and use of these resources. A case in point can be found in the news and material produced on 4 June on the situation in the Middle East and the Obama speech at Cairo University mentioned before. The SER group of special envoys produced specific coverage for the internet, which complemented what was planned for the radio station: chronicles, photo galleries, video interviews, reports on everyday life there, and sound updating and indexing.

The COPE website backs images with a visual approach based on photos and videos of the two main news stories, to the detriment of text, sound and other graphic elements. The three main items are given in 143 to 853-word texts, with no hypertext links or key words in the body of the story – there were only six of these in the twenty-seven items analysed. Each of the news items analysed contained a photograph, but they did not always have associated audio/video. The conclusion is that the production, composition and audio and visual composition and edition on www.cope.es are open to improvement, as is its hypertextuality. On www.rtve.es, multimedia resources are used in its news content and in the whole structure. Photographs – for example, on 4 June 2009, rtve.es issued a gallery of fifty photos on the subject of the search for the Air France plane which had disappeared in the Atlantic on 1 June , recordings of interviews or audiocuts of their interviewees on the Radio Nacional programmes, and videos produced by the group's different TV channels are frequently online together with the scripts of the news items. This criterion is used across the board, even in live broadcasting the images and sounds of certain events are used, as in the above-mentioned Obama speech. Apart from live coverage of the images and sounds of the speech, www.rtve.es also offered a minute-by-minute chronicle sent by a reporter who gave a rapid summary of Obama's message, using Twitter.

As for Onda Cero, it also makes use of multimedia formats to handle the news in depth, by means of the sources and resources of the Antena 3 audiovisual group. The audio cuts offered on this website are from the Onda Cero radio programmes. In addition, same special multimedia contents are produced by the web of the antena3noticias.com group, to which it is linked. The hypertextual and multimedia configuration of the Punto Radio site is practically non-existent, with the exception of some limited interactive options – which will be explained in the next section. So the Punto Radio website simply presents text contents – between fifty-three and 589 words long– and there is a complete absence of image, sound, video, graphic elements or documents linked to its online news.

## Interactive news

The SER, COPE, Onda Cero, Punto Radio and Radio Nacional channels still face the challenge of giving greater news content interactivity to their websites. This means personalizing the search for news, fostering user participation in the news stories, encouraging dialogue between the editor and the user and establishing synergies with other participative techniques, such as surveys, forums, chatrooms, blogs, e-mails, text messages and multimedia messages. The analysis carried out shows surprisingly little use of these options, as the encouragement of interactivity and the diversification of techniques are precisely the most highly developed resources by Spanish radio online in the last three seasons, as per Moreno, Martínez-Costa & Amoedo (2008). The only increase has been in the possibility of news-sharing through social networking. The SER site includes the usual means of interactivity with the public: user comments, surveys and the possibility of sharing news on social networks. The introduction of user comments is not very frequent and only appears for those news items with a major social impact, generally on topics linked to the economy. The users' response to surveys is greater, particularly when linked to economic topics. The sharing of news with other users and social networks has increased on the SER channel during the 2008–09 season, from five (Technorati, Del.icio.us, Digg, Meneame, Yahoo), to thirteen social platforms: Menéame, Digg, Del.icio.us, Wikio, Reddit, Enchilame, Facebook, Fresqui, Google, Stumbleupon, Live, Myspace and Twitter. At the same time, each item can be automatically shared on at least three networks.

The user of the COPE site can make comments on the news, and can also share items with other people or with the channel's web community, through the social platforms and networks at Del.icio.us, Facebook, Technorati, Yahoo and Menéame. But we see no dynamic dialogue in this participation technique. However, the classification and ranking of 'The Latest/Most Watched/Most Listened to/Most Commented/Most Shared' is available, and is one of the essential elements for interactivity and participation on this channel. The interactivity strategy on the Punto Radio news site is much more limited. The user may only make comments on the news items and since 2009 has been able to share this content through Facebook, MySpace, Twitter, Menéame, Delicious, Fresqui, Windows Live, Google, Technorati, BlinkList and MSN Reporter. These are the only two means of participation linked to the Punto Radio website. But we must say that no comments were registered on any of our samples.

Finally, neither at www.rtve.es nor www.ondacero.es can the user post comments on the news published. However, the reader can e-mail all the texts and many of the videos published by rtve.es and ondacero.es. Web-user participation and opinion on rtve.es was possible in the case of the live coverage of President Obama's speech in Cairo on 4 June. The rtve.es users on Facebook were able to publish their opinions on the social network. Between 12noon and 1 p.m., thirty people gave their opinions during the broadcast.

Finally, www.ondacero.es permits user-sharing through Del.icio.us, Technorati, Digg and Menéame, while www.rtve.es permits Del.icio.us, Digg, Facebook, Fresqui and Menéame.

## Conclusions

The internet opens doors to the enrichment of the news services that the radio has always offered through traditional broadcasting. A talk radio network website can be a reference point for current affairs – both general and specialized, as well as a platform which allows for listening on demand and promotion of news contents and entertainment on the channel's main magazines and programmes. The number of news items that each channel includes on its website has stabilized over the 2008–09 season. The news offer of Spanish talk radio online varies between thirty items on SER, twenty-two on COPE, twelve on www.rtve.es, five on www.ondacero.es and two simple headlines on the Punto Radio homepage. The channels' topic strategy has also changed over the 2008–09 season: SER has increased its sports coverage, in detriment of society and economy news. COPE offers a greater number of society items, includes local news and has reduced news on politics. And on the Radiotelevisión Española website there is also a significant increase in society news and the sports and economic news items remain unchanged.

As for the updating of news contents, the channels SER, COPE, Onda Cero, Punto Radio and Radio Nacional are facing the challenge of improving the online edition of their news contents, plus a constant updating in accordance with the development and follow-up of each news story, to benefit from the synergy with the production and broadcasting times of their radio news bulletins. This challenge is usual in other traditional media, such as newspaper newsrooms, which work online with the editorial concept of a 'continuous deadline', and it brings them closer to traditional talk radio. This synergy with the radio is clear at the moment of summing up the morning's news, the main news bulletin broadcast at 2 p.m., which unites and summarizes the morning's news continuity. At least two of the three main news items on the web appear on the homepage for these programmes. On the contrary, in the hourly bulletins breaking news, urgency and brevity are more important. In some cases there is no coincidence between the first items online and the main topic on the bulletin.

On the subject of narrative and multimedia resources, although there has been improvement over the period analysed, the news websites tend to use lengthy blocks of hypertext, their text and audiovisual items are not very well organized and they have few narrative and documentary links. Therefore, the talk radio networks need to make greater efforts to integrate the contents and to consolidate their own internet narrative styles. The SER website is worthwhile viewing as a point of reference as it is careful to update its contents and multimedia narrative, especially in the area of sound. The COPE follows the same line, but gives greater weight to video and image rather than sound. Onda Cero, on the other hand, makes less use of the updating of news and multimedia design. Radio Nacional has improved its strategy on the use of the RTVE group's contents and multimedia treatment. And finally, Punto Radio simply has a symbolic news website.

Improvement has also been seen in the interactivity options on all channels. There has been an increase in the offer and visibility of the social networks, as options to communicate, share and receive information between the users, who only send comments and respond to the suggested surveys when the topics have direct repercussion on society. All in all, talk radio has acquired a fresh news dimension online, which goes further than radio continuity. This new dimension is transforming the production routines of news radio stations, and may give greater credibility and consistency to the news service brands – and to the channel brands themselves – in society and on the interactive communications market.

## Notes

1. The set of ninety samples – forty-five from the Web and forty-five from radio– should be considered within the current affairs context of 12 December 2008, 24 April 2009 and 4 June 2009. This logically determines the main topic classification of the news content at each time analysed on these dates.
2. See on this subject, the research work on radio content on the internet carried out by Ala-Fossi, Lax, O'Neill, Jauert & Shaw (2007); Menduni (2007, 2002); Bonini (2006); Neumark (2006); Delys & Foley (2006); Ren & Chan Olmsted (2004); Priestman (2004, 2002); Wall (2004); Hamula & Williams (2003); Moody, Greer & Linn (2003); Pitts & Harms (2003); Randle & Mordock (2002); Evans & Smethers (2001); Hendy (2000, 2000b); Tacchi (2000) and Lind & Medoffn (1999), among others.
3. As for Amoedo, Moreno and Martínez-Costa (2008), all radio broadcasters for the Spanish area have updated their websites over the last three seasons, with the intention of promoting interactivity with the listener. In addition, most of these networks are upgrading their professional teams and radio content production structures for the internet.

## References and further reading

Ala-Fossi, M., Lax, S., O'Neill, B., Jauert, P. & Shaw, H., 'The Future of Radio is Still Digital – But Which One? Expert Perspectives and Future Scenarios for the Radio Media in 2015', presented at the *52nd Convention of the Broadcast Education Association (BEA)*, Las Vegas, Nevada, USA, April 18–21, 2007.

Amoedo, A., Martínez-Costa, Mª.P. & Moreno, E., 'An Analysis of the Communication Strategies of Spanish Commercial Music Networks on the Web: los40.com, los40principales.com, cadena100. es, europafm.es and kissfm.es', *The Radio Journal – International Studies in Broadcast and Audio Media*, 6:1, 2008, pp. 5–20.

Bonini, T., *La radio nella rete. Storia, extetica, usi sociale*, Milan, Ed. Costlan, 2006.

Coyle, R., 'Ether to 01–Digitizing Radio', *Convergence*, 12:2, 2006, pp. 123–27.

Delys, S. & Foley, M., 'The Exchange: A Radio Web Project for Creative Practitioners and Researchers', *Convergence*, 12:2, 2006, pp. 129–35.

Evans, C. L. & Smethers, J. S., 'Streaming Into The Future: A Delphi Study of Broadcasters Attitudes Toward Cyber Radio Station', *Journal of Radio Studies*, 8:1, 2001, pp. 5–27.

Hamula, S. R. & Wnmouth, W., 'The Internet as a Small-Market Station Tool', *Journal of Radio Studies*, 10:2, 2003, pp. 262–69.

Hendy, D., 'A Political Economy of Radio in the Digital Age', *Journal of Radio Studies*, 7:1, 2000, pp. 213–34.

Hendy, D., *Radio in the global age.* Cambridge: Polity Press, 2000.

Lind, R. A. & Medoff, N. J., 'Radio Stations and the World Wide Web', *Journal of Radio Studies*, 6:2, 1999, pp. 203–21.

Martínez-Costa, Mª.P., Moreno, E. & Amoedo, A., 'Estrategias de comunicación de las cadenas generalistas españolas en la red: análisis comparativo de www.cadenaser.com, www.cope.es, www.ondacero.es, www.puntoradio.com y www.rne.es en las temporadas 2006–2007 y 2007–2008', *Actas y Memoria Final del Congreso Internacional Fundacional Asociación Española de Investigadores en Comunicación*, Facultad de Ciencias de la Comunicación, Santiago de Compostela, Spain, January 30 to February 1, 2008. Menduni, E., 'Four Steps in Innovative Radio Broadcasting: From Quicktime to Podcasting', *The Radio Journal*, 5:1, 2007, pp. 9–18.

Menduni, E., *La radio territorio e percorsi di un mezzo mobile e interactivo.* Bologna: Baskerville, 2002.

Moody, A., Greer, J. & Linn, T., 'Public Radio Station Websites & Their Users', *Journal of Radio Studies*, 10:2, 2003, pp. 255–61.

Moreno, E., Amoedo, A. & Martínez-Costa, Mª.P., 'Radio and the Web: Communication Strategies of Spanish Radio Networks on the Web (2006–2008)', *Ecrea 2008 Barcelona*, Barcelona, November 18–21, 2008, http://www.ecrea2008barcelona.org/guide/download/984.pdf. Accessed 18 March 2009.

Neumark, N., 'Different Spaces, Differents Times – Exploring Possibilities for Cross-Platform Radio', *Convergence*, 12:2, 2006, pp. 213–24.

Pitts, M. & Harms, R., 'Radio Websites as a Promotional Tool', *Journal of Radio Studies*, 10:2, 2003, pp. 270–82.

Priestman, C., 'Narrowcasting and the Dream of Radio's Great Global Conversation', *The Radio Journal*, 2:2, 2004, pp. 77–88.

Priestman, C., *Web radio: Radio production for the internet streaming.* Oxford: Focal Press, 2002.

Randle, Q. & Mordock, J., 'How Radio is Adapting Weather to the Web: A Study of Weather Strategies on Local News/Talk Radio, TV, and Newspaper Home Pages', *Journal of Radio Studies*, 9:2, 2002, pp. 247–58.

Ren, W. & Chan–Olmsted S., 'Radio Content on the World Wide Web: Comparing Streaming Radio Stations in the United States', *Journal of Radio Studies*, 11:1, 2004, pp. 6–25.

Salaverría, R., *Redacción periodística en the internet.* Pamplona: Eunsa, 2005.

Tacchi, J., 'The Need for Radio Theory in the Digital Age', *International Journal of Cultural Studies*, 3:2, 2000, pp. 289–98.

Wall, T., 'The Political Economy of the Internet Music Radio', *The Radio Journal*, 2:1, 2004, pp. 27–44.

Wilson, J., '3G to Web 2.0? Can Mobile Telephony Become an Architecture of Participation', *Convergence*, 12:2, 2006, pp. 229–42.

# Chapter 8

Lost and Challenged Contents: Music Radio Alternatives and Cultural Practices

Vesa Kurkela and Heikki Uimonen

D igitalized communication technology has strongly influenced not just the number of stations but also the contents of radio programming. Theoretically speaking, the current radioscape consists of innumerable channels, enabling limitless possibilities of more diversified music, content and services than ever before. With the aid of new technology, radio listening has become almost ubiquitous: devices such as cellular phone podcasts liberate radio listening from the constraints of time and space.

In practice, the change in the radioscape has not been as profound as one would imagine. The number of channels has not increased considerably since the 1990s, and the content of broadcast music has by no means been diversified. In fact, a diverse musical content fits the idea of hit music radio quite poorly. In formatting their musical content these radio stations typically rely on a few artists seen as would-be breakers or on nostalgic hit tunes. Nor is radio listening essentially more ubiquitous or mobile than in the end of the analogue era, in the 1980s. Some examples of the most popular mobile equipment of the time, Walkman cassette recorders, also had radio listening functionality. Moreover, internet radio did not necessarily make radio listening more ubiquitous, since until recent years, the use of computer has mostly been sedentary with fixed cable connections. Today, however, mobile broadband networks and smartphones are significantly changing the situation. In the near future, a greater number of music radio stations or compensatory music services will probably move into the internet, which is increasingly mobile and ubiquitous in essence. The question is how fast will all this happen.

This chapter discusses the reasons why innovation technology seems to be incapable – in this specific case and generally – of changing cultural practices overnight. The variables explaining this can be found in legislation, radio economics and the capacity of programme production. Cultural change is also slowed down and controlled by the habits of radio listening and leisure time in general. Everyday habits seldom change easily or in a short period of time.

In addition, our paper discusses the way in which the new digital communication environment has influenced radio content. In order to test our hypotheses we carried out a survey among two groups, one of them consisting of music professionals and the other of music students. The main object of the survey was to study the stability of listening habits and the changing mediascape in Finland today. Our main argument is that, despite the changes in online communication, old listening habits and the insufficient availability of new technology prevent the domesticating of the new, internet-based music services. We will also study how music radio is defined and identified in the era of new mobile technology.

Music radio has no doubt consolidated its place in the mediascape. At the same time the role of radio as an on-line transmitter is becoming increasingly blurred. In this process of change digital technology has a central position: due to the new technology we can listen to music on numerous music radio channels or from collections of recordings compiled in advance. When this can be done with a single item of equipment, it is no wonder that the role of radio as a broadcasting medium will be redefined in the future.

## New technology and changes to music radio

In spite of all the promotion and excitement around new technological innovations, we argue that radio broadcasting was more thoroughly influenced by the radical cultural transformations that occurred on the eve of the digital era. The most important was the globalization of American-style music radio. The hegemony of classical music and popular education, which European public service radio had relied on, was replaced by Anglo-American popular music and commercial business cultures. As a consequence, rock music lost its position as the expression of rebellious youth. It was amalgamated with the hegemonic culture and neutralized into harmless and easy-to-listen radio content, thus becoming suitable for almost any radio channel. To be a little controversial, rock music today is part of the musical establishment: it is brought to kindergartens and elementary schools, so that children are brought up as compliant consumers of rock. Today, the main content of music radio is African American music and especially pop and mainstream rock. This very same musical content has dominated the European radioscape since the 1980s, for more than a quarter of a century.

Although musical content has remained almost the same, there are some demographic changes among the radio listeners. Originally rock music radio was part of a lively and active youth culture, almost a mass movement. Today, according to the radio scholar Michael Keith, radio companies are facing enormous challenges owing to the loss of young audiences (Keith 2009). The overall trend is similar to that seen in the Finnish radio culture. Judging by public expressions of opinion at least, the young seem to be quite indifferent to the radio channels repeating the same hit songs and using relatively limited play lists in music broadcasting. Most likely this is a generation issue: most adolescents are accustomed to listening to hit music and one-sided music radio – the idea of a full-service radio station is virtually unknown to them. On the other hand, they are used to listening to music on the internet and to finding whatever they need – with or without charge.

Music is no longer the only factor uniting youth – if it ever was. Or, if it still is 'connecting people', the people have been fragmented into adherents of numerous musical genres and at the same time expanded into a global network of internet users. On the other hand, the well-branded music programmes of the popular mainstream, such as the globally known Idols, seem to attract audiences of almost all tastes, ages and social groups. This popular mainstream is also a central content of most music radio stations. Those complaining about changes in music radio are mostly middle-aged music lovers, whose musical ideals derive from the golden days of their youth and have been rudely by-passed in the streamlining of music radio channels. The average middle-aged music listeners are happy with nostalgia radios that play the music from their youth. However, the passive attitude of young audiences can be considered more dangerous to the future of music radio than the dissatisfaction of middle-aged listeners. Almost all former innovations and reforms in the Finnish radioscape have had their origins in the discontent with prevailing practices or the activity of the youth. A well-known example of this is a programme called Rock Radio and its penetration into the arena of public broadcasting in the early 1980s (Kurkela & Uimonen 2007).

From a business perspective the changes in music consumption in Finland have been remarkable, and have followed technological innovations closely. The sales of vinyl recordings peaked in 1984, of music cassettes in 1989 and of CDs in 1992. In the first years of the new millennium record sales have decreased almost every year. Especially the young consumers have increasingly moved to internet services, while record companies have failed to provide an alternative to peer-to-peer downloading: so far selling music on the internet does not look like a success story (Alanen 2009). There is also a remarkable change in the content of music sales via the internet: previously the share of single records was about 5% of the total phonogram sales, but now singles almost dominate the market in internet downloading (Alanen 2009). Internet buyers seldom download complete albums; single tracks are a typical way of buying music on the net.

## Spotify – an alternative to music radio?

The music industries seem to be very keen on new ways of doing business on the internet, and most likely with good reason. The Swedish music streaming service Spotify provides music via the internet. The service is different from conventional music services due to the method of dissemination: the users are not downloading the music files on to their computers, but listening online. There are competing streaming services, such as Deezer in France, and in July 2009 Microsoft announced plans to launch its own music streaming service. The name Spotify is composed of the words 'spot' and 'identify'. Daniel Ek and Martin Lorentzon founded the service; the development was started in 2006 and it was launched on 7 October 2008. The headquarters of Spotify are in the United Kingdom, and its research and development wing is located in Stockholm. The parent company in Luxemburg has forty-five employees (Wikipedia 2009; Kinnunen 2009: 14). Spotify allows the customer to listen to music for free. However, its 'beta version' comes with visual and aural advertisements and information on the service is provided between the music tracks. Alternatively, the user can pay what is called a premium for a day, a month or a year, and then enjoy the service without the ads. Currently the expanding Spotify is available in eight European countries, including Germany, Sweden, Norway, Finland, the United Kingdom, France and Spain. In May 2009 Spotify listed 3 million songs. This means that listening to the whole Spotify catalogue would take twenty years (Spotify 2009; Macmaa 2009; Kinnunen 2009: 14)

Spotify consists of many features that resemble music radio. It contains a special 'Radio' operation that plays tracks from new and old albums in accordance with the user's preferences. The user can select one or several of eighteen fundamental popular music genres, mainly African American music, and then limit the selection to one or several decades. The Radio operation creates an automatic selection and plays one track per album in succession. The result is a complete non-stop programme of music radio, without interruptions from any DJ. Furthermore, Spotify songs are listed by the popularity of individual tracks: the more frequently listened songs are positioned higher on the play list. This causes an incidental listener to select them first, which of course helps the song to keep its high position. An interesting feature is the listeners' ability to create their own playlists and share them with their friends. All music tracks from all possible record companies and countries are not available, due to the agreements between Spotify and certain countries. The service is also mobile. Thanks to an agreement between Spotify and Apple, online music became available to listening devices such as iPhones in August 2009. By now, Spotify's revenue is already higher than that of iTunes. In addition, the service gives recording companies the option to promote their music free of cost (Spotify 2009; Kinnunen 2009: 14). In Sweden, lawsuits paved Spotify's way to success. The new law on internet piracy allowed copyright holders to obtain the IP addresses of internet users who were suspected of copyright violations. Furthermore, the Pirate Bay trial was extensively covered by the media. Spotify quickly became an alternative to file sharing. It already has one million users among the nine-million population of Sweden. According to the Finnish newspaper *Helsingin Sanomat*, the number of Spotify users is already four million (Barnett 2009; Alroth 2009).

What is the actual musical content of the Spotify service? Generally speaking, the supply is overwhelmingly abundant, and it is quite difficult to pinpoint a single musical genre that is absent. Alongside the major genres the supply includes somewhat marginal types of music, even in the field of ethnic music. However, certain geographical areas of world music are represented by only a few tracks (e.g., Bulgaria, Romania and Finland) and some locally important popular styles, such as the Bulgarian chalga, are totally missing. It must be noted, though, that the same styles and traditions are very poorly available even in commercial internet music libraries, such as Contemporary World Music (2009) or Smithsonian Global Sound (2009). The biggest gaps in the Spotify supply are related to some prominent names of rock and pop music. Some labels and artists consider that Spotify pays too small a remuneration for music that sells steadily without any internet promotion. Accordingly, the original recordings of the following top artists are poorly represented or completely missing in Spotify: The Beatles, Michael Jackson (back catalogue reissues only), Led Zeppelin, Metallica, Pink Floyd and Frank Zappa (availability checked on 2 September 2009). Furthermore, many artists and recording companies have decided to withdraw some of their music which had previously been available, and this has caused Spotify to announce that 'the artist or label has chosen to make this track unavailable'.

However, cover versions of the music of the above-mentioned artists are extensively available. For instance, there are almost 3000 cover tracks from the Beatles. There seems to be a very good reason why original Beatles songs are not accessible via Spotify. In September 2009 the *opera omnia* of the group was released as a series of remastered albums. If the original songs were available on the internet for free streaming, the number of potential buyers would be considerably smaller than it is now. Composers and songwriters have criticized Spotify, saying that the remuneration for artists is insufficient. Magnus Uggla, a Swedish musician with a long career, argues that his six-month remuneration from Spotify is on the same level as a busker's daily earnings. It is somewhat contradictory that Uggla's record company, Sony, paid 3000 euros for a share of Spotify with the market value of about 250 million euros. Uggla decided to withdraw his music from Spotify, thus following Bob Dylan, who made his recordings unavailable to all streaming services, such as Deezer, Last.fm and we7 (Alroth 2009).

Streaming is not based on music downloading. From the copyright perspective, the musical works are not actually sold, but hired for broadcast listening. For instance, when using Apple's iTunes the users download the music to their computers. Services such as Spotify give an opportunity for listening without downloading. In this sense Spotify resembles a music radio station more than a record shop. Due to this difference Spotify remunerations are considerably smaller compared to internet music sales. The agreements concerning streaming are signed between the record companies and the streamers. In due course, the record companies forward the royalties to the artists. According to a representative of Sony Finland, the sum paid for listening to a single track is very small and therefore the artist's share is even smaller. A Spotify spokesman is of the opinion that it will take the company 'up to two years' to grow big enough to become a 'material revenue generator for artists' (Barnett 2009; Alroth 2009).

According to Jari Muikku, manager at the Finnish Composers' Copyright Society Teosto, the pricing of music streaming is still incomplete and the remuneration is proportionate to the financial success of the streaming service. The share of the artists and labels is based on the streaming duration of each musical track as well as the turnover of the service company. Nevertheless, the market value of the company is not a good basis for defining the royalties of music streaming, since 'the market values will not be realized before the company is sold or when substantial dividends are given'. However, in August 2009 a representative of the music industry stated: 'If Spotify's user base and advertising revenues continue to grow at their current rate, the music industry is looking at a really significant new revenue stream in about six months' time' (Barnett 2009; Alroth 2009).

Ano Sirppiniemi, another representative of Finnish Teosto, supposes that, at least partly, Spotify was originally launched without remuneration contracts (2009)[1]. The deals were first made with the big labels, and smaller Finnish labels, for example, made their contracts with Spotify in the first half of 2009. Indeed, Spotify has signed agreements with the four largest record companies in the world. Sony, EMI, Warner and Universal were followed by the Independent Online Distribution Alliance (IODA). IODA brokers for independent labels and thus brings two million indie tracks to Spotify (Kinnunen 2009: 14).

From the artist's perspective, licensing music online is quite problematic. In accordance with the publishing contract the labels and their publishers have licensing rights for a range of public uses of the music without the artist's permission. Actually the publisher's main mission is to increase the public performances of musical works and find new ways and methods for public use. If the deal with the labels proves to be difficult or takes too much time, the streamer can test the copyright system by 'crashing'. In other words, the service simply makes the music available online. This is followed by a possible court case or arbitration with the record company in order to reach an agreement on the remuneration (Sirppiniemi 2009). All this resembles the early years of Finnish commercial radio stations in the late 1980s, when the remuneration practices were unclear and unsettled. The radio companies paid only nominal sums for airing music. This was to indicate that they accepted the principle of copyright fees but not the sums claimed by copyright organizations. Negotiations and court proceedings took several years because the parties did not reach an agreement concerning the price of radio music (Veima 2009)[2].

Spotify's business is based on paying copyright revenues, although the fees are relatively small at the moment. Their business strategy seems to be to get the free users hooked on the service so firmly that they will buy the premium subscription after getting tired of irritating advertisements. The service is especially suitable for young people. They are used to getting music free from the internet, but on the other hand they have been acclimatized into a mediascape where they or their parents pay the monthly subscription for mobile phone use. Another source of income for Spotify are the advertisements. They appear to be irritating on purpose, and it seems that users are compelled to listen to them increasingly if they are listening to music for free for a long period.

## Changing listening habits in Finland in 2009 – a preliminary survey

Internet services such as Spotify anticipate changes in our listening habits. In order to get at least a tentative picture of the current situation, a minor case study was carried out among music researchers, musicians and students (Kurkela & Uimonen 2009). Our presupposition was that these people would form the vanguard when it comes to active music listening and innovations in the field. A small survey among music professionals and music students was carried out on 25 August and 9 September 2009. The questionnaires were filled in by a group consisting of twenty-two professional researcher-musicians, eleven of them male and ten female, aged between twenty-eight and sixty-three. The average age was thus 41.3 years. Another questionnaire was presented to a group consisting of twenty- four university students, seven of them male and seventeen female, aged between eighteen and fifty. The average age of the second group was 27.2 years. Among other related issues, radio-listening habits and the use of compensatory ways of listening to music were inquired about.

The professionals mainly listened to the radio as background while doing something else: driving, commuting, cleaning, cooking and so on. To a lesser extent, individual programmes such as radio plays and concerts were listened to. However, individual programmes aired by the public funded YLE (Finnish Broadcasting Company) and the commercial Radio Helsinki were mentioned, as well as a semi-nationwide radio chain airing Finnish schlagers and pop. The respondents in the student group also listened to the radio in the background in similar situations as the professionals. The channels listed were more diverse. They included not just the previously mentioned stations, but also Groove FM, Classic Radio, Voice, NRJ, Nova, Radio Rock, Radio Suomipop, Radio Dei, Auran Aallot, Radio 957 and Iskelmäradio. The large number of channels implies surfing between the channels. The listening was sometimes involuntary, as stated by a twenty-four-year-old male who had to listen to the radio at his workplace. What is striking is that 50% of the students (thirteen in number) listened to the radio very little or hardly at all. This echoes the US finding mentioned above that young people under twenty-five years of age are quite uninterested in listening to the radio.

All but three of the professionals had used portable listening devices since the 1970s. These included compact cassette recorders, cassette Walkmans, portable CD players, MiniDiscs, laptop computers, mobile phone radios and iPods. All except two respondents in the student group had used at least one of the devices as well. Eight individuals among the professionals (38%) had not changed their listening habits with the portable listening devices and new technological innovations. The remaining informants were using their laptops and iPods to listen to music on the train or while travelling or jogging. They searched for radio programmes on the internet and listened to them not only during leisure time but also at the workplace. Even if the possibilities of music listening were manifold, they were not necessarily utilized. A forty-four-year-old male pointed out that he listened less to music than 'twenty years ago'. On the other hand, a forty-eight-year-old male no longer purchased records due to the MSN Music and Spotify services. A forty-five-year-old female thinks of the radio receiver as connected to a certain location, which is why she does not listen to music on her cell phone. Thirteen students answered that their listening habits have not changed. It must be remembered, though, that some of them were virtually born with the mobile technology and the internet, so that they have not experienced similar changes as the middle-aged respondents have.

Eighteen professionals used the internet music services such as Spotify, Youtube, Myspace, YLEn Elävä arkisto (The YLE Living Archive), iTunes and classical music channels. A twenty-eight-year-old female complained that the American web radios are not available due to 'a change of the law'. The services are utilized for nostalgic music listening/watching, for teaching and research and for work and entertainment purposes. The respondents used Spotify and Deezer mainly to find new music, to monitor the success of Finnish ensembles abroad, in listening to records they already own or getting to know 'classics' so far by-passed. Music recommended by friends and Spotify's genre radio were also listened to. All but one of the students used the above services, plus one called the Prog archive, for the purposes mentioned above. Nine professionals (43%) used Spotify to listen to new music or music already acquired, although Spotify had not replaced radio or record listening. They felt that the advantages of the new service were the extensive collections of music and the easy-to-use interface. The disadvantages were the irritating advertisements, but they were considered intentional by the provider: they were used to lure the listeners to buy non-commercial services and to use the chargeable premium option. Some respondents listened to music before purchasing the record and thus were happy to avoid buying 'bad records'. A forty-eight-old male said that Spotify replaced not just the buying of the records but the MSN service as well. A forty-year-old-male used Spotify instead of the municipal music library. However, at the same time he wondered who would actually pay the musicians. A social use of Spotify was represented by DJ turns at parties: according to a thirty-year-old woman, tunes were retrieved from the service and then played to the rest of the partygoers.

Nine students (38%) also used Spotify. The pros and cons were similar to those reported by the professionals. In addition, the availability of minor labels was greeted with joy, though the gaps in the supply were considered irritating. A thirty-five-year-old female answered that Spotify replaces background sound from the radio or television at home. A twenty-one-year-old male did not value the service as such, but instead preferred to listen to music from 'real' recordings. Another twenty-one-year-old male pointed out that owing to its ease of use and speed, the service was replacing the illegal downloading of music.

Both professionals and students bought between zero and two hunderd items of vinyls and CDs per year. The records were acquired while travelling abroad, from Finnish record shops and music festivals for personal use and as presents. The internet was used to buy not only CDs but also vinyl LPs and singles. However, relatively little or no music was downloaded: a forty-four year-old male had stopped using Finnish downloading services, and two of the respondents used the downloading opportunity in their profession. A twenty-year-old male student used Pirate Bay to download records not available in other formats; a twenty-three-year-old female answered that 'the money that used to be spent for a few records per month was now spent in support of Spotify'.

Six professionals shared their own music or that of others via the internet. The most popular distribution channels were Myspace, Facebook, Youtube and iLike. Also, 50% of the respondents had learned about the internet music services from their friends and relatives, the other half from the internet and music journals. Only three student respondents agreed that they used peer-to-peer networks in order to search for 'hard-to-find music' or 'ripped versions' of cassettes. Thirteen respondents had heard about the internet services from their friends or relatives. Concerning the impact of the internet on acquiring or listening to music, the professionals' opinions differed. They considered that the internet supply will change listening habits by making the listening more diverse and making it easier to get to know new artists. However, they were more sceptical as to whether the internet would change their music acquisition. A thirty-five-year-old female said that the internet would reduce the 'waste purchases'; a thirty-one-year-old female considered the records as objects. She also mentioned that sleeve art was important to her, which is why she does not listen to music only via the internet. The respondents considered that listening was increased by its ease of use and low price. A thirty-eight-year-old male stated that listening to music via the internet will increase, since music on the internet is free of cost.

A forty-four-year-old male said that he had given up music listening and if he listened at all, he concentrated only on his existing collection. A thirty-five-year-old female considers that finding information about live concerts is part of using the internet for music purposes. A fifty-four-year-old male forecast that music radio will disappear and that the record industry will have to find new ways of doing business in the future. Radio was considered a more flexible medium because the internet was not suitable for mobile listening (soon after the survey was taken, Spotify was introduced to iPhones). A thirty-year-old female considered opting for the monthly payment to Spotify, as long as the copyright and revenue issues are settled in the future.

To a large extent the students were in agreement with the professionals. A twenty-three-year-old female wanted to visit the record shops in order to fill her record shelf; a twenty-one-year old male bought more records inspired by the internet listening services. The collections of the municipal music library were also mentioned (perhaps a Scandinavian phenomenon?). A twenty-one-year-old female was the only respondent who struggled to reduce listening to music via the internet because music sounded better when listened to with 'proper equipment'. What remained obscure was whether the perceived difference in sound quality was related to the internet music itself or to the listening equipment used. There might not be too many listeners who have an internet connection attached to their hi-fi equipment. And if they had, would they notice the difference between the high-fidelity or 'packed' sound of music?

## Remarks and conclusions

It can be concluded that at least the music professionals have adapted to the use of the internet as a medium for new music services. Unfortunately this survey does not reveal how common the innovations have become among laypersons. On the other hand, the rapid expansion of Spotify could mean that professionals' attitude to new technology is more or less the same as that of other internet users or music listeners. The respondents stressed that they discovered new music with the help of Spotify. Listening to the radio does not meet this need because formatted stations rely mainly on old and nostalgic music. Furthermore, music radio is not an interactive online service and thus it effectively prevents the musical preferences of an active and avid listener affecting the playlist. Spotify encourages these preferences, and for music professionals this kind of information is self-evidently an important part of their work. It is worth noting that hardly anyone paid attention to the sound quality of the internet music. One might assume that broadband-mediated music has reached a level where even the professionals are satisfied. If this is the case, one of the biggest obstacles to disseminating music via the internet has been removed.

Because of their newness, Spotify and the other streaming services are not necessarily known to the vast majority of music consumers. Our case studies among the music professionals of today and tomorrow really cannot verify or falsify the assumption that music streaming could replace music radio in the future. However, it is evident that the new internet services have managed to stir things up a bit. The growing popularity of streaming is bound to cause record sales to drop even more. Hit music radio stations are threatened as music streaming in mobile devices becomes more common. In a few years it might be interesting to look back and see who managed to ride the gravy train in the music business. If someone did not get on board, was it the record industry and the hit music radio stations which are essentially connected to them? Perhaps it took too long for the hesitating record companies to establish their internet music shops, not to mention winning the court cases in pirate and peer-to-peer network trials. Now there are new applications such as Spotify which are redefining the listening and consumer habits of the public. Public service radio is probably becoming resigned to its fate and at the same time finding its niche on the internet in diversifying its services with the help of their vast archive of material. The use of the internet for the purposes of listening to music includes the acquiring of physical records and retrieving information about music events. Some of the internet music listeners still want to deal with the tangible artefacts such as records and their sleeves. This tactility and the record as an aesthetic entity will help the record markets to survive. On the other hand, this is more or less involved with record collecting which is related not only to music listening but also to extra-musical values.

The copyright and revenue debate around the Spotify music service resembles the perennial dispute related to music and broadcasting. Whenever there is a new innovation or business application in broadcasting, old and established practices are challenged and confused for some time. The identical arguments were presented when music radio stations were introduced in Europe; also the internet applications raised opinions about the copyright issues. The criticism concerning the matter is self-evidently presented not just by the music makers, but also the other beneficiaries such as publishers and producers. Philosophically the situation is a very interesting one. Broadcasting is genuinely a business dealing with immaterial rights; the delivering of actual goods is not a part of it. The records, sheet music or even the packed strings of digital bytes in the internet music stores are not delivered from a seller to a buyer. In addition, broadcasting continues to disseminate music very broadly to an audience unattainable by record sales. It might be a little challenging for the consumers to think that the delivery of something immaterial could be compared to the selling of more tangible or digital goods.

In addition there is reason to assume that every time there are strong opinions or criticism concerning copyright revenues, new interesting modes of music business are about to emerge. Sometimes new business practices lead to the courtroom, which is not unheard of in the history of music publishing. In early twentieth-century modern music publishing, the related legislation and moneymaking especially in the United Kingdom and in the United States came into conflict and thus had to constantly define their boundaries in courts and by precedents (Coover 1985). The history of radio has also been a history of disagreements about revenues. And evidently, when there is a disagreement about money, someone definitely stands to gain from it, be it only the lawyers.

## Notes

1. Sirppiniemi A., Telephone interview by Heikki Uimonen, 18th August 2009.
2. Veima, M., Interview with the former CEO of the local radio station Radio 957 in Tampere, Finland, by Heikki Uimonen, 11 March 2009.

## References and further reading

Alanen, A., 'Miljardin klusteri. Kasvu keikoilla ja peleissä', *Tieto & trendit*, 2009, pp. 4–5, 28–33.

Alroth, J., 'Musiikkipalvelu Spotify on vastatuulessa', *Helsingin Sanomat*, 2009, 24th August.

Barnett, E., 'Spotify to make "significant" revenue for UK record labels "within six months", *Telegraph* (2009) 25th August, http://www.telegraph.co.uk/technology/6086013/Spotify-to-make-significant-revenue-for-UK-record-labels-within-six-months.html. Accessed 21 September 2009.

Contemporary World Music, *Music online: Contemporary World Music* http://womu.alexanderstreet.com/. Accessed 21 September 2009.

Coover, J., *Music publishing, copyright and piracy in Victorian England. A twenty-five year chronicle*, 1881–1906. London & New York: Mansell Publishing, 1985.

Keith, M., 'The Absence of Social Impact Curricula in Radio Studies', keynote in *The Radio Conference 2009*, York University, Toronto, Canada, 27 July 2009.

Kinnunen, A, 'Spotify Challenges the Traditional MP3 Business', *Blue Wings*, September 2009, p. 14.

Kurkela, V. & Uimonen, H., 'Usko, toivo ja petollinen rakkaus. Rock-kulttuuri ja suomalaisen radiopolitiikan muutos' in M. Mantere & H. Uimonen (eds) *Etnomusikologian vuosikirja 19*, Helsinki: Suomen Etnomusikologinen Seura, 2007, pp. 9–28.

Kurkela, V. & Uimonen, H., 'A case study of music listening, radio and the Internet carried out by Kurkela & Uimonen', 25th August & 9th September 2009.

Macmaa, 'Spotify–musiikin ilmainen aarrearkku', *Macmaa*, http://macmaa.com/2009/05/27/spotify-musiikin-ilmainen-aarrearkku/. Accessed 1 June 2010.

Smithsonian Global Sound, *Smithsonian Institution*, www.folkways.si.edu. Accessed 21 September 2009.

Spotify, http://www.spotify.com/en. Accessed 21 September 2009.

Wikipedia, 'Spotify', en.wikipedia.org/wiki/Spotify. Accessed 21 September 2009.

# Chapter 9

## Music Radio in the Age of Digital Convergence: A Case Study of the Catalan Context

Josep Maria Martí, Xavier Ribes, Maria Gutiérrez, Luisa Martínez and Belén Monclús

# Introduction

Music radio in Spain is suffering from stagnation, mainly reflected in the ageing of its potential listenership and the way its strategies for development are leading to the homogenization of formats, a process which is being reinforced by the consolidation of morning shows and late shows. Apart from sharing similar programme schedules, they are also adopting similar approaches in fostering audience participation as a programming genre. This chapter aims to present some of the most significant information extracted from the research project titled La Ràdio i els Joves: Problemàtica actual i tendències de futur (Radio and Young People: Current issues and future trends), conducted by the l'Observatori de la Ràdio a Catalunya of Universitat Autònoma de Barcelona. The study is framed within the Catalan broadcasting ecosystem, being the most suitable environment for some really productive research in order to deepen and explore the causes of youth alienation from music radio and to put forward alternatives to redefine the digital environment. Moreover, the penetration of the internet into the media diet of young people aged between fourteen and twenty-four years becomes a relevant, key phenomenon for programming strategies, either parallel or complementary to the delivery of broadcasting content over the airwaves.

The reason for choosing Catalonia as the context of the research lies in the level of innovation there, which has achieved international recognition thanks to some of the projects established within the public radio framework. The methodology we have used is defined through quantitative and qualitative parameters as follows:

- Data analysis taken from the EGM survey results (General Media Survey), of EGM Catalunya Ràdio, a private organization responsible for the publication of audience data for Spanish state broadcasting, and the Baròmetre de la Comunicació i la Cultura, an organization which depends on participation of the main operators and that also measures the media diet of the Catalan population. Both surveys have become a referential framework for broadcasting programmers and they allow the development of an accurate picture of changes to the audience in quality terms.
- A research team to conduct a telephone survey of cultural and broadcasting consumption involving one thousand subjects was established. The sample has been built according to the guidelines of the Institut d'Estadística de Catalunya (IDESCAT) (Catalan Institute of Statistics), corresponding to the distribution of the population aged between fourteen and twenty-four in 2007.[1]

- The organization and creation of two focus groups, each of them centred on a different age demographic (fourteen to eighteen and nineteen to twenty-four-year olds, respectively).
- Personal interviews, according to Delphi format patterns, with those responsible for programming sections of music stations, both public and private, operating under Catalan territory.

Before proceeding, we must explain that the results obtained and presented in this chapter are part of the first stage of our research, which was based on quantitative data.

## The ageing of the music radio audience

Youth disaffection with radio as a communication medium, as the audience surveys reveal, has reached music radio as well. The analysis of the cumulative data gathered and presented by EGM Ràdio Catalunya[2] during the calendar year 2008 reveals that the average age of listeners to music radio in Catalonia is around thirty-eight years. The most recent audience results, shown in Chart 9.1, corresponding to the second EGM survey in 2009, reveal a slight audience increase in all age demographics, but it will take some time to determine whether it represents a real recovery of youth audiences, since for more than a decade this lack of interest has been steadily maintained, both in the Catalan territory and across the Spanish State, as we are going to demonstrate later on. Certainly, listening to the radio did decline in the younger demographics between 2004 and 2007.

**Chart 9.1:** Changes in the audiences of music radio stations in Catalonia, divided by age groups (2004–09)

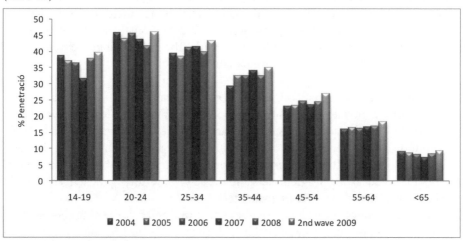

(Percentage penetration)
Cumulative audiences from February to November, Monday to Sunday, among people aged fourteen years and older in Catalonia.
*Source*: Original chart, based on EGM Ràdio Catalunya data.

**Chart 9.2:** Average age profile of radio listeners in Catalonia (2001–09).

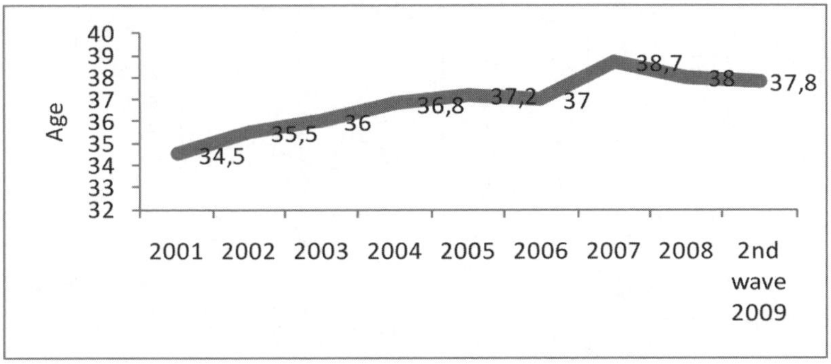

Cumulative audience from February to November, from Monday to Sunday, among people aged fourteen years and older in Catalonia.
*Source*: Original chart, based on EGM Ràdio Catalunya data.

In general terms, music radio is facing a constant loss in its audience, partly among young listeners as shown in Chart 9.2. A more detailed approach to changes in the audiences of thematic radio stations, seen from the socio-demographic variable of age, makes asserting this tendency easier (Huertas 2008: 95), even though we should note that all major follow-up percentages are to be found in the population demographic aged between fourteen and forty-four years. In addition, having studied in depth the profiles, Huertas asserts that only four stations present higher rates in the fourteen to nineteen-year-old demographic, according to the data gathered by the EGM Ràdio Catalunya for the period from February to November 2008. These are 40 Principales (13.5% of twenty to twenty-four-year olds), Flaix FM (8.5% of twenty to twenty-four-year olds), Ràdio Flaixbac (7.3% of fourteen to nineteen-year olds) and Máxima FM (5.1% of twenty to twenty-four-year olds). All four radio stations reach larger percentages between fourteen and twenty-four-year –olds; thus their audience profile is the youngest in the market. In fact, this gives Máxima FM an average audience of 27.5-year olds and 40 Principales an average of 32.5 years. That is to say, both stations have an average audience age situated in the demographic from twenty-four to thirty-four-years old. This tendency does not substantially vary in the second survey wave of 2009.

Table 9.1 shows in a very detailed fashion the profile of radio listeners in Catalonia, and the tendency towards ageing of that audience.

**Table 9.1:** Thematic music stations by age group in Catalonia (2008 and 2009).

| Age | 40 Principales | | Cadena Dial | | RAC 105 | | Flaix FM | | M-80 | | R. Flaixbac | | Europa FM | | Cadena 100 | |
|---|---|---|---|---|---|---|---|---|---|---|---|---|---|---|---|---|
| | 08 | 09* | 08 | 09* | 08 | 09* | 08 | 09* | 08 | 09* | 08 | 09* | 08 | 09* | 08 | 09* |
| 14–19 | 10.9 | 10.0 | 1.5 | 1.1 | 1.5 | 2.0 | 8.2 | 10.6 | 0.9 | 0.8 | 7.3 | 6.6 | 4.2 | 4.6 | 2.0 | 2.8 |
| 20–24 | 13.5 | 14.4 | 2.6 | 2.0 | 1.7 | 2.6 | 8.5 | 9.1 | 2.0 | 2.0 | 6.0 | 6.5 | 3.7 | 4.7 | 2.2 | 3.5 |
| 25–34 | 11.5 | 11.9 | 4.3 | 3.7 | 2.6 | 4.0 | 4.8 | 5.6 | 2.2 | 2.5 | 3.7 | 3.6 | 4.3 | 4.4 | 3.4 | 4.5 |
| 35–44 | 6.9 | 7.8 | 4.3 | 4.0 | 3.3 | 4.6 | 2.5 | 3.1 | 3.1 | 2.5 | 1.4 | 1.8 | 2.2 | 2.8 | 3.1 | 3.2 |
| 45–54 | 4.3 | 4.3 | 3.1 | 2.8 | 3.6 | 4.8 | 1.2 | 1.6 | 2.1 | 2.5 | 1.4 | 1.1 | 0.9 | 1.2 | 1.7 | 2.0 |
| 55–64 | 1.3 | 1.4 | 2.2 | 2.4 | 1.7 | 2.7 | 0.3 | 0.3 | 0.8 | 1.0 | 0.5 | 0.3 | 0.3 | 0.2 | 0.9 | 0.8 |
| <65 | 0.4 | 0.3 | 0.6 | 0.6 | 0.5 | 0.6 | 0.2 | 0.1 | 0.2 | 0.2 | 0.1 | 0.1 | 0.1 | 0.1 | 0.2 | 0.3 |
| Age average | 32.5 | 32.6 | 40.0 | 40.6 | 41.8 | 40.8 | 29.2 | 29.3 | 38.9 | 39.0 | 29.4 | 29.5 | 31.4 | 31.5 | 36.5 | 35.3 |

| Age | Kiss FM | | Máxima FM | | R. Tele Taxi*** | | Radio RM** | | Radiolé | | RADIO 3/ RNE 3 | | iCat fm | |
|---|---|---|---|---|---|---|---|---|---|---|---|---|---|---|
| | 08 | 09* | 08 | 09* | 08 | 09* | 08 | 09* | 08 | 09* | 08 | 09* | 08 | 09* |
| 14–19 | 0.9 | 0.6 | 4.1 | 4.3 | 0.7 | — | 0.1 | — | 0.6 | 0.7 | 0.1 | 0.2 | 0.1 | 0.2 |
| 20–24 | 1.8 | 2.2 | 5.1 | 5.4 | 0.9 | — | 0.3 | — | 0.6 | 0.6 | 0.5 | 0.4 | 0.4 | 0.7 |
| 25–34 | 3.1 | 3.5 | 2.3 | 2.4 | 1.3 | — | 0.5 | — | 0.5 | 0.5 | 1.1 | 1.2 | 0.8 | 1.0 |
| 35–44 | 3.7 | 3.9 | 0.8 | 1.1 | 1.6 | — | 0.6 | — | 0.6 | 0.6 | 0.6 | 0.6 | 0.5 | 0.7 |
| 45–54 | 1.9 | 2.4 | 0.4 | 0.4 | 2.4 | — | 0.9 | — | 0.7 | 0.7 | 0.5 | 0.4 | 0.4 | 0.7 |
| 55–64 | 0.8 | 1.1 | 0.1 | 0.1 | 4.7 | — | 1.3 | — | 0.8 | 0.9 | 0.3 | 0.2 | 0.2 | 0.1 |
| <65 | 0.2 | 0.2 | 0.1 | 0.1 | 3.7 | — | 0.5 | — | 0.4 | 0.5 | 0.2 | 0.2 | 0.0 | 0.0 |
| Age average | 38.0 | 37.9 | 27.5 | 27.9 | 55.0 | — | 50.0 | — | 45.8 | 45.2 | 40.1 | 39.5 | 38.1 | 36.7 |

Cumulative audiences by daily average from February to November, from Monday to Sunday among people aged fourteen and older in Catalonia.

*The data for 2009 belong to the second wave, therefore, they are provisional data for 2009.

***There is no information available concerning 2009 of Grup Tele Taxi radio stations (Radio Tele Taxi i Radio RM).

*Source:* Original chart, based on EGM Ràdio Catalunya data and Huertas (2008: 101).

Unlike the previous information, Table 9.1 only refers to a shorter period, namely 2008 and the second wave of 2009. However, in order to understand the scale of this progressive disinterest of the youngest audience demographic towards radio, it is necessary to pause a moment and look at the changes in listening to music broadcasting which have been ongoing for many seasons. Chart 9.3 reflects this tendency according to the EGM Ràdio Catalunya information from 2006 to 2009. It is worth highlighting the perceived upturn observed in some radio stations in 2008, with regard to listeners aged between fourteen and nineteen, while there has been a slight decline in the twenty to twenty-four-year old demographic. However, it is in this last demographic where this general tendency to increase has been detected in most of the radio stations and/or music radio stations, with the exception of Cadena Dial, according to the information in the second wave of 2009. On the other hand, the situation is not as homogeneous as it seems as far as the youngest audiences are concerned, since there are some radio stations that have experienced declines in their audiences, such as 40 Principales (0.9 percentage points), Ràdio Flaixbac (0.7 points), Cadena Dial (0.4 points) and M-80 (0.1 point). The rest of the stations have experienced an increase.

**Chart 9.3:** Changes to the audiences of the thematic music radio stations in Catalonia, in the age groups from fourteen to nineteen and from twenty to twenty-four years old.

(2006–2009)

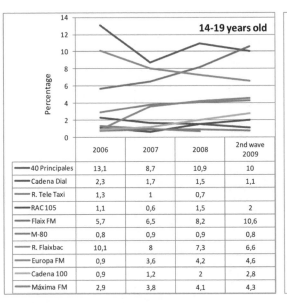

| | 2006 | 2007 | 2008 | 2nd wave 2009 |
|---|---|---|---|---|
| 40 Principales | 13,1 | 8,7 | 10,9 | 10 |
| Cadena Dial | 2,3 | 1,7 | 1,5 | 1,1 |
| R. Tele Taxi | 1,3 | 1 | 0,7 | |
| RAC 105 | 1,1 | 0,6 | 1,5 | 2 |
| Flaix FM | 5,7 | 6,5 | 8,2 | 10,6 |
| M-80 | 0,8 | 0,9 | 0,9 | 0,8 |
| R. Flaixbac | 10,1 | 8 | 7,3 | 6,6 |
| Europa FM | 0,9 | 3,6 | 4,2 | 4,6 |
| Cadena 100 | 0,9 | 1,2 | 2 | 2,8 |
| Máxima FM | 2,9 | 3,8 | 4,1 | 4,3 |

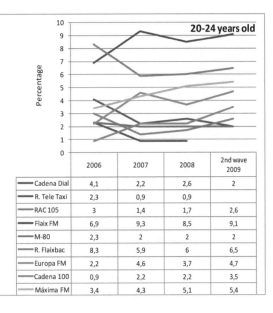

| | 2006 | 2007 | 2008 | 2nd wave 2009 |
|---|---|---|---|---|
| Cadena Dial | 4,1 | 2,2 | 2,6 | 2 |
| R. Tele Taxi | 2,3 | 0,9 | 0,9 | |
| RAC 105 | 3 | 1,4 | 1,7 | 2,6 |
| Flaix FM | 6,9 | 9,3 | 8,5 | 9,1 |
| M-80 | 2,3 | 2 | 2 | 2 |
| R. Flaixbac | 8,3 | 5,9 | 6 | 6,5 |
| Europa FM | 2,2 | 4,6 | 3,7 | 4,7 |
| Cadena 100 | 0,9 | 2,2 | 2,2 | 3,5 |
| Máxima FM | 3,4 | 4,3 | 5,1 | 5,4 |

Cumulative audiences by daily average from February to November and from Monday to Sunday, among people aged fourteen years and above, in Catalonia.
*Source*: Original chart, based on EGM Ràdio Catalunya data and Huertas (2009).

**Chart 9.4:** The crisis in music radio consumption by young people in Catalonia, by station (2004–08).

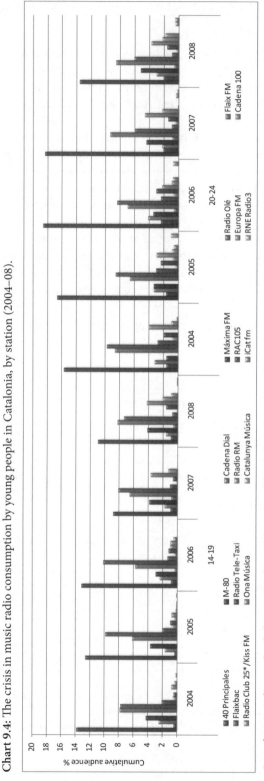

Cumulative audiences by daily average from February to November, from Monday to Sunday. (Radio Club 25 sold its frequencies to Kiss FM in 2007.)
*Source:* Martí & Monclús (2008).

Nevertheless, both the stagnation and the ageing of the music radio audience in Catalonia have been notable for some seasons, as can be observed in Chart 9.4. On the one hand, this chart broadens the range of the thematic music radio stations, since it includes total listening to music radio stations in Catalonia, and not only those which enjoy the largest audiences, but it also includes the periods 2004–05 for the purposes of comparison. It can also be observed that the majority of the youth audience is concentrated on three or four radio stations which inevitably have undergone striking and constant losses in their listenership.

However, the disaffection of the young Catalan population towards listening to the radio can be traced back more than ten years, and this provides clear evidence of an important audience decline of 17.5 points in the fourteen to nineteen year-old demographic, as well as one of thirteen points among the age group of twenty to twenty-four-year olds for the medium of radio overall. These are percentage points which will be difficult to regain in today's highly competitive media environment, as Chart 9.5 shows. Thus, quite apart from the way the information is presented, this suggests a significant crisis, enough for programmers to start planning new strategies that must consider the diet of culture and media of these age groups among potential listeners. In conclusion, the volume of listeners in these age groups has been declining season after season in general terms, and whatever slight increase can be detected seems like a 'blip' in the latest figures.

**Chart 9.5:** Changes in radio listening by the fourteen to twenty-four-year-old age group in Catalonia (1996–09).

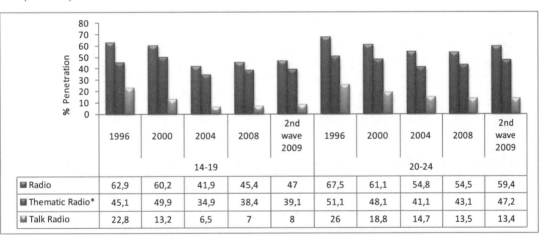

| | 14-19 | | | | | 20-24 | | | | |
|---|---|---|---|---|---|---|---|---|---|---|
| | 1996 | 2000 | 2004 | 2008 | 2nd wave 2009 | 1996 | 2000 | 2004 | 2008 | 2nd wave 2009 |
| ▪ Radio | 62,9 | 60,2 | 41,9 | 45,4 | 47 | 67,5 | 61,1 | 54,8 | 54,5 | 59,4 |
| ▪ Thematic Radio* | 45,1 | 49,9 | 34,9 | 38,4 | 39,1 | 51,1 | 48,1 | 41,1 | 43,1 | 47,2 |
| ▪ Talk Radio | 22,8 | 13,2 | 6,5 | 7 | 8 | 26 | 18,8 | 14,7 | 13,5 | 13,4 |

*EGM Ràdio Catalunya including music radio and news formats in the thematic radio category.
*Source*: Original chart based on the EGM and *EGM Ràdio a Catalunya* information.

Following its music radio analysis among the youngest audience demographic, in 2008 the Baròmetre de la Comunicació i la Cultura[3] reported that the average reach of radio among the population was 54.3%, placing radio in fourth position, preceded by the internet with 64.1%, external communication 66.4% and television as the leader with an unassailable 91.1%. Table 9.2 presents the general distribution of media audiences according to age group. This information allows us to appreciate that the share of radio in the media diet is 8.3 percentage points higher in the twenty to twenty-four age group than the fourteen to nineteen year olds, whereas the share of TV and the internet are 4.7 points and 2.8 points lower, respectively.

**Table 9.2:** Total media audience, fourteen to twenty-four-years old (2008).

|                                | 14–19 | 20–24 |
|--------------------------------|-------|-------|
| Newspapers                     | 33.3  | 43.4  |
| Supplements                    | 9.7   | 13.3  |
| Total magazines                | 66.2  | 66.6  |
| Weekly magazines               | 36.5  | 36.9  |
| Fortnightly monthly magazines  | 15.3  | 6.1   |
| Monthly magazines              | 48.1  | 48.1  |
| Others                         | 5.5   | 7.6   |
| Internet                       | 65.6  | 62.8  |
| Radio                          | 50    | 58.3  |
| TV                             | 93.5  | 88.8  |
| Exterior                       | 65.3  | 67.4  |

Percentage share of all media among people aged fourteen years old and above in Catalonia.
*Source*: Original chart from data in *El Baròmetre de la Comunicació i la Cultura* (FUNDACC 2008).

Moreover, the decline in radio is less severe than in television and the internet. The information provided by the Culture and Media Department of the Catalan Autonomous Government and Catalan Institute of Statistics (see Table 9.3), also supports this premise, emphasizing at the same time the importance in their diet of such cultural activities as listening to music and the significant role acquired by the computer as an entertainment tool and one for cultural consumption.

**Table 9.3:** Cultural habits and entertainment activities of the Catalan population aged 15–29 (2006).

| Cultural habits | % | Other cultural habits | |
|---|---|---|---|
| **Reading and writing** | | Library | 67.1 |
| Newspapers | 90.1 | Museums | 55.8 |
| Books | 85.1 | Historical buildings | 50.9 |
| Magazines | 82.8 | Exposition | 40.1 |
| Write | 32.2 | Record offices | 15.2 |
| **Music** | | Associations | 32.4 |
| Listening to music | 99.6 | **Entertainment Habits** | **%** |
| Concerts | 68.1 | **Activities** [1] | |
| **Staging Arts** | | Family/friends meetings | 28.4 |
| Cinema | 91.1 | Sport practice | 16.5 |
| Theater | 46.3 | TV/video | 15.3 |
| **Audiovisuals** | | Study/classes | 14.6 |
| TV | 97.6 | Walk about | 11.8 |
| Video/DVD | 95.0 | Computer | 10.0 |
| Radio | 71.8 | Bars | 100.0 |
| **Information Technologies** | | Reading | 5.6 |
| Internet users | 94.6 | Sleep/rest | 4.9 |
| Computer users | 82.8 | House chores/Cooking | 1.6 |
| Videogames | 59.2 | | |

[1]Activities carried during the working day, spare time and the weekend prior to this survey. Respondents were allowed to provide up to ten answers.
*Source*: Fundació Audiències de la Comunicació i la Cultura (2008).

Though all these factors are relevant to the slow, constant radio audience decline is increasingly becoming an important issue for programmers. Even the better-positioned radio stations have been losing listeners every season. This is affecting the whole group of operators, and although some stations present some signs of improvement in their results, this should be interpreted as a result of particular and isolated circumstances. This can be read into the increase of Flaix FM's increase in listenership during 2008 can be attributed to this.

**Table 9.4:** Changes in total listening to the top five music radio stations in the ranking from Monday to Sunday from 2006 to 2009 (in thousands).

| Station | 2006 | 2007 | 2008 | 2nd wave 2009 |
|---|---|---|---|---|
| 40 Principales | 394 | 379 | 363 | 389 |
| Cadena Dial | 169 | 177 | 171 | 165 |
| Radio Tele Taxi | 175 | 162 | 147 | – |
| RAC 105 | 157 | 142 | 137 | 207 |
| Flaix FM | 144 | 145 | 166 | 220 |

*Note*: The EGM outcome in 2009 does not consider Radio Tele Taxi. Cadena 100 occupies the 5th position in the 2nd wave in 2009 with 164,000 listeners.
People aged fourteen years and above in Catalonia.
*Source*: Original chart from information in Huertas (2008) and *EGM Ràdio Catalunya* (February–November).

From a quantitative point of view, these are logical results due to the fact that radio does not occupy a prominent position in the media diet of Catalan youngsters, and this has serious consequences for music radio. However, if listening to music ranks first in their regular cultural habits, even surpassing TV, the internet and cinema, why are youngsters not interested in music radio?

### Young people's broadcasting preferences

In order to state which broadcasting pattern is preferred by Catalan youngsters aged between fourteen and twenty-four, they were asked to name the radio station they would listen to most often. The answers were classified according to the following variables:

- talk radio, which logically embraces the group of radio stations with all audiences' content;
- music radio, referring to the thematic music stations;
- specialized radio, including thematic non-music stations, and
- don't knows, for those answers which clearly demonstrated ignorance of what they listened to.

It was necessary to enlarge the categories to 'others' (local stations with mixed content) and 'without any preference' (some of those polled revealed that they felt indifferent to the stations), although these responses were very few in number. The outcome is to be seen in Chart 9.6.

**Chart 9.6:** Programming type preferred by Catalan youngsters aged fourteen to twenty-four years.

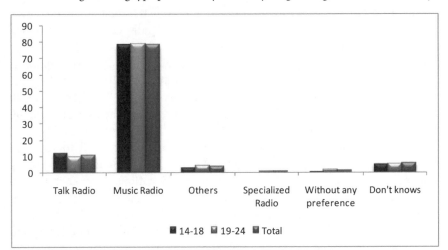

*Source*: Original chart.

From Chart 9.7 it is evident that thematic music radio is the preferred choice of teenage Catalan listeners. The EGM Ràdio Catalunya survey indicates that every broadcasting season is equally significant, but by using a different analytical method, it arrives at a similar conclusion. However, this analysis of young people's general behaviour shows different nuances when the information is closely observed from a gender perspective.

**Chart 9.7:** Programming type preferred by Catalan youngsters aged fourteen to twenty-four years, according to gender.

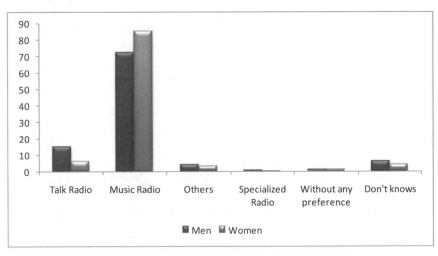

*Source*: Original chart.

From the point of view of gender, it can be observed that women listen to thematic music radio stations more often (85.1%) and their interest in the talk radio genre is down to 6%. On the other hand, men, although choosing music radio (72.3%), also tune in to radio stations with generalist programming (15.2%). It has to be said that radio consumption is slightly different according to the station, although both genders agree in naming the same operators. For men, the order of preference is headed by Flaix FM (26.9%), followed by 40 Principales (16.6%) and Ràdio Flaixbac (8.4%). In the case of women, the list starts with 40 Principales (29.4%) and is followed by Flaix FM (19%) and by Ràdio Flaixbac (12.5%).

From the point of view of age, music radio similarly stands out in the two surveyed groups achieving 78.5% among teenagers aged fourteen to eighteen years and 78.9% among those aged nineteen to twenty-four years. The three preferred stations were: Flaix FM, 40 Principales and Ràdio Flaixbac, but with different orders of preference. Teenagers aged fourteen to eighteen tune into 40 Principales (22.7%) more often, whereas the teens aged nineteen to twenty-four years go for Flaix FM (24%). Flaix FM is also the second (21.7%) in preference in the age demographic fourteen to eighteen years; 40 Principales (23%) was the most preferred station among young people aged nineteen to twenty-four. Ràdio Flaixbac occupies the third position in both the groups, with a percentage rate of 12.9 (for those aged fourteen to eighteen years) and 8.8 (for those aged nineteen to twenty-four years). A clear and manifest coincidence has been detected in the analysis between the favourite music stations and those which broadcast the music the young listeners like the most, a situation which can be interpreted as an expectation and interests' adjustment, in spite of the fact that the crisis in thematic music radio is currently indisputable.

If the most preferred radio content among young people is music, other options, such as news, humour and finally sports, cannot be underestimated as is clear from Chart 9.8. In all, recognizing this might open the way to new methods of broadcasting and development.

According to the chart, apart from music teenagers aged nineteen to twenty-four years display a greater interest in other types of content, unlike the younger ones. As far as age is concerned, other behaviours can be observed; we list them as follows:

- Music accounts for the majority of the broadcasting preferences of teenagers aged fourteen to eighteen years.
- In the second age demographic (from nineteen to twenty-four), the range of most-preferred content widens. Thus, together with music content, we find news, information and humour. This third group of content is one of their top preferences, since the impact of music is smaller in the case of the youngest listeners.
- Unlike music, the rest of the most-preferred content shows significantly low percentages overall. In this sense, the appearance of participation as a broadcasting genre has to be highlighted, since it features prominently in the schedules, contrary to the playlists of these stations.

**Chart 9.8:** Most preferred broadcasting content among Catalan youngsters aged fourteen to twenty-four years and nineteen to twenty-four years.

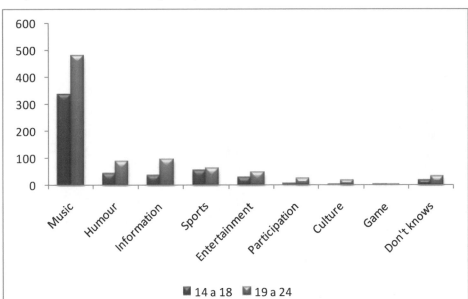

*Source*: Original chart.

From the perspective of gender, as shown in Chart 9.9, the analysis suggests the following points:

- The young male listener presents a wider range of expectations since, apart from music, he consumes sport (13%), humour (11%) and news (9%). This might explain male listening to generalist radio being superior to female listening at 9.2%.
- The association of radio and music has a significant appeal among young women who listen to radio, which consequently reveals less interest in other types of content, since information and news rank 10%.
- The gender differences in the rest of the content is not very significant, and in some cases, as is the case of culture (2%), the percentage is not the same. In the case of women, humour stands out above the rest, but in any case, it does not surpass 10%.

**Chart 9.9:** Most-preferred broadcasting content among Catalan youngsters aged fourteen to twenty-four years, by gender.

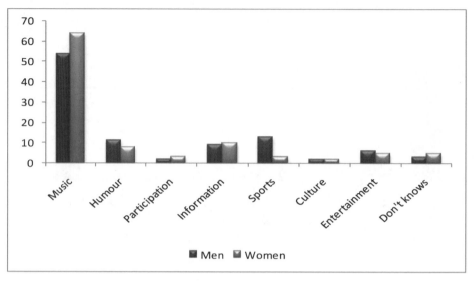

*Source*: Original chart.

## What does radio broadcasting offer to young people?

We have found that musical content stands out from the rest as regards the broadcasting consumption of Catalan youngsters. However, this interest does not seem to prevent the steady decline in the young audiences of radio stations. If we pay closer attention to the formats that shape the thematic music radio stations' offer, a fundamental factor arises: the format could partly be the explanation for the disinterest that Catalan youngsters express towards radio. Music radio which is broadcast in Catalonia is mainly framed in the Adult Contemporary (AC) format, which includes a significant number of radio stations that are basically targeted at an adult audience. In other words, at people older than twenty-four. Therefore, we can conclude that there is a mismatch between the music preferences of the youngest audiences and the broadcasting material offered in the market.

**Table 9.5:** Format changes to music and thematic networks in Catalonia, 1999 and 2008.

| 1999 | 2008 |
|---|---|
| **Music List** | |
| 40 Principales, Hot 70, Radio Club 25 | |
| **Adult Contemporary (AC)** | |
| M-80, Flaixbac, RKOR, Ona Música, Cadena 100, RAC 105 | M-80, Ràdio Flaixbac, Cadena 100, RAC 105, Europa FM, Kiss FM, GUM FM, Styl FM, Próxima FM |
| **Crossover** | |
| | 40 Principales (Music charts and AC) |
| **Oldies** | |
| | Èxits FM |
| **Folklore** | |
| Cadena Dial, RM Radio, Radio Tele Taxi | Cadena Dial, RM Radio, Radio Tele Taxi, Radiolé |
| **Classic Music** | |
| *RNE Radio 2*, Sinfo Radio, *Catalunya Música* | *Radio Clásica (RNE)*, *Catalunya Música* |
| **Dance Music** | |
| Flaix FM | Flaix FM, Máxima FM |
| **Beautiful Music** | |
| Ràdio Estel | Ràdio Estel |
| **Non-commercial Music** | |
| | iCat fm |
| **Mixed Formats** | |
| *RNE Radio 3*, *Catalunya Cultura* | *RNE Radio 3*, Rock & Gol |

*Note*: Public stations shown in italics.
*Source*: Martí & Monclús (2008).

According to our information, Catalan youngsters aged fourteen to twenty-four years, prefer to listen to three types of format: Crossover (40 Principales), Dance Music (Flaix FM) and Adult Contemporary (Ràdio Flaixbac). This diversity has to be interpreted from the radio stations' schedules, in which all of them coincide in presenting morning shows and late shows that combine news, humour and participation. Moreover, during the day, musical content is usually from the playlist, and there is very little speech and much more music. However, it has to be highlighted that only dance music could be considered as the music format conceived for the youngest audiences, instances of which were found only in Flaix FM *and* Máxima FM. The other stations are obviously searching for an older and wealthier listenership: this factor is especially important in the radio market in Catalonia, sustained primarily by the private sector.

## The 'radio-young people-internet' triangle

Thematic music stations have taken to the internet through their websites; where apart from offering information about the station's programme content, they also provide some other features. According to the information provided by the Culture and Media Department of the Catalan Autonomous Government and Catalan Institute of Statistics (Table 9.3), young people have assimilated the internet into their consumption of culture and entertainment. So it was important to find out to what extent young people knew about the radio's presence on the web. Paradoxically, it was found that more than a quarter of the surveyed young people (27.6%) are completely unaware of the radio stations' websites: only 72.4% would be able to identify radio stations that have a presence on the web. This lack of knowledge might be one of the reasons why less than half (46.7%) of the youngsters visit radio web pages, as shown in Chart 9.10. Then, generally 53.35% of young people do not visit the stations' web pages

**Chart 9.10:** Awareness and use of radio stations' websites.

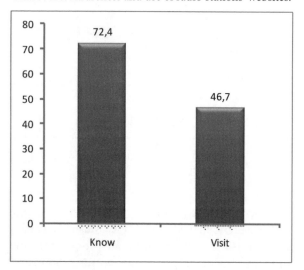

*Source*: Original chart.

Apart from the young visitors, 71.8% (that is to say, 33.56% of the total amount) claimed to visit the web pages 'sometimes' or 'almost never'. Only 28% of the visitors (13.08% of the total number of young people) can be considered faithful listeners, mainly because they are those who openly claim to visit broadcasting websites 'very often' or 'often', as can be seen in the information gathered in Chart 9.11. This low fidelity is undoubtedly related to the low levels of product relevance stemming from content restricted to little more than basic, live simulcasting on the website and the lack of additional content in this type of service.

**Chart 9.11:** Visits to radio station websites.

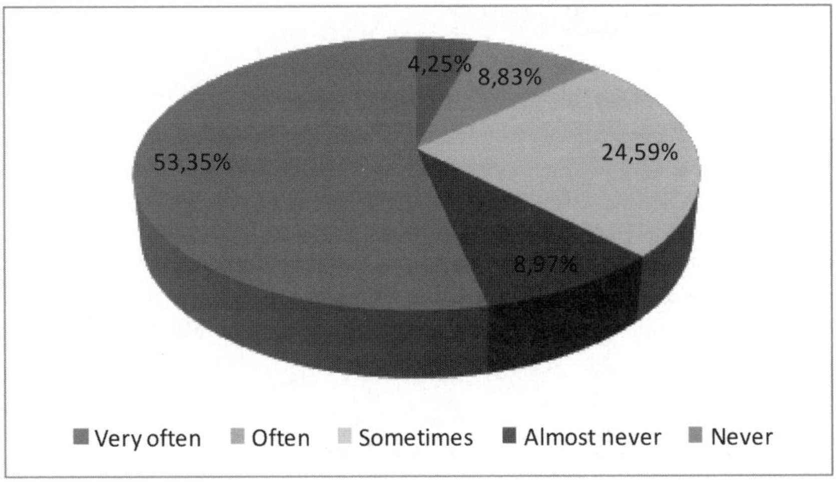

*Source*: Original chart.

The number of visits to radio web pages that young people have made in the thirty days prior to the survey are noteworthy: the total falls to 9.3% for the fourteen to nineteen years demographic; and is down to 12.1% for the twenty to twenty-four-year-old demographic, according to the information provided by the *Baròmetre de la Comunicació i la Cultura* in 2008. If we consider broadcasting consumption via the internet, shown in Chart 9.12, we also find that those listeners represent 35.6% of those surveyed. In this, boys rank higher (39.8%) than girls (31.3%).

**Chart 9.12:** Internet radio listening.

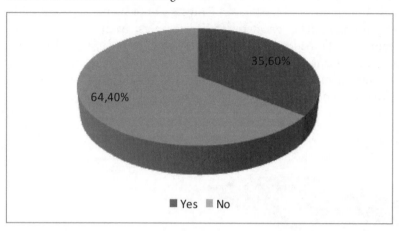

*Source*: Original chart.

It is noteworthy that the age distribution seems to favour the eldest sector (Chart 9.13). The percentages shown indicate 38.7% of the cyber-listeners are aged between nineteen and twenty-four years, as compared to 30.8% in case of those aged between fourteen and eighteen.

**Chart 9.13:** Internet radio listening frequency according to age groups.

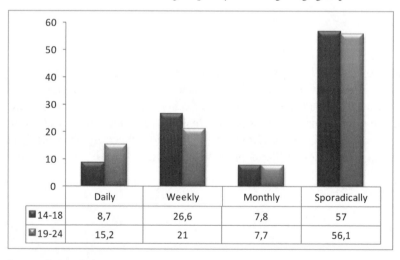

| | Daily | Weekly | Monthly | Sporadically |
|---|---|---|---|---|
| 14-18 | 8,7 | 26,6 | 7,8 | 57 |
| 19-24 | 15,2 | 21 | 7,7 | 56,1 |

*Source*: Original chart.

According to 56.4% of bitcasters consumers, internet radio listening can be considered sporadic. Only 22% of this group admit listening to internet radio weekly. By comparison, 13% of this demographic admit to listening to internet radio daily. If bitcasters make up only 35.6% of the total surveyed, young people who are faithful to internet radio would not even reach 5% (4.62%).

**Chart 9.14:** Frequency of internet radio listening, according to gender.

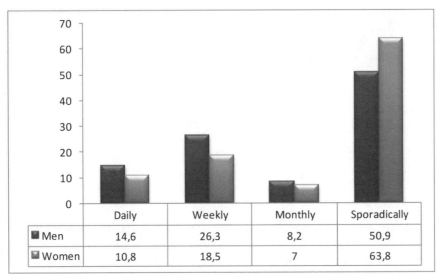

| | Daily | Weekly | Monthly | Sporadically |
|---|---|---|---|---|
| ■ Men | 14,6 | 26,3 | 8,2 | 50,9 |
| ☑ Women | 10,8 | 18,5 | 7 | 63,8 |

*Source*: Original chart.

In terms of gender (Chart 9.14), men (39.8%) are more inclined to listen to internet radio than women (31.3%) and the frequency of listening is also higher in the case of men. If we observe internet listening by age demographics we find 38.7% of the oldest say that they use the internet to listen to broadcasting, against 30.8% of the younger ones. Similarly, the nineteen to twenty-four-year-old group is more faithful (15.2% listen to internet radio on a daily basis) than the fourteen to eighteen-year-old group (only 8.7% claim they listen to radio through the web on a daily basis). Here the lifestyle difference between these two age demographics, which is related to their online broadcasting consumption, needs to be highlighted.

**Chart 9.15:** Different types of internet radio consumption according to gender.

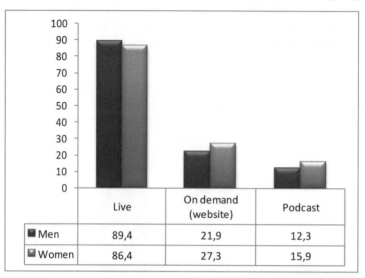

| | Live | On demand (website) | Podcast |
|---|---|---|---|
| Men | 89,4 | 21,9 | 12,3 |
| Women | 86,4 | 27,3 | 15,9 |

*Source*: Original chart.

One of the other issues we analysed was the type of listening taking place (Chart 9.15): 88.1% of those who listen to internet radio use live online broadcasting; 24.2% listen to songs or radio extracts from the website (radio on demand), and only 13.8% of cyber-listeners use the podcast option (meaning, in general terms, they download the programmes and consume/listen to them later). The most significant differences are to be found between women who, in this case, take a more active stance than men. Whereas 27.3% of the women use radio on demand, only 21.9% of men use this service. Women also consume more podcasting (15.9% of the girls as against 12.3% of boys). If we analyse live listening and on-demand modality by age (Chart 9.16), the consumption pattern is virtually identical. The most significant difference is to be found in the use of podcasts. The group comprising eighteen to twenty-four-year olds is keener on this type of radio listening (15.8% ) than the younger group of fourteen to eighteen-year olds (10.1% ).

**Chart 9.16:** Internet radio consumption according to age group.

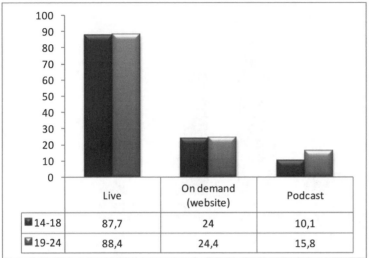

| | Live | On demand (website) | Podcast |
|---|---|---|---|
| ◼ 14-18 | 87,7 | 24 | 10,1 |
| ◼ 19-24 | 88,4 | 24,4 | 15,8 |

*Source*: Original chart.

Different times of the day reveal different preferences insofar as listening to the radio on the web is concerned (Chart 9.17). There are no noticeable differences between 6 am and 12 noon or during the early afternoon between 12 noon and 4 p.m. However, in the late afternoon, between 4 p.m. and 8 pm, the number of women listening (57.2%) exceeds men by 8% (49%). This tendency is reversed during the evening between 8 p.m. and midnight, when there are 16.5% more men (51.6%) listening to the radio than women (35.1%). Finally, during the very early morning between midnight and 6 a.m., once again women (5.8%) exceed men (2.8%) by only 3 points.

**Chart 9.17:** Time of day for internet listening, by gender.

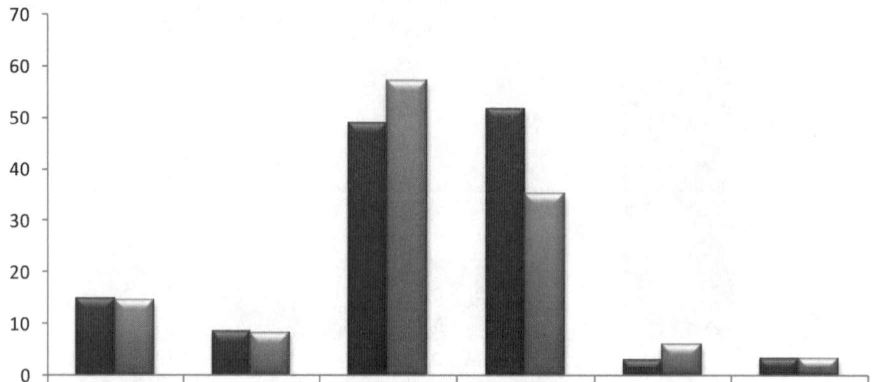

| | Morning (6 am-12 pm) | Midday (12 pm - 4 pm) | Afternoon (4 pm - 8 pm) | Night (8 pm- 12 am) | Early morning (12 am - 6 am) | Any time |
|---|---|---|---|---|---|---|
| Men | 14,7 | 8,2 | 49 | 51,6 | 2,8 | 3,1 |
| Women | 14,5 | 7,9 | 57,2 | 35,1 | 5,8 | 3,2 |

*Source*: Original chart.

Internet radio consumption is more prevalent during working days (Chart 9.18). In fact, 35.9% of those who claim to listen to streaming radio declare that they do not listen in that way at weekends or during holidays. Conversely, only 6.4% declare that, although they listen to internet radio, they do not listen to radio during the week. Regular listening sessions last from fifteen to sixty minutes, both on working days (47.2%) and during public holidays (28%). We also found sessions of one or two hours during the working week (20.5%) and holidays (15.4%). Listening sessions shorter than fifteen minutes make up 11.9% of the amount of listening on working days and 7.9% during the holidays. It should be borne in mind that 10.1% of cyber-listeners claimed to listen to internet radio more than two hours per day on working days and 9.7% of the listenership listen for more than two hours during holidays.

**Chart 9.18:** Internet broadcasting consumption in hours.

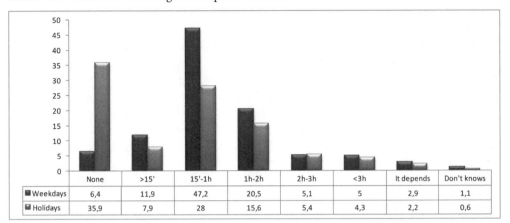

| | None | >15' | 15'-1h | 1h-2h | 2h-3h | <3h | It depends | Don't knows |
|---|---|---|---|---|---|---|---|---|
| Weekdays | 6,4 | 11,9 | 47,2 | 20,5 | 5,1 | 5 | 2,9 | 1,1 |
| Holidays | 35,9 | 7,9 | 28 | 15,6 | 5,4 | 4,3 | 2,2 | 0,6 |

*Source*: Original chart.

Another issue of interest which has evolved from the information obtained from the qualitative research is the presenter speech listeners would like to skip when they tune into radio for listening to music. Listeners were annoyed at the voice of the presenter and preference for the presenter to not speak at all was very pronounced. For this reason, the figure of the presenter, at least in the Catalan radio environment, has currently fallen into disuse. Young people also made clear to us that not only do they use the internet for listening to music but also to keep themselves updated with music news and for downloading. It can be stated that, in a way, music scheduling, for a long time within the gift of the presenter, is now taking place on the web, where in a very passive fashion and without any previous conception, it provides cyber-listeners with access to the current trends in new music and is thus becoming a reference point for them.

## Conclusions: the digital environment, a new opportunity?

No doubt the converging of the radio with the internet is the most suitable strategy to counteract, on the one hand, the loss of audience in thematic music stations, and on the other, to generate an increase in the number of cyber-listeners. However, in the light of the data assembled, bearing in mind that later qualitative research will enable us to better clarify some previously suggested trends, the situation is so complex that the simple action of creating a corporate website does not necessarily create an emotional link with the radio station, which automatically enhances audience loyalty. First, we must consider the absence of broadcasting formats specifically conceived and shaped for this audience demographic.

The majority of the thematic music radio stations, mostly the private ones, have opted for the Adult Contemporary format, which due to its characteristics, will not easily appeal to the twenty-four-year-old demographic.

On the other hand, we have stated that the lack of awareness of thematic radio's role in the web is very significant, given the high percentage of young Catalan people surveyed who have defined themselves as cyber-listeners. But they certainly know what they search for and how to profit from it as a means of downloading music, purchasing new music and loading them into their digital playback devices. Therefore, with this kind of use, thematic music radio is reduced to a showcase where the broadcaster-consumer selects the podcast he or she likes. Evidently, this is one of its uses, but not the only one. Furthermore, together with a more diverse offer and considering streaming and the type of consumption as a variable (among others), thematic music stations have made an effort to clearly define their products and promote their brands. It is unlikely they will reach their potential audiences if radio decides to work in partnership with an obsolete medium that has nothing to contribute. Only from this point of view, can it be understood why radio has lost its prescriptive character, a very important quality in its former avatar.

The results of our qualitative research will enable us to reinforce some of the assertions made from the quantitative data obtained. Although the results of the focus group are not entirely representative, we have found, for example, that radio has not lost its prescriptive function among the younger demographic in the population. In the light of this information, we believe that the main goal is the integration of radio into the daily lives of young people. The situation is still complex and deserves special attention. In fact, the creation of a stable audience has become very necessary for the survival of this medium.

## Notes

1. The last available census.
2. The General Media Survey, *Estudi General de Mitjans* EGM, conducted by the Asociación para la Investigación de Medios de Comunicación AIMC Association for the Media Investigation has become a referential framework about the Spanish population's Media consumption. The information provided becomes highly important for the radio stations, and mostly because they condition their programming policies and strategies. Since 2003 the AIMC conducts a specific EGM for the area of Catalonia, *EGM Ràdio Catalunya*, which consists of 25,000 interviews among the over fourteens in Catalonia. The survey is divided into three annual 'waves'.
3. The *Baròmetre de la Comunicació i la Cultura*, fostered by the Fundació d'Audiències de la Comunicació i la Cultura (FUNDACC Audiences' Foundation for Culture and Media), is a Media survey that deals with media and cultural diet within the Catalan-speaking territories. Instituted in 2004, FUNDACC has become the second referential point for those Media which broadcast in Catalonia. For further information see http://www.fundacc.org/fundacc/es/.

## References and further reading

Asociación para la Investigación de Medios de Comunicación (AIMC), *Estudio General de Medios - EGM Ràdio Catalunya*, Madrid: AIMC, 1996–2009.

Barea, P., 'Hábitos de recepción de la Radio en el País Vasco', *ZER*, 6:1 1999, pp. 153–78.

European Broadcasting Union, *Public Youth Radio in Europe*, Geneva, Estrategic Information Service of EBU, 2008.

Fundació Audiències de la Comunicació i la Cultura (FUNDACC), *La dieta mediàtica i cultural dels joves*, [Online], 2008, http//fundacc.org/fundacc/ca/dades/informesespecials/contentMain/0/text_files/filela_dieta_mediatica_i_cultural_dels_joves_%20dades.pdf. Accessed 1 October 2008.

Glevarec, H., 'Youth Radio as Social Object: The "social meaning" of "free radio" shows for young people in France', *Media Culture Society*, 27:3 2005, pp. 333–51.

Gutiérrez, M., 'La programació radiofònica a Catalunya' in J. M. Martí, B. Monclús. coord, *Informe sobre la Ràdio a Catalunya, 2008*, Bellaterra, Servei de Publicacions de la Universitat Autònoma de Barcelona, 2009, pp. 71-88.

Huertas, A., 'El consum radiofònic' in J. M. Martí, B. Monclús eds, *Informe sobre la Ràdio a Catalunya, 2006–2007* Barcelona, Observatori de la Ràdio a Catalunya, Departament de Comunicació Audiovisual i Publicitat, Universitat Autònoma de Barcelona, 2008, pp. 69–90.

—— 'El consum radiofònic: Davant la barrera psicològica del 50 per cert' in J. M. Martí, B. Monclús. eds, *Informe sobre la Ràdio a Catalunya, 2008* Bellaterra, Servei de Publicacions de la Universitat Autònoma de Barcelona, 2009, pp. 89–106.

Martí, J. M., Monclús, B., 'Music Radio 2.0: Construction within the Web Society Framework. The Way Youth Aret Tansforming the Conventional Musical Radio Format', in Proceedings of *The Communication Policies and Culture in Europe. II ECREA European Communication Conference* [Online], 2008, http://www.ecrea2008barcelona.org/guide/abstract.asp?id_callfor=400&id_seccion=13&id_subseccio=113. Accessed 10 Febuary 2009.

McClung, S., Pompper, D., Kinnally, W., 'Appealing to Abandoning Adolescents: Radio Use Motivation Factors and Time Spent Listening', in Proceedings of *The Annual Meeting of the International Communication* Association [Online], 2005, http//www.allacademic.com/meta/p11786_index.html. Accessed 1 November 2008.

Ribes, X., 'Informe especial: La radio catalana a Internet, 2006–2007' in J. M. Martí, B. Monclús eds, *Informe sobre la Ràdio a Catalunya, 2006–2007* Barcelona, Observatori de la Ràdio a Catalunya, Departament de Comunicació Audiovisual i Publicitat de la Universitat Autònoma de Barcelona, 2008, pp. 99–113.

# Chapter 10

Whatever You Say, Say Nothing: Analysing Topics on *Liveline*

Frank Byrne

T his chapter attempts to address the question, 'What are the main characteristics of today's radio content?' by considering the content of one radio format in a particular national context. Through that exercise it suggests a number of theoretical avenues that might be useful in a wider consideration of how categories of content make it to the airways. Specifically, we will explore the subject matter being talked about over a two-year period in an Irish phone-in programme, *Liveline*. Initially the main reason for undertaking this was to provide a context for a more detailed conversational analysis of the *Liveline* programmes. It allows us to estimate how representative those 20 programmes are of the generality of topics being covered over the longer period.

New technology offered a handy source for the data. Since early 2007 each day RTE Radio 1 posts a podcast of the programme to its website and offers a one- or two-line description of the contents.[1] We simply categorized these for all the normal programmes between 1 July 2007 and 30 June 2009.[2] We offer a couple of provisos. I do appreciate that I am at the mercy of how the station elected to describe the topics but having listened to a considerable sample of the programmes, I was reasonably satisfied as to their broad accuracy. Secondly, after a few false starts, I settled on the seven broad categories, which for me represented a common sense and practical way of grouping the topics, but I would be the first to concede that these would clearly be open to contestation.

Some of the topics were dealt with briefly involving only one or two callers; others played out over a number of programmes. Where the station posted them as separate podcasts, we counted them separately. To borrow a term from blogging, we counted 879 'threads' over the two-year period and assigned them to the categories below.[3]

| | |
|---|---|
| 1. Consumer watchdog and complaints department | 262 |
| 2. Ombudsman – complaints about officialdom | 157 |
| 3. Requests for help and offering cautions | 21 |
| 4. Sharing personal troubles and experiences | 87 |
| 5. Social/cultural/civic standards and values | 229 |
| 6. Identity – construction of the self and others | 48 |
| 7. Quirky, complex, difficult to categorize | 75 |
| | |
| Total | 879 |

Similar work had been carried out on talk radio previously. Higgins and Moss (1982) plotted the topics on Australian Radio news bulletins. Norma Ellen Verwey (1990) undertook macro analysis of phone-in content in both Canada and the United Kingdom. Also, in the United Kingdom Anthony Wright (1979) schematized the content of phone-in calls to three local radio stations over a twelve-month period. Similar but smaller scale work was done by Sara O'Sullivan (2000a) in an Irish context when she categorized the topics on a different, more youth orientated and more tabloid phone-in based show, *The Gerry Ryan Show*.

Content is but one element of discursive exchange; one that I suspect is sometimes overlooked for being almost too obvious but, in terms of my background concern about what enters the public sphere, it is useful to know, not only how we are deliberating but what we are actually talking about. Joke Hermes (2006) speaks of content having meaning because it has a narrative quality: 'What's the story?' we say. Seyla Benhabib notes that the 'struggle over what gets included in the public agenda is itself a struggle for justice and freedom' (1992). What we're talking about matters.

This chapter will offer a brief note on the programme in question. *Liveline* is broadcast each weekday from 1.45 to 3 p.m. after the lunchtime news programme on RTE Radio 1, Ireland's national public service broadcaster. After the breakfast show it is the second most listened to programme, attracting a listenership of over 425,000 daily. Joe Duffy, its regular presenter, describes it as a space where people are allowed to tell their history, make a point or challenge injustice. It is somewhat unusual among PBS phone-ins in that it eschews studio experts, guests and politicians and it ostensibly relies for its material on calls from the public. That said, it broadly conforms to Lunt and Lewis's (2008) description that 'the content of such programmes is mainly made up of the experiences, thoughts, ideas and actions of the public mediated by the programme host and rendered into a program structure through a variety of devices'.

The focus of this research has been to examine how this modicum of access by non-professional, non-expert voices, can impact on the democratic process. In this particular instance, it was important to explore how these specific issues made their way into the mediated public sphere. Having assembled this admittedly roughly filtered data and agreeing with Anthony Wright (1980) that 'all of life (and death) is here, I was struck by two avenues of enquiry. The first led to the question, 'what shaped this material?' Why were some topics included and others not? Why did some receive more attention than others? The second avenue led to speculate on some of the theoretical strands that these concentrations and clusters of topics suggest – possibly a case of plots in search of a character!

So, what elements influence the thematic content of what we listen to? We might consider this first question under three broad headings:

1. the discursive context of time and place;
2. the parties to the programme;
3. the medium.

In terms of context, it is reasonable to infer that this list of topics would be different in a timeframe other than the present and different again in a different location. Ireland has been described as, 'a late modernizer, a latecomer to modernity' (Share, Tovey & Corcoran 2007) and we might add a latecomer to post- or even late modernity. Some of the implications of this will be teased out a little further on but we do understand when Paddy Scannell (1989) refers to the 'shifting borders of what could be talked about'. When Anthony Wright (1980) listed the factors that shaped the list of topics he catalogued, he mentioned publicity campaigns by groups and the ready availability of authors and of politicians, especially in the 'silly season'. They do not apply in any significant way to *Liveline* but he also mentions the publication of reports by organizations and the material in the newspapers of the day and both of these would also seem to have had an impact. The connection between 'topic' and 'topicality' is obvious; the programme feeds off whatever is current, noticed and signalled in some ill-defined intertextual soup.

The global recession and economic downturn is reflected in increased concerns with prices and loss of investments and with the services of financial institutions. The downstream effect of government belt tightening is best illustrated by the volume of concerns with healthcare provision. The programme has become a virtual counter-public sphere for campaigns around the scarcity of hospital beds, public healthcare provisions for cancer patients and the plight of cystic fibrosis sufferers. A hard-hitting and frankly horrific report last May on what has been described as the 'systemic abuse' meted out to children in religious-run residential institutions during the 1950s, 1960s and the 1970s became the trigger for a succession of harrowing programmes devoted to the stories of survivors.

In the course of the programme, the host of the show underlined the importance of an awareness of what is being covered elsewhere in the media. He also remarked on the impact that the rhythms of the year can have on content. The agenda can be different if Parliament is in session or children are in school. Holiday travel highlights difficulties with airlines and seasonal concerns about bonfires and fireworks, with students celebrating and the crassness of Christmas all come around on an annual basis.

It seems on the surface that the list of topics does not portray an overt Irishness but we would suggest that there is an overarching process of community building and in Billig's terms, 'banal nationalism' underpinning all of them. 'Callers share a world of lived experience', according to Higgins and Moss (1982) and in this case we understand that it is 'our' financial institutions, 'our' police force, 'our' issues with addiction or vandalism that are being discussed among ourselves. Religion almost invariably signifies Catholicism. 'The Border' relates to only one divided island. Nowadays, 'the border problem' thankfully is less likely to be about armed struggle and more about price differences.

The players – listeners, callers and the programme team, also known as the producers – also shape the agenda. Listeners, unless they become callers, do not impact directly on the programme content; but much as the programme may sound like a conversation with callers it is ultimately a transmission to listeners. If listeners are no longer interested, attentive, entertained or engaged the programme fails. If the topics are not those they want to hear or do not inspire enough of them to call, the programme fails. On their behalf and for their sakes both callers and presenter cooperate in being interesting and relevant. The demography of the listenership is reflected in the contents. Joe Duffy has characterized the *Liveline* audience as middle class. He could have added middle aged and middle Ireland. The young and the disadvantaged find other outlets to air their concerns, outlets that are not as reverent or as staid as the national PSB broadcaster. Little adolescent angst, authority bashing or radicalism is evident in this list. It is a matter of concern to Duffy who confesses that it is an uphill struggle to encourage such callers but unless listeners are tacitly aligned with the interests of callers they will drift away.

Callers therefore share the demographic characteristics of the general listenership. They are mainly listeners whose levels of engagement or interest have spurred them to become active in their own meaning making in what John Tebbutt (2006) calls 'the performance of opinion'. Attention has been drawn to the performative nature of calls – categorizing them for example as expressive, confessional or exhibitionist – but I would rather concentrate here on the opinions. The observation would be that callers simply want to make a point without sounding foolish. In this they supply the bulk of the content; they tell the stories of their misfortune; they rant about a rip-off or argue for their version of a more civilized world.

The producers of *Liveline* are often criticized because they *produce* the programme. The argument goes that the programme projects itself as a platform for the man or woman in the street and that any adulteration or embellishment of this is somehow not playing by the rules and diminishing the promise of access and the democratic potential of the show. There is a certain naïveté in this contention. Turned on its head it seems to expect that the slot be left vulnerable to repetition, irrelevance, incoherence, libel, or worst of all, silence. Verwey (1990), in her Canadian research, notes the not very inspiring example where callers were taken on a first-come-first-served basis.

Producers have a range of short-term priorities. The most urgent, according to Brian O'Neill (1993), is to fill a time slot with sound content. Beyond that they hope to attract the maximum audience. They do this by being interesting and entertaining – whether via controversy, sympathy, humour or coaxing callers to tell their stories – and finally they have to avoid the pitfalls – the offensive, the boring, the libellous, the incoherent and the inappropriate. Only then can they reflect on any strategic civic potential as a platform, a forum or a worthy campaign rallying point.

So yes, they employ a raft of devices. Having a blank running order two hours before airtime is a sobering prospect. There has to be a provocative opener; there has to be fallback material if calls are slow; decisions have to be made about the calls on offer. Seventy-five minutes of empty air is a daunting stretch especially if there is no expert or guest or music with which to fill it. It would be akin to a lecturer walking into a lecture theatre five days a week with no idea who would turn up or what the title of the lecture was.

Yes, they seek to generate topics; yes they look to previous callers and contacts; yes there is selecting and coaching as calls come in. Certainly they aim for variety, drama and balance.

Always they wait for what they describe as the 'magic call', that call which will light up the switchboard and incite or enrage or engage callers and listeners. Whatever the balance between caller-originated topics and studio-originated topics, the fact remains that the programme is caller driven; unless callers respond and engage and develop topics that go nowhere. It is reasonable to suggest that the programme content is shaped in the tension between the professional production priorities and the freer agenda of non-professional callers.

The very fact that the phone-in is on radio with its specific auditory codes also has repercussions. The format has been tried with little success on TV. Radio clearly precludes complex visual explorations but in recent months *Liveline* is using its website to allow callers to post images relating to their calls. Right now you may view a dilapidated and dangerously neglected playground; the unstewarded crush at the entrance to an Oasis concert and the littered state of beaches near Dublin. Radio is a relatively old technology and the phone is even older but in recent years the phone-in has expanded its reach via newer technologies. Throughout the programme texts and e-mails are invited. The series producer tells us that the new skill demanded of studio personnel, is to quickly persuade timid texters and e-mailers to speak on air. Higgins and Moss (1982) have characterized radio as a dramatizing medium where all content is shaped towards dramatic reflexivity. There were always pictures on radio and radio feeds off stories. The programme host talks of not closing off stories even if a resolution has been available early in an exchange. The story is more important than the closure.

We turn now to a glance at the various categories of call and some tentative thoughts about some theoretical perspectives they suggest (see Appendix 1). The first and biggest category, at a fraction below 30% of all threads, is that designated as 'Consumer Watchdog and Complaints Department'. In fact, looking across categories, complaining and negativity are very much a feature of the phone-in – an observation noted by other commentators (Verwey 1990, Higgins & Moss 1982,). *Liveline* is subjected to a degree of criticism on this account, being branded in the popular press as, 'Whineline' or a 'Wingefest' but it might also be borne in mind that the right to complain is fundamental to democratic expression. Slavko Splichal frames this as a natural and civil right, part of a larger right of expression and publication (2002). He cites John Milton's 1644 text Areopagitica in which he encouraged, 'the utmost bound of civil liberty' under conditions where 'complaints are freely heard, deeply considered and speedily reformed'. John Keane (1991) cites Montesquieu's assertion that 'the right to grumble and complain [...] helped liberate England from the heavy silent fear of despotism'. *Liveline* may not attain the ideal of deep consideration or speedy reform but it may be the case that those who complain about complaining are unaware of the irony of their position and of the taint of elitism.

Having acknowledged the right and importance of complaint, we wonder how it is used. Not exactly profoundly, is the answer. We witness the citizen as the consumer of goods and services. We see the demands for individualistic satisfaction and lifestyle choices. Each feels entitled to a stake in the fruits of neoliberalism. As O'Sullivan (2000b) reminds us, 'commodification is a central component of modernity' and whether we chose to view contemporary Irish society in terms of late modernity or of post modernity, both paradigms share a common element – the practices of consumption (Tovey & Share 2003). If we can get a refund on the budget airline tickets, we are free. Furedi (2004) contends that we are living in an era of Therapy Culture. The language of therapy and psychology has entered the mainstream – we have become conversant in our daily exchanges with self-esteem, trauma, stress and syndromes. This, he maintains, has led us to focus on our own vulnerability and oriented us to 'social networks and institutions through a culture of litigation and complaint, leading to a depoliticization of public life' (Lunt & Pantti 2007).

This leads us neatly to complaints about officialdom where we are prompted to question how they frame conceptions about where we believe the responsibility for the welfare of individuals lies. At a first glance we are inclined to see these callers as being part of what John Thompson (1995) describes as 'a new demagoguery of distrust' or what Murray Levin (1987) calls a 'barometer of alienation' (1987) from the democratic state. In Marshall's (1950) terms, callers are claiming their entitlement to Social Citizenship – the right 'to live the life of a civilized being, according to the standards prevailing in the society' (Dahlgren 1995). Subsidized private health care should not mean that public patients have to wait for two days on a gurney in an Accident and Emergency corridor or for two years for their hip replacement. Further, drawing on Foucault's theories of governmentality, Lunt and Lewis (2008) in the face of the growing hegemony of neoliberal individualism in civic life, become concerned with the shift from government to governance. Questions of social and political responsibility, they say, are again devolved to the level of the consumer-citizen. They also point to another useful body of theoretical work in Axel Honneth's (1996) thinking on the Politics of Recognition. Honneth identifies the citizen's self respect as 'a matter of viewing oneself as entitled to the same status and treatment as every other person' and that human dignity entails the 'capacity to raise and defend claims discursively' (Honneth 1996). Failure by the state to recognize this dignity by the denial of rights and identity or by the withdrawal of social supports, results in the routine disrespect experienced by individuals. The phone-in remains one of the few mass media sites available to citizens to defend their claims discursively and in public and to afford a capacity for solidarity.

All of the categories of topics involve stories and narrative – tales of woe at the hands of impersonal bureaucracy, self-effacing anecdotes about being ripped off by unscrupulous con artists, reminiscences and memories of a gentler world and the recounting of testimony of harsher experience in a different world where good manners and common decency have been eroded. It is clearly not Habermasian deliberation that is the dominant discursive mode in the phone-in; it is storytelling. You can't argue with a good story! Paddy Scannell (1989) tells us that if public figures are entitled to opinion, private figures are entitled to experience. Stories frame and order our experience and legitimize our group identities (Higgins & Moss 1982; Fitzgerald & Housley 2002; Riessman 2008). Narrative, as Dahlgren (1995) says, is everywhere.

This category dwells on a particular subset of narrative – those confessional, victimage, troubles-telling stories that are also prominent on TV talk shows. Sara O'Sullivan (2000) locates these stories within Giddens' (1991) idea of the self in the modern world as a reflexive project – the capacity to keep a particular narrative going. Of more particular interest to our concern here is her plotting of the space that Irish talk radio has provided in the journey 'from silence to openness' – an illustration of Scannell's shifting boundaries of what could be talked about. She outlines the contribution that radio made in the latter half of the twentieth century in facilitating social change in a traditional, mainly Catholic, society. Personal intimate stories, stories whose time had come, stories about topics that were previously taboo entered the public sphere. Issues long locked in private worlds – cold, abusive marriages, confused sexualities, mental illness – were broached and then aired with increased frequency. She suggests that in the new millennium the urgency and impact of this seismic cultural shift have diminished and our data seem to support this. Had we taken this count of topics in the 1980s or early 1990s the preponderance of personal stories would have been different in nature. However by the turn of the century, as we have seen, concerns have moved to issues of choice, lifestyle and service. O'Sullivan (2000) confirms, 'The talking points during 1998 and 1999 on *Liveline* were property prices, traffic, tribunals and other political scandals'.

While victimage stories, as Dahlgren (1995) reminds us, invite involvement they deflect attention from issues of power. However in one particular instance, *Liveline*'s intensive airing by those who suffered shamefully as children in religious-run institutions has led directly to improvements in their legal support and the provision of compensation.

Many of the headings in the category on standards and behaviour bear out Joke Hermes' contention that programmes like these are, 'deeply invested in the setting up of norms and rules of appropriate demeanour' (2005). The themes of callers to *Liveline* are not that dissimilar to those noted by Murray Levin in the US – the loss of power, the dangers of urban living, the decay in manners and morals, the decline of ethical values in the young, the rise in drug abuse and the fall in religious practice. He talks of the essential character of a nation being revealed 'in the seemingly petty habits of daily life, the amenities and routines of everyday existence by which people civilize or brutalize each other' (1987). Higgins and Moss also identified and developed this strand of thematic and tonal flow, which they characterized as violence/fear/intimidation in a world that is perceived as increasingly more anxious, pressurized and disordered – the risk society (1982). Modernity is about staving off hazard, we are told, and the phone-in is not above feeding bouts of moral panic. Recurrent threads relating to the increased prevalence of knife attacks or the antics of joyriders and boy racers or threads which reinforce a gangland construction of crime, serve simply to impose an artificial distance between 'us' and 'them'.

Because of the case made for their normative potential, discussions under the heading of popular culture fall into this category also. We will not do justice to commentators like van Zoonen, Hermes or Leurdijk except to note their contention that talk about sport, 'reality' TV, fandom, celebrities and popular fiction affords a postmodern platform where excluded groups can gain admission to a public arena. Phone-ins and talk shows allow for the admission of new topics and, possibly more importantly, new ways of talking about them. Here is a foundation for cultural citizenship whether we subscribe to Peter Dahlgren's liberating schema or Toby Miller's darker, more determinist, version.

These are some of the things we talk about and a selection of the reflections they inspired but what do we say when we say nothing? Commentators on discourse (Cook 1989; Mills 1997) submit that omission, absence and silence can be as significant as speech in considering the import of discourse. Absence can point to the devaluation of subjects, which are not considered important in a culture. It may reflect areas of social taboo or private no-go areas. The imperative to non-articulation may be as strong in discursive terms as the drive to publicize. There is a whole realm of investigation for another time and place into what is not being said on Irish talk radio. All we shall do here, in conclusion, is fly a few kites with few strings attached. These are but some of the discursive gaps that spring to mind:

- We have already commented on the absence of the voices of 'youth' and of pockets of the disadvantaged class.
- In spite of the dramatic change in what was a singularly homogeneous population, and where over the course of 25 years over 10% of the current population were not born in Ireland, non-Irish accents are rarely heard.
- The global and the international seem to generate little attention. Indeed much as issues relating to the environment and global warming seem to have inserted themselves into the wider public sphere in recent decades, they have little direct presence in this list of topics.
- For a country whose identity for much of the twentieth century was defined by its ambivalent relationship to militant nationalism, it is as if the 'Troubles' never happened. Even that euphemism points to a consensus of reluctance to engage with voices deemed unpalatable in 'modern' Ireland. A government broadcasting ban on Republicans in the 1980s and 1990s possibly normalized this state of mind.
- As a discursive mode, there is very little genuine debate – plenty of talk, no discussion. The historian Professor Joe Lee sees this absence of intellectual discussion as something of a national failing and Livingstone and Lunt believe the phone-in is a lost cause if we are seeking Habermasian rational critical debate. Part of our wider research is attempting to identify what elements of deliberation can be identified in *Liveline*.

These are offered merely as food for thought.

What has been attempted above is some rudimentary quantitative research based on the programme's own podcast postings. Through this an effort has been made to discern some patterns and themes, which can throw light on the society in which they are produced and received. Andra Leurdijk (1997), referring to discussion programmes agreed that they 'generally do not provide much analytical depth or historical background, their strength lies exactly in these confrontations between concrete daily experiences and the more abstract logics of political and academic discourses. In fact, most talk shows are more like a collage of views and examples and anecdotes coming from different individuals'.

The phone-in topics offer an insight into the contradictory ways people experience their social realities. They happen on radio and therefore they have an element of institutional talk but that said, I would argue that there is a greater proximity between the talk of the phone-in and everyday talk. These topics reflect more closely the topics of the dental waiting room, the hairdresser, the dinner party or the local pub than the discourses of the news or the political interview or the radio documentary. We agree, too, with Peter Dahlgren (2006) when he suggests that the individual's role as a citizen emerges in various ways from within informal everyday speech. He says:

'It is via meandering and unpredictable talk that the political can be generated, that the links between the personal and the political can be established. The looseness, open-endedness of everyday talk, its creativity, potential for empathy and affective elements, are indispensable for the vitality of democratic politics'.

That other modes of access, vox pop, the media practice of inserting fragments of often anonymous public opinion into news and documentary programmes, derive from the Latin tag *vox populi, vox dei* – the voice of the people is the voice of God. For all its limitations, the phone-in would appear to offer a more structured and extensive platform for the voice of the public. It would make no claim to approximating to the voice of God, either in legitimizing political decisions or in arriving at a consensus on the common good. Nevertheless the suggestion here is that it should not be ignored as a resource to interrogate the temper of our times.

## Appendix 1

| Cat | S1 | S2 | Thread Category | # | Sub | Total |
|-----|-----|-----|-----------------|-----|-----|-------|
| A | | | **Consumer watchdog and complaints department** | | | 262 |
| | A1 | | Prices | | 31 | |
| | A2 | | Loss of earnings/deposits/investments | | 21 | |
| | A3 | | Warnings re scams and con-artists | | 22 | |
| | A4 | | Business owners complain | | 23 | |
| | A5 | | Service complaints | | 165 | |
| | | A51 | Financial institutions | 26 | | |
| | | A52 | Airlines and airports | 25 | | |
| | | A53 | Gigs and events | 24 | | |
| | | A54 | Treatments and therapies | 16 | | |
| | | A55 | Claiming prizes and vouchers | 11 | | |
| | | A56 | Builders, furnishings and gardens | 9 | | |
| | | A57 | Restaurants, hotels, caterers | 7 | | |
| | | A58 | Miscellaneous service complaints | 47 | | |
| B | | | **Ombudsman – complaints about officialdom** | | | 157 |
| | B1 | | Courts, sentencing, the legal system | | 12 | |
| | B2 | | The Health Service | | 59 | |
| | B3 | | Welfare payments and entitlements | | 15 | |
| | B4 | | The behaviour of politicians | | 14 | |
| | B5 | | Education and schooling | | 11 | |
| | B6 | | The police | | 8 | |
| | B7 | | Local Government actions and services | | 9 | |
| | B8 | | Taxation | | 6 | |
| | B9 | | Miscellaneous official services | | 23 | |
| C | | | **Requests for help and offering cautions** | | | 21 |
| D | | | **Sharing personal troubles and experiences** | | | 87 |
| | D1 | | Addiction | | 8 | |
| | D2 | | Physical/sexual/institutional abuse | | 23 | |
| | D3 | | Financial hardship/unemployment | | 13 | |
| | D4 | | Grief and loss | | 16 | |
| | D5 | | Troubled/missing young people | | 7 | |
| | D6 | | Miscellaneous hardships | | 20 | |
| E | | | **Social/Cultural/Civic standards and behaviours** | | | 229 |
| | E1 | | Antisocial behaviours | | 150 | |
| | | E11 | Attacks and assaults | 43 | | |
| | | E12 | Theft and burglary | 26 | | |
| | | E13 | Gangland related | 9 | | |
| | | E14 | Bullying, intimidation | 11 | | |
| | | E15 | Poor taste/offensive/bad manners | 22 | | |

| Cat | S1 | S2 | Thread Category | # | Sub | Total |
|-----|-----|-----|-----------------|-----|-----|-------|
| | | E16 | Littering, vandalism | 7 | | |
| | | E17 | Discrimination – ethnic/gender | 6 | | |
| | | E18 | Miscellaneous misbehaviours | 26 | | |
| | E2 | | Discussion of religious/moral issues | | 22 | |
| | E3 | | Political issues | | 12 | |
| | E4 | | Protests and industrial action | | 12 | |
| | E5 | | Popular culture | | 33 | |
| | | E51 | Sport | 13 | | |
| | | E52 | Celebrity and entertainment issues | 8 | | |
| | | E53 | Media | 7 | | |
| | | E54 | Art | 5 | | |
| **F** | | | **Identity – Constructing the self and the other** | | | **48** |
| | F1 | | International events | | 10 | |
| | F2 | | Cross-border issues/boundaries and differences | | 13 | |
| | F3 | | Historical events | | 7 | |
| | F4 | | Personal reminiscences – micro history | | 9 | |
| | F5 | | Celebrations and tributes | | 9 | |
| **G** | | | **Quirky, complex, difficult to categorize** | | | **75** |
| | | | **Grand total threads** | | | **879** |

## Notes

1. The podcast has become a very useful tool for radio research, making storage, retrieval and analysis of radio programmes much simpler than before.
2. Non-phone-in 'special' programmes were not included in the count.
3. Podcasts of the programme and all the material for this chapter can be seen or heard at http://www.rte.ie/radio1/podcast/podcast_liveline.xml.

## References and further reading

Annenberg, P. P. C., *Call-in political talk radio: Background, content, audiences, portrayal in mainstream media Philadelphia*. University of Pennsylvania, 1996.

Benhabib, S. 'Models of Public Space: Hannah Arendt, the Liberal Tradition, and Jürgen Habermas' in C. Calhoun (ed.) *Habermas and the Public Sphere*, Cambridge: MIT Press, 1992.

Billig, M. *Banal Nationalism*, London, Sage, 1995.

Cook, G., *Discourse*. Oxford: Oxford University Press, 1989.

Dahlgren, P., *Television and the public sphere: Citizenship, democracy and the edia*. London: Sage, 1995.

Dahlgren, P., Doing Citizenship: The Cultural Origins of Civic Agency in the Public Sphere. *European Journal of Cultural Studies*, 9, 2006, pp. 267 – 286.

Duffy, J., 'Do the Poor only Come Out at Christmas? The Media and Social Exclusion', in D. Kiberd (ed.) *Media in Ireland: Issues in Broadcasting*, Dublin: Open Air, 2009.

Fitzgerald, R. & Housley, W., 'Identity, Categorization and Sequential Organization: The Sequential and Categorical Flow of Identity in a Radio Phone-in'. *Discourse & Society*, 13, 2002, pp. 579–602.

Furedi, F., *Therapy culture: Cultivating vulnerability in an uncertain Age*. London: Routledge, 2004.

Giddens, A., *Modernity and self-identity*. Cambridge: Polity, 1991.

Hermes, J., 'Citizenship in the Age of the Internet'. *European Journal of Communication*, 21, 2006, pp. 295–309.

Hermes, J., *Re-reading Popular Culture*. London: Blackwell, 2005

Higgins, C. & Moss, P., *Sounds real: Radio in everyday life*. St. Lucia: University of Queensland Press, 1982.

Honneth, A., *The struggle for recognition: The moral grammar of social conflict*. Cambridge: MIT Press, 1996.

Keane, J., *The Media and democracy*. Cambridge: Polity Press, 1991.

Lee, J., 'Democracy and Public Service Broadcasting in Ireland', in D. Kiberd, (ed.) *Media in Ireland: The Search for Diversity*, Dublin: Open Air, 1997.

Leurdijk, A., 'Common Sense versus Political Discourse: Debating Racism and Multicultural Society in Dutch Talk Shows'. *European Journal of Communication* 12, 1997, pp. 147–68.

Levin, M. B., *Talk Radio and the American Dream*, Lexington, Lexington Books, 1987.

Lunt, P. & Pantti, M., 'Popular Culture and the Public Sphere: Currents of Feeling and Social Control in Talk Shows and Reality TV', in R. Butsch (ed.) *Media and Public Spheres*, Basingstoke: Palgrave Macmillan, 2007.

Lunt, P. & Lewis, T., 'Oprah.com: Lifestyle Expertise and the Politics of Recognition', in *Women and Performance: A Journal of FeministTheory*, 18, 2008, pp. 9–24.

Marshall, T. H., *Citizenship and social Class*. Cambridge, Cambridge University Press, 1950.

Miller, T., *The well-tempered self: Culture and the postmodern subject*. Baltimore: Johns Hopkins University Press, 1993.

Mills, S., *Discourse*. London: Routledge, 1997.

Milton, J., *Areopagitica and other Political Writings*. Indianapolis: Liberty Fund, 1996.

O'Neill, B., 'Producing the Arts Show: An Ethnographic Study of Radio Producers at Work', *Irish Communications Review*, 3, 1993.

O'Sullivan, S., 'Understanding Irish Talk Radio: A Qualitative Case Study of *The Gerry Ryan Show*', Dublin: University College Dublin, 2000a.

O'Sullivan, S., 'Talk Radio', in E. Slater and M. Peillon (eds) *Memories of the Present: A Sociological Chronicle of Ireland 1997–1998*, Dublin: IPA, 2000b

Riessman, C. K., *Narrative methods for the uman sciences*. Los Angeles: Sage, 2008.

Scannell, P., 'Public Service Broadcasting and Modern Public Life', *Media, Culture and Society*, 11, 1989, pp. 135–66.

Share, P., Tovey, H. & Corcoran, M. P., *A sociology of Ireland*. Dublin: Gill & Macmillan, 2007.

Splichal, S., 'Rethinking Publicness: The Precedence of the Right to Communicate', *Javnost – The Public*, IX, 2002, pp. 83–105.

Tebbutt, J., 'Imaginative Demographics: The Emergence of a Radio Talkback Audience in Australia'. *Media, Culture and Society*, 2006, 28, pp. 857–82.

Thompson, J. B., *The media and modernity*. Cambridge: Polity, 1995.

Tovey, H. & Share, P. *A sociology of Ireland*. Dublin: Gill & Macmillan, 2003.

Van Zoonen, L., *Entertaining the citizen*. Lanham: Rowman and Littlefield, 2005.

Verwey, N. E., *Radio call-ins and covert politics*. Aldershot: Avebury, 1990.

Wright, A., *Local radio and local democracy: A study in political education*. London: IBA, 1979.

# Part III

Community

# Chapter 11

Online Community Radio, an Alternative Model: Analysis of Characteristics, New Formats and Contents

Pascal Ricaud

## Introduction

The term 'community radio' is little used or appreciated in France. Elsewhere, and in particular in the Anglo-Saxon countries and *chez* our Quebecois cousins, this term is regularly understood and used by radio stations for immigrant or minority communities. In France – where the nation state built itself and strengthened itself around an identity and around a unique language – our republican and universal tradition almost forbids us to use this term, which connotes a compartmentalised, exclusive communitarianism. One speaks more readily of radio stations which are 'free', 'associative' or 'of proximity', the latter meaning very local. The problem also stems from the fact that in France we tend to only apply the title to stations of the regional and immigrant communities.

We classify 'community' radio stations among those which have an alternative agenda or which address a specific section of the population that has been neglected or ignored in the past by the traditional mass media. These alternative radio stations are as follows:

- those of immigrant communities (multi-community or inter-community), such as Radio Trait d'Union which is meant for only one community, or AYP FM (broadcast and online), which is the associative radio of the Armenian diaspora ;
- regional community radio, such as Radio País and Gure Irratia, which use regional languages, including Breton, Basque and Gascon, and sometimes multi-community radio stations, for example Radio Pays in Paris;
- militant radio, involved in social actions, more often located in cities, among them Radio Libertaire, Radio Zinzine, Radio Canut and Radio Galère;
- stations helping weak, vulnerable and minority groups, such as Vivre FM and Euro FM.

This chapter presents a research project, studying several online web community radio stations using a comparative approach: their editorial projects, experimental formats and programmes, the new forms of audience participation they use and the levels of approval by their audiences. We studied radio stations for regional and immigrant communities and some involved in social and localized actions. Even though we will provide other examples, we will mainly focus on complementary case studies of AYP FM and Radio Armenie for the Armenian community in France, and Vivre FM for disabled persons. Our other examples will include those of some regional communities in France which we have been studying since 2005 and which are only on the internet.

## New *reliances*: distribution models, formats and content adapted for isolated and dispersed audiences

The internet offers new opportunities for diversification, segmentation and interactivity in radio. If these radio stations are addressed at scattered communities, or diasporas, they can widen and diversify their audiences. For such a restricted and dispersed audience, the internet is more suitable than FM broadcasting. It is no coincidence that websites aimed at different diaspora and web radio stations targeted at them developed in very similar ways. On the Vivre FM website, apart from musical programmes, other genres such as news, practical information, cultural programming, and so on are not very different from formats we can see elsewhere, but their content clearly caters to their audience. For instance, cultural programming includes shows and exhibitions taking place in buildings or places which are easily accessible to disabled persons. The aim is to make listeners' everyday lives easier. Vivre FM is most noteworthy for its mission of *reliance sociale* (social linking), a traditional function undertaken by different media,[1] which is all the more important in this case for audiences who are too often in a situation of exclusion or marginalization. However they must also encourage, even militate for *reliance* to neighbourhoods and to the public infrastructure. On the website, the accent is on contacts, on the forum and on the creation of links between listeners. It is essential for disabled persons to be able to connect more directly with each other, so that the exchange of information and experiences plays an important part in the improvement in everyday life and facilitates better control of their direct environment, and all this has been possible owing to the internet.

Advertising is directly related to the initiatives and organizations for disabled persons and it relies on a principle of solidarity. Examples include the national committee for the coordination of action for disabled persons, Mutuelle Intégrance, which works for people with disabilities, the chronically dependent and old people under medical care; it works in tandem with the magazine *Etre*, which publishes information about disability. Vivre FM ('the difference *versus* indifference') belongs to the national association for the prevention of disability and for information about disability, but the station is also linked to organizations and media organizations dealing with these same issues. To ensure this function of social reliance through the production of social reports in the media, we have a parallel system of mediators using signage through interactive media to provide simultaneous written, audio and symbolic commentaries. A number of organizations, including associations and public bodies for prevention and information, monitor and report on *reliance* (Bolle De Ball 2003).

On AYP FM we can distinguish various levels of discourse, that is, of engagement which also corresponds to an audience more or less involved in militant action, be it social, cultural or political. The programming switches between information, culture and programmes of reflection and debates. We also found, just as in Basque associative radio stations for example, a space for expression and for stronger political assertion, as characterized by the programme *l'avis du Nors*. Beside the *social reliance* (notably, again, to create a link with the original community in Armenia), the aim is to allow each person to retain a link with their identity, in all its complexity, taking into consideration all the layers of which it is composed. This is *reliance* on oneself. According to Bougnoux (1995) 'each of us lives at least double life, either individual or collective and massive', and we share past or present territories of collective imagination. If we compare AYP FM to Radio Armenie, we can see rather quickly that the latter offers a more heterogeneous programme, with more dissimilar programmes and programming items, including news, cultural, musical, religious and practical help programmes, which are unrelated to the Armenian identity, culture and history.

This format situated half way between thematic radio and generalist radio can perhaps be partly explained by the station's limited resources, meaning it is less professional and survives essentially on donations, some of them being made online. This format and the solidarity expressed by the listeners of Radio Armenie can also explain the intent of the station, which was launched in 1983: it was launched at the right moment in the context of globalization to occupy a privileged place by enabling communication in minority languages which were at that point perceived to be threatened with extinction. By welcoming Assyros-Chaldeans and Greeks to tune in to their station, they support this cause. From the presentation of their mission we realize that the Armenian community that first settled in the Rhône-Alpes area not only wanted to reinforce the presence of a public micro-space but also to occupy a place in a wider public sphere which is multicultural and includes various identities and territories. The Armenian minority considers Radio Armenie to be trying to represent both the regional community and the diaspora, apart from presenting Armenia in all its diversity. Its approach can be described as 'citizen wise', the radio choosing as a priority social communication and popular education, by organizing debates about problems concerning citizens. This approach and the content of Radio Armenie programmes, offer a synthesis and an interesting transversality of militant and community radio stations' various missions, even if the internet radio site reveals that Armenia is right at the heart of its preoccupations, and for example they might include an online press review from a correspondent living in Erevan.

This transversality also supports its relationship to our typology of community radio, which relies essentially on two points: the nature of the audience and the objectives of the radio station (even though often only partially fulfilled) and how the station is adapted to this audience. Online interactivity with the listeners is limited to the 'your reactions' feature, but it is not on this level that the links with the local audience are reinforced; it is on the spot and through online and FM programmes that the connection with the local audience is made. Online community radio stations are useful and sometimes necessary for some associations and communities because they can respond to the objectives of *reliance: reliance on oneself* (psychological), *social reliance* and *reliance on the world* (notably cultural). This happens through three key notions evoked by Marcel Bolle de Ball (2003) which we shall quote here, because they are truly representative of the missions and the roles played by community radio stations:

- identity, inherent in reliance on oneself;
- solidarity (or fraternity), inherent in reliance to others; and
- citizenship, inherent in reliance to the world.

These are the three keywords which really illustrate editorial projects, programmes and relationships that these radio stations have developed with their listeners: identity, solidarity and citizenship.

## Radio citizenship or radio militancy?

These radio stations, contrary to the themes-associated radio stations in particular, are not only characterized by their accessibility to specific publics which can express and appropriate themselves by co-producing or by animating, for example, programmes. They play a central role through participation, mobilization, accompaniment and the impulse of collective actions of specific audiences belonging to particular communities (regional or immigrant) and/or to associations with a cultural or social vocation participating in social movements or protest movements.

Vivre FM broadcast radio programmes on FM in Paris-Ile de France from 5.30 a.m. to 5.30 p.m., and they are non-stop online. The internet allows the station to mitigate a singular and questionable decision of the French regulator, the CSA, to give Vivre FM a digital frequency shared with Radio Campus. The CSA, when distributing digital frequencies in 2009 confirmed, even though the availability of frequencies was increased, the sharing of a frequency with Radio Campus (broadcasting from 5.30 p.m. to 5.30 a.m.) already decided on the 9th of September 2003, in a previous round of frequency distribution. The president of Vivre FM, Jean-Michel Sauvage, declared that 'the increased availability of digital frequencies allowed at last the granting of satisfaction to our companions of the airwaves, too often considered to be second class citizens'. He added that the CSA's decision 'may reinforce [...] this view, which can only lead to the normalisation of exclusion and marginalisation'. If this type of decision reinforces the links and solidarity between listeners and their radio station, and between the listeners themselves, it creates an even greater feeling of injustice and insecurity. The internet cannot adequately fill the gap created by forcibly maintaining inaccessibility for different sorts of people (the blind, the elderly, those in need of special medical care and so on). On Vivre FM, the question of citizenship, and feeling like second-class citizens who are not integrated or are badly integrated into the life of the city is right at the heart of the current debate.

We are not identifying or recognising here a particularly complex issue around citizenship, although it is quite different to issues of citizenship for the able-bodied. However, we always find this feeling of 'minoritization' or marginalization.[2] These people live in a suburb that it is social, mental or geographical. There feeling of alienation/marginalization is aggravated when it concerns important moments in their lives. In two minutes and seven seconds a podcast to Vivre FM covers, for example, difficulties met by disabled persons in polling stations, emphasizing in particular the obstacles disabled people face and the measures in place organized according to the type of disability.[3] This example really illustrates a legitimate aspiration: the one of a public autonomy (Habermas 1997). Such autonomy depends on the guarantee of a right to political participation, including the right to vote, which is so fundamental in our representative democracies. Nevertheless, it is more often the question of 'private autonomy' which is discussed. If, by 'private autonomy', Habermas (1997) means the 'private use of subjective liberties' – for example the right, often claimed by radio stations using a regional language, to use these languages overtaking the *stricto sensu* frame of home – it is not a case of secondary freedoms, but of fundamental freedoms.

Let us take the example of accessibility to school, to the right to education, and especially the acceptance of children with special needs in secondary schools with a special inclusion unit. One school headmaster perceived the need for citizen action and an opportunity to teach solidarity to the pupils in his establishment. On 3 September 2009, solidarity and citizenship were placed at the heart of an on-air campaign running through programmes and other content. This solidarity was expressed towards the radio station through online listener donations, using PayPal. For all the community radio stations, calls for donations increasingly involve the internet. This solidarity and commitment is expressed in different ways, including co-distribution of information and the use of educational content. Gure Irratia (Basque radio) for example, seeks through the internet listeners who would like to become local correspondents for the station in their own villages or towns in Labourd, the former province of the Basque country in France. They also seek volunteer presenters and offer audio modules of downloadable courses in the Basque language for Basques, living in the Basque country of France, in Euskal Herria or diaspora.

The programme *l'Avis du Nors* on AYP FM is produced by young militants of FRA NorSeround, the post-1945 movement of young Armenians born in France. This militant group held its first meeting in 1947 at the SFIO centre of the former French socialist party. This programme is also broadcast on Radio Armenia and heard on FM in Lyon, one of the principal Armenian neighbourhoods in the Paris region and in Bouche du Rhône, as well as on the internet (radioarmenie.com). This means that with the two FM radio stations the programme can reach most Armenians in France.[4] However, the ambition of FRA NorSeround is twofold: it refers at the same time to their original country because they have been uprooted from their homeland, and also to the welcoming country where they have re-rooted. This was conceived from the start to communicate and make Armenian actuality understandable for young listeners to the radio station. *L'Avis du Nors* has, since then, covered very different subjects ranging from the assassination of Hrant Dink to all-year-round cultural events in Armenia and France, not forgetting the main national debates which sometimes have a universal impact, such as the proposal of law about DNA tests or the tragic events in Darfour (norseround.fr). We are undecided between the desire for distinction and affirmation of the original identity and the desire for integration implicit in the appropriation of French citizenship. Such an editorial line and such content in community radio stations are not characterized by identity withdrawal, which means Daniel Bougnoux (1995) was right when he said that modern communication could be favourable to the plurality of both belonging to one identity and adapting to another.[5]

The online associative radio stations and the community web radio stations – although present in a utopian space without a map or physical borders – remain attached to territories, sending back at the same time:

- in de-territorialized identities reactivated through a collective maintained imagination (historic broadcasts), cultural and religious identity, the practice of a vernacular language; and
- in re-territorialized identities – resulting more from a process of hybridization than of acculturation – trying to make a synthesis between the original identity and that of the host country, through universal values, a reference for citizenship and successful integration, (in the way that the programme *Entreprendre* on AYP FM tells success stories of Armenian entrepreneurs) and the use of a common language.

Community radio stations hesitate between 'citizenship radio stations' and 'militant radio stations'. Their radio project is at least based on a mission of social communication (for example, multi- or inter-community), such as Radio Trait d'Union and Radio Pays in Paris or Radio Orient, which wants to be 'a link between the Orient and Occident'. At best, their ambition is to offer a space for expression, celebration, conservation (through collective memory) and demands for a specific community (such as the Armenian AYP FM or the Basque Gure Irratia). For the latter examples, the internet is an additional way to create a space for listening, of meeting for communities scattered throughout the world, and to preserve a common-voiced memory with such features as an online archive system or podcasting.

### Towards a convergence between media public space and communicational reason on web radio stations and online radio stations?

Whatever the radio project may be (regionalist, separatist, related to an identity or social movement for example) it is always related to a will to adapt the public word, or to allow a particular public to express itself. This step, participative and based on the principle of a collective appropriation of the listener-actor and even the producer of content, can be traced back to the 1970s as principles which have today been further developed on the internet. These radio stations contribute, apparently, to the current evolution of the media public space. An essential duality lies in on the one hand the emergence of micro public spaces, and on the other hand homogenization which can be seen today notably through the example of online radio stations and in the emergence of new community forms of expression (online communities).

The media public space, including with the emergence of online media and of the 'blogosphere', assumes a wider dimension, provided that interactivity is implemented in ways which allow action, contribution and the right to reply – or in essence, the participation of internet users in discussions and debates around subjects in society. More specifically, in the case of community media, it corresponds to the possibility of discussing subjects with a polemic, traumatic, symbolic dimension for these communities. These communication media represent the main communal space of representation and debate for regional communities, immigrants, minorities and structured social movements. Nevertheless, they are partial public spaces in the way that they are more or less exclusive and are seldom organized around contradictory debates. These new media contribute to the emergence of new forms of expressing citizenship, participation and social appropriation of mediatized public space, but it is a restrictive public space without deliberative approach or links with spaces of political decision.

So, we can safely state that online debates in France are dominated by technology 'for its own sake' and by a certain approach to consultation and argumentation that has crystallized in the course of a decade the opposition between participative and representative democracy, and more specifically, a territorial problem area concerning the redefinition of the procedures and the actors in the decision-making process. On the first point, many online debates have suffered as a result of a lack of reflection on the protocols, the context within which they are established, the context of collective decision making and of a common vision. So, it is not a matter of trying to reduce the particularities and the disadvantages of the communication systems and media existing on the web, but of integrating them to a more general and fundamental reflection of relationships between *doxa* and *episteme*, of stakes and contexts playing a role at this level, and finally, to use the knowledge we have of these systems to conceive a protocol which is 'deeply' deliberative, where, notably, the *doxa* will be right in the heart of the process of production of a shared opinion and shared propositions (Natali, Ricaud and Kiely 2006).

## Notes

1. R. Clausse (1963) already distinguished between the social functions filled by newspapers, the function of social reliance allowing to break their isolation, and to create functional links. For the author, the notion of reliance evoked the idea of social membership, and finally of recognition.
2. Vivre FM asked the CSA to prepare a re-examination of its file, considering that it has 'a vocation of public utility'. It wishes that its listeners can benefit from a full programme and they 'do not become, besides the multiple already lived discriminations, a radio public' completely apart' (Leroi Thibault, *RadioActu*, 5/6/2009, http://www.radioactu.com/actualites-radio/107957/vivre-fm-la-station-demande-une-frequence-pleine-en-numerique/).
3. See http://www.handirun-cfm.org/spip.php?article159.
4. As many as 350,000 Armenians have settled in France. They constitute the largest Armenian community in Europe, arriving in several waves of immigration, not only from Armenia after

the Armenian genocide of 1915 under the Ottoman Empire but also at the end of the 1940s from Palestine or from the Eastern European countries, and then from the Lebanon, from Iran or Turkey after 1975. Within the community, it would often be usual to speak about several diaspora and not just one. This is particularly true for the Armenian community.

5. 'Is it too much to expect from modern communication that it does not facilitate either the tribal fold or the abstract universalism, but pluri-membership and rotating identifications' (Bougnoux 1995).

## References and further reading

Bolle De Ball, M., 'Reliance, déliance, liance: émergence de trois notions sociologiques', *Sociétés*, 80, 2003, pp. 99–131.

Bougnoux, D., 'Expression identitaire et communication moderne' in J. P. Saez (ed.) *Identités, cultures et territoires*, Paris: Desclée de Brouwer, 1995, pp. 101–113.

Clausse, R., *Les nouvelles*, Bruxelles, Editions de l'Institut de Sociologie, 1963.

Dayan, D., 'Médias et diasporas', *Cahiers de médiologie*, 3, 1997, pp. 91–97.

De Certeau, M., *L'invention du quotidien: 1– arts de faire*, Paris: Gallimard, 1990.

Habermas, J., *Droit et démocratie*, Paris, Gallimard, 1997.

Morin, E., *Introduction à la pensée complexe*, Paris, ESF, 1990.

Natali, J. P., Ricaud, P., Kiely, G., 'Public Opinion and Governance: E-Deliberative Situations [EDS] – A Tool To Gather and Analyse the Views of Participating Citizens', in *Workshop 'e.government'*, 2e *International Conference of TIC*, 6 p., Damas: ICTTA, 24–28 April 2006.

Ricaud, P., 'Les radio stations communautaires, de la FM à Internet', in J. J. Cheval (ed.) *La radio, paroles données, paroles à prendre, Médiamorphoses*, 23 2008, Paris: INA Armand Colin, pp. 45–48.

## Chapter 12

New Technologies and the Facilitation of Participation in Community Radio Stations

Rosemary Day

Early adopters of any new communications technology tend to adapt the technology to meet their own needs and so contribute to its development, discovering unforeseen potential that benefits those who come to use the technology later. It seems that this will be the case with the current crop of new communications technologies within community radio. In 2009, social networking sites such as Facebook and Twitter were being used by a small number of participants in some Irish community radio stations. They were used to garner and cultivate audiences for individual shows in much the same way that commercial stations, celebrities and product promoters attract an audience, fans or customer base. So they provide examples of one-way and very simple two-way flows of communication. Some early signs of more innovative exploitation of the potential that social networking sites can offer community media projects were observed but these were neither well developed nor widespread. Tentative experimentation in providing for multi-flows of communication and for the facilitation of participation in meaningful and useful ways was primarily being undertaken by students in campus community radio stations, with new immigrants and younger managers showing the way in a few urban and rural geographically based stations.

This research project was a logical extension of an earlier investigation into how Irish community radio stations foster and facilitate participation in their stations and community projects (Day 2009). The potential of social networking sites, when linked to mobile phone technology, seems to have the capacity to promote two-way dialogue and multi-flows of communication that are more dynamic than traditional, one-way flows of information. If realized, such multi-flows of communication could and should assist community radio stations in the recruitment of volunteers, in maintaining a real and immediate two-way dialogue with them, in creating new communication flows within the community served and in facilitating participation in the station at the most meaningful and powerful of levels, these being participation in ownership, management and programme making (Day 2009).

Traditionally community radio stations have employed a number of strategies to recruit, train and care for volunteers, ensuring their participation is meaningful and beneficial. In Ireland, these include training courses, mentoring systems and the appointment of coordinators to care for volunteers, among others (Day 2009). The social benefits that the facilitation of participation bring to individuals and to communities are many and Irish community radio stations bear witness to this fact. Irish community radio stations seek to empower women (McGann 2007), to combat the marginalization of disadvantaged sectors of the community (Byrne, Galliano and Murray 2007), to provide adult education (Stanton 2007) and to facilitate the work of community development projects (Unique Perspectives

2003; Day 2007). Community radio stations do not exist solely to broadcast. They have social and sometimes political agendas and use broadcasting as a means of achieving their aims of community building, empowerment and social justice. Working in a manner which forsters community development necessitates the facilitation of participation by members of the community served at all levels and this project set out to investigate the extent to which Irish community radio stations were employing new technologies in 2009 to assist them in the facilitation of such participation.

## Participation

The term 'participation' itself can cause confusion. Some people believe that any engagement by, or involvement of, citizens within the mass media constitutes participation, no matter how fleeting, mediated or insignificant. However this is clearly not the case for community media activists who value participation for the social and personal benefits that accrue as part of its facilitation for the individuals involved and for the community as a whole. White's distinction between 'genuine participation' and 'pseudo participation' is useful in identifying what community media activists really mean by participation (White 1994). She maintains that 'pseudo participation' is tightly controlled, heavily mediated and is facilitated for reasons such as the provision of cheap and popular programming or the projection of an image of inclusivity and localness. 'Genuine participation' on the other hand, is enabling, relatively unmediated and provided for its own sake (White 1994). Commercial media and public service broadcasters in general tend to work at the level of 'pseudo participation' while community media aim for 'genuine participation'. 'Genuine participation' leads to social benefit in the community in terms of the empowerment and conscientization of individuals, the strengthening of community ties and the progression of community development goals.

In my earlier work (Day 2009), I investigated the notion of 'genuine participation' and asked to what extent Irish community radio stations were facilitating this. To answer that question I needed a framework that would help to identify, if not quantify, the type and quality of participation that was being facilitated. It was necessary to distinguish between the types of participation that other media provide, as opposed to those facilitated by community media for whom participation is a core aim and end in itself beyond the levels of broadcasting. It became clear just how important it is to do this during the course of this research, when many of those actively involved in community radio stations were found to believe that the facility for dialogue provided by social networking sites was sufficient in itself to fulfil the aim of enabling participation. Technicians in particular did not imagine or seek to enable any deeper or more meaningful type of participation. McCain and Lowe (1990) provide a starting point to help differentiate between different types of participation. They propose a hierarchy that ranks citizens' involvement in the media as occurring on three levels in ascending order: access, participation and self-management. This can be expanded into a framework of seven cumulative levels to tease out the quality or form of participation enabled in descending order, as shown in Table 12.1.

A framework for participation in media.

| Level | Category | Type | Provided by |
|---|---|---|---|
| 7 | Full and active participation | Ownership by community | Community media |
| 6 | Self-management | Management and decision making, open to community, unmediated by outside groups | Community media |
| 5 | Participation | Schedule, programme planning, autonomous production after training by station, open to community | Community and access media |
| 4 | Mediated participation | Producing and presenting programmes | Public service, commercial and community media |
| 3 | Controlled participation | Presenting programmes with professional producers | Public service, commercial and community media |
| 2 | Controlled access | Speaking on air | Public service, commercial and community media |
| 1 | Reactive access | Responding to content broadcast | Public service, commercial and community media |

*Source*: Day 2009.

Most broadcast media offer access and participation up to level 3, 'controlled participation'. The facilitation of 'controlled access' and 'controlled participation' makes sense for all broadcasters, be they public, private or community. All radio stations, regardless of category, need to build links with their target audiences. Such participation often provides cheap programming and it sometimes makes for a riveting broadcast when someone breaks down on air or attacks another caller (Higgins and Moss 1982; Shingler and Wieringa 1998) but it is rarely beneficial or empowering for the participants. Some public service and commercial radio stations offer 'mediated participation' (level 4) where members of the public are selected and trained to produce and present programmes. This can provide a useful service for both the community and the station; however, it is provided primarily for the station's benefit rather than for the development of the community. Only access and community media allow for the 'genuine participation' we see at level 5 and usually it is only community media who can, or want, to provide for 'genuine participation' at levels 6 and 7, enabling the exercise of self-management and ownership. It is only at the top-three levels that participation is offered for the benefit it can provide the community, rather than merely as a means to a business-driven end, for example to extend audience reach in order to increase profits.

Larger audiences and higher profits are welcome by-products for any broadcaster, including community radio stations. However, community media aim to facilitate citizen participation in their projects, both on and off the air, to empower individuals and to connect them to others in their communities. They seek to do this in ways that enable members of their communities to work together so as to improve the quality of life of those communities. Community-development practice stresses the need for this to come from within the community and to be controlled by the members of the community (Rubin and Rubin 1992). It can be fostered by community development workers and other agents of social change but it must be led and most importantly owned and controlled by the community itself. This requires the facilitation of 'genuine participation' at levels 5, 6 and 7 in the areas of programme planning and production, in management and decision making and in ownership. It is extremely difficult to maintain the facilitation of this type of participation and most community radio stations fail to do so adequately. The more successful stations recognize this and constantly review and revise the strategies they employ to facilitate participation. However, many Irish community radio stations, and those who work in them, do not recognize the difference between different types of participation and the important implications of this, and they struggle to achieve their goals as a result (Day 2009).

## The research project

The aim of this small research project was to ascertain the extent to which Irish community radio stations had discovered the potential that new communications technologies could offer them to provide for participation in their projects at the higher levels of 'genuine participation' in 2009. The research was conducted over six months and consisted of a simple questionnaire, a focus group, individual interviews with managers and basic observation or monitoring of popular social networking sites and of stations' websites. Five stations were found to use new communications technologies to some degree to facilitate participation. At first it seemed that stations were not using the newest technologies at all. However, this changed from month to month with more technologically aware, usually younger, participants in stations setting up their own pages on Facebook and beginning to establish a presence there for their shows. The five stations were Cork Campus Radio, Flirt in Galway and Wired Fm in Limerick (all student community radio stations) and two small, rural stations on the Atlantic seaboard, Connemara Community Radio in Galway and Raidió Corca Baiscinn in Clare.

Two major reasons for the slow adoption of social networking tools emerged clearly from the focus group and interviews. Technicians from many stations, both paid and voluntary, found that the concept of participation itself was alien to them. They were excited by what new technologies could do but did not demonstrate any understanding of the value of facilitating participation as a goal in itself. There is a clear need for a process of conscientization within this group in stations. It was equally clear that older managers and members of boards of management, who do not use social networking sites themselves, could not conceive of the potential that these sites have to offer their stations in the future. Their resistance came from an insistence that communication should be personal and immediate and remain rooted in the community. This stems from a lack of understanding of just how personal and immediate social networking is for those who are engaged in it and how technologically assisted networking enhances relationships that are rooted in real communities such as young professionals and students. Again, there is a clear need for education in this area and some dialogue between technicians and managers in each station would reap benefits for community radio projects across the country. The result of such a dialogue would led to the conscious adaptation of new communications technologies to make the facilitation of participation more targeted, immediate and regular and consequently make it more meaningful and effective. It would ultimately promote community radio stations' core aim of building the community served.

The lack of awareness of the importance of participation and a lack of understanding of how and why it should be facilitated meant that as late as the autumn of 2009, most community radio stations in Ireland were using new communications technologies in the same manner as commercial and public service counterparts. They used the internet sites and facilities such as Facebook and Twitter to attract and to cultivate audiences. They used the internet sites to communicate with members of their communities in one direction. Oftentimes, this limited forum was merely used to advertise and to give information, although occasionally social networking sites were used to engage in a limited form of dialogue to keep people listening and to encourage feedback and some general comments. However, they did not actively engage members of their communities at the levels of broadcasting, managing and exercising their rights and responsibilities as owners of the stations.

For most of the first decade of the twenty-first century the adoption of new technologies by Irish community radio stations was poor. This was due to the lack of finance, the rate of development of the technologies themselves, the age and education levels of many of the participants in community radio stations and the lack of time to experiment or to learn new skills for volunteers who were already busy broadcasting and engaging in community work in their spare time. As late as 2009, high-speed broadband was still not available in every area where community radio stations are broadcasting. In others, poor literacy and low incomes meant that the internet was not being used by the majority of the population. Websites were created for community radio stations from the late 1990s onwards but these generally remained static and quickly became boring and irrelevant. They remained no more dynamic than electronic noticeboards and even at this were rarely updated. Stations made no effort on their websites to communicate with the members of their own communities in a way that was different from the way they presented themselves to the casual web browser. By 2008 text lines had been introduced into nearly every station but these were mainly used in the same way that commercial and public service broadcasters avail of them, for members of the public to send in requests and for simplistic feedback on content. They were not being used to connect listeners to each other or to invite them to participate in the day-to-day management and long-term policy planning of stations. There was little evidence of new communications technologies being embraced and utilized to promote multi-flows of communication that could be exciting. There was less evidence of any experimentation with communication at meaningful levels that could lead to 'genuine participation' that could be powerful. There was no evidence of any attempt to develop multi, micro-public spheres that could be truly dynamic both socially and politically.

After this slow and disappointing start, the situation has undergone rapid change and development and some station managers reported seeing the benefit of actively engaging with new communication technologies. Two stations in 2006 used the internet to interface with emigrants from their communities. One of them, Connemara Community Radio, has had offers of financial assistance from emigrants in New York who depend on the website for local news, in particular for the death notices. Although this demonstrates greater involvement between the station and some members of the community, the result, in terms of production, is still at the level of information provision and is largely an example of uni-directional communication. The interesting change was the adoption of social networking sites by student stations and the two most useful and popular in 2009 were Facebook and Twitter.

Most of the activity was still at the level of individual pages and postings and operated as simple one- and two-way flows of communication. Students created pages and tweets to advertise individual shows and presenters and to provide an opportunity for some dialogue with fans. While this was interesting and enjoyable, it was no different from the way they were being used by any other medium or celebrity. However, there were some signs that student stations were beginning to adapt the technology to serve more important community radio goals. The three student stations, Cork Camps Radio, Flirt in Galway and Wired in Limerick, were each using social networking sites to bind their volunteers together and Flirt was showing signs of beginning to engage students through Facebook and open blogging to participate, to some extent, in planning and decision making in the station.

Student stations are ideally placed to lead the way as they are the only communities in Ireland served by community radio stations that use new technologies daily and for long periods of time. Students spend a lot of time on Facebook, and it is because they already use social networking sites to connect with each other that they have no difficulty visiting and contributing to station pages on a regular basis. In other communities, where people rarely connect to the internet and where Facebook is not a routine and daily function in ordinary life, it is difficult to see how stations could get them to log on or to imagine why the members of those communities would want to. However, this situation is bound to change and when the rest of the population depends on the internet, on social networking sites and on their mobile phones for more than just accessing information, texting and talking, their community radio stations will need to engage with these new technologies and to use them as organizational tools to involve members of their communities in decision making, planning and policy-making. Social networking sites have the potential to be open to all and to provide opportunities for participation on an equal playing field, much as Habermas hoped for in providing 'ideal speech situations' (Habermas 1962). However, as with all ideal constructs, this is still only imagined by some. Student stations in Ireland had not yet discovered how to do this through the use of new technologies in 2009 and other stations lagged even further behind but at least student community radio activists were beginning to experiment with social networking as a tool for the facilitation of communication that flows in more than one direction.

One example of how social networking can be used as a formal organizational tool that improves communication and builds relationships between volunteers was provided by Cork Campus Radio. All volunteers are required to set up a page on Facebook during their induction and as part of their formal training. They are encouraged to make this a distinct page, separate from their own personal pages. They use these pages as commercial broadcasters do, to post their play lists and to engage with their audiences as individuals. However, they move up the participation hierarchy outlined in the framework for participation in the media by trying to consciously create what their station manager terms 'a cloud'. All these pages are interlinked and the conversations and discussions that are carried out on them are station related. This, they have found, helps them to get to know each other and was introduced after an internal evaluation found that there was a gulf between the student volunteers and the board of management and poor connectivity and communication between the students themselves. The station manager reports that whereas student presenters frequently only knew the presenters who came on air immediately before and after them and did not engage in the station outside their own show, the interactions and exchanges on Facebook have led to students having prior knowledge of and communication with each other when they meet at station social functions. They reported that they felt more a part of a team and that they felt that there was less of a clique running the station as a result of their engagement on Facebook. This is a long way from being an example of active participation in station management but it is a step forward. The difficulty for managers in breaking down the operation, or the perception of the operation, of cliques within stations was observed and noted in my earlier research (Day 2009: 175). This layered, yet transparent, set of interactions, of multi-flows of communication in fact, seems to provide one way of countering this problem.

Cork Campus Radio also uses the activity on individual pages and the collective interaction between them in the 'cloud' to update the station website collectively. Their website became a more vital and energized, interactive space for communication within and for the station as a result. Although the manager only updated his own news once a fortnight, student volunteers had begun to use Twitter for headlines on this site as well in the usual manner and found the immediacy and brevity it offers ideal for maintaining a fresh and lively approach. The Twitter headlines on the website were changed by volunteers who had access to the station's mobile phone on a daily basis and this was reported as increasing activity, interest and engagement by students in the site significantly.

The staff at Cork Campus Radio were still using e-mail for contacting volunteers in 2009 and they used their text line for emergencies but they used Facebook for the business of managing schedules, for programme planning and for ensuring that everyone knows what everyone else was doing on air. This does not provide for participation at level 5 of the framework 'schedule, programme planning and autonomous production' of itself but it does assist and supplement the other work practices and strategies that do.

Cork Campus Radio's station manager reported that he found it easier to interact and engage with his volunteers in 2009 than he did in former times when he depended mainly on texts and on e-mail. He believes that because of Facebook and Twitter he is in immediate and constant contact with students. He can see who is online at any given time and he knows more about what students are interested in and what they are doing and they can talk to each other and to him more immediately and effectively than heretofore. This means he can manage them more effectively, although it does not yet provide opportunities for them to participate more effectively in management.

Flirt in Galway had advanced further in 2009 in their use of social networking sites as a way of connecting their volunteers with each other and with the station. They provide an early example of a community radio station in Ireland exploring new technologies to attract and engage the participation of members of their community in station management itself. They did all that Cork Campus Radio were doing – their presenters had and used their own Facebook pages, blogs and Twitter but they created a single page on Facebook for the station and gave the station a quirky personality for students to interact with. 'She' is called 'Raidió Gaillimh' and you can become friends with 'her'. This is more integrated than Cork Campus Radio's 'cloud' and is a smart, self-aware effort to tie volunteers in more closely with their station and with each other. 'Raidió' has a blog, written mainly by the young station manager who updates it daily. She uses it sometimes to spark off debates about management issues but she uses it as an organizational tool for management more often so that all volunteers know what is being planned and can have some input in or influence on it before it becomes practice.

The two smallest and most isolated, rural, community radio stations in Ireland, Connemara Community Radio in North West Galway and Raidió Corca Baiscinn in South West Clare were also beginning to use new technologies in 2009 but to different degrees. Individual presenters in both stations had Facebook pages and blogs relating to their programmes but the lack of broadband and the lower income and education levels of many in their target communities meant that this was not a widespread practice. While the manager of Connemara Community Radio was keen on trying any means of improving the rates and quality of participation, he was suspicious of new technologies, seeing them as a replacement for, or even a block to, 'real' or face-to-face communication. In the case of his community, primarily older people, without broadband, living in an isolated, disadvantaged, rural area, this resistance is valid; people there do not use Facebook and Twitter to communicate with their neighbours. The opposite is true for members of student communities as they live on and through social networking sites.

Raidió Corca Baiscinn transmits in a very similar area and community but they were in the process of introducing significant uses of new communications technologies in

2009. They developed a new, more dynamic website early in the year and they put a link specifically for volunteers on the front or home page. Broadband had recently been rolled out in their transmission area and they began streaming and podcasting in the autumn. Their young station manager believes that as people take advantage of broadband to fulfill other needs on a regular basis, Raidió Corca Baiscinn should take advantage of that activity and link local internet users into their website and project. The station began to have a presence on Facebook in the summer and the staff were eager to explore the possibilities it might offer. Raidió Corca Baiscinn has a coordinator (for volunteers) who is supported by a team of trainers to recruit, train and care for volunteers and they believe that Facebook and Twitter could be really useful but only once people in their target communities begin to use them. As they are run as part of a community development initiative and target the most disadvantaged members of their community first, this is likely to take some time.

In the meantime, and similar to the experience of Connemara Community Radio, they find that emigrants in New York and elsewhere are beginning to get in touch with each other as they discover their more dynamic, audio-supported web page. The potential usefulness of social networking for members of their diaspora is obvious. Whether the community radio station decides to devote energy to facilitating the 'genuine participation' of these emigrants or not is debatable but it is a possibility provided, for the first time, by the development of new communications technologies.

## Conclusions

The rate of uptake of internet and mobile phone technology in Irish community radio stations beyond the use of static websites, e-mail and texting was found to be disappointing. The reasons for this are multifaceted and include the poor telecommunications infrastructures and the low income and education levels of most of the communities served by Irish community radio stations. The facilitation of participation itself was overlooked on two counts. Firstly, the belief of many older community radio activists that new communications technologies would fail to enable personal and meaningful communication resulted in the avoidance of any sustained engagement with new technologies. Secondly, the lack of understanding by station technicians, both paid and voluntary, of the crucial importance of participation for community projects also contributed to the lack of experimentation with new communication technologies; technologies that are almost certain to facilitate 'genuine participation' if used and adapted consciously and creatively.

Some exceptions were observed – these included some individual presenters, some new immigrants and some younger managers in stations who were using social networking sites to promote their own shows and agendas but there was no evidence in any of these cases of any attempt to facilitate 'genuine participation'. Rather they provide examples of one-way and simple two-way flows of communication that did not facilitate genuine participation in the programming, management and ownership of the community radio stations. It was only the student community radio stations that offered any evidence of the exploitation of the potential that social networking sites offer to community radio stations to attract, facilitate and foster the participation of members of the community in the station at the higher levels of the framework proposed.

New communications technologies that enable dialogue were available to Irish community radio stations in 2009 but were not energetically explored for their potential to facilitate 'genuine participation'. The adoption and adaptation of these new technologies will depend on the rate of the use of the internet and newer mobile phone technologies within the target communities over time. In order for any of these new technologies to be useful to a community radio station in recruiting new participants and in supporting them in that participation, members of those communities must be comfortable with the technologies and must already be using them. Younger people tend to be early adopters and adapters of newer technologies. Students in particular are IT literate and embrace new challenges and opportunities. They communicate and interact through digital technology and it is no surprise, therefore that the initial, admittedly limited, experiments in using social networking sites to facilitate participation in 2009 were to be found in student community radio stations and in stations led by younger people.

Most Irish community radio stations however, serve communities where the rate of internet usage was still limited, infrequent and uncommon in 2009. This was found to be related to age, educational achievement, financial resources and poor telecommunications infrastructures. Given that the majority of Irish community radio stations work from a community development ethic (Unique Perspectives 2003; Day 2007) we can hardly expect that the poorest, most marginalized members of society will be in a position to use these new technologies in the immediate future.

In the meantime, it is up to the young, well educated, technologically able community radio activists of the student stations to explore further the potential to facilitate 'genuine participation' through new technologies. If they lead the way in using social networking sites to facilitate 'genuine participation' simply and effectively, other community radio stations will follow happily when their communities are ready.

## References and further reading

Byrne, J., Galliano, S. and Murray, C., 'Empowerment through Community Radio: NEAR Fm as Example', in R. Day (ed). *Bicycle Highway: Celebrating Community Radio in Ireland*, Dublin: The Liffey Press, 2007, pp. 69–88.

Day, R. (ed.) *Bicycle highway: Celebrating community radio in Ireland.* Dublin: The Liffey Press, 2007.

Day, R., *Community radio in Ireland: Participation and multi-flows of communication.* Cresskill: Hampton Press, 2009.

Habermas, J., *The Structural Transformation of the Public Sphere: An Inquiry into a Category of Bourgeois Society*, Cambridge: Polity Press, 1983/1962.

Higgins, C. S. and Moss, P. D., *Sounds Real: Radio in Everyday Life,* St. Lucia: University of Queensland Press, 1982.

McCain, T. & F. G. Lowe, 'Localism in Western European Radio Broadcasting: Untangling the Wireless', *Journal of Communication* 40:1, Winter, 1990, pp. 87–101.

McGann, N. 'Women in Irish Community Radio', in R. Day (ed.) *Bicycle Highway: Celebrating community radio in Ireland.* Dublin: The Liffey Press, 2007, pp. 89–104.

Rubin, H. J. and Rubin, I. S., *Community organizing and development*, 2nd ed. Boston: Allyn and Bacon, 1992.

Shingler , M. and Wieringa, C., *On air: Methods and meanings of radio*. London: Arnold, 1998.

Stanton, P. 'Adult Education through Community Radio: The Example of Community Radio Castlebar', in R. Day (ed.), *Bicycle highway: Celebrating community radio in Ireland*, Dublin: The Liffey Press, 2007, pp. 105–12.

Unique Perspectives, *Community Radio in Ireland: Its Contribution to Community Development: A Report for the Community Radio Forum.* Dublin: CRAO, 2003.

White, S. A., 'Introduction – The Concept of Participation: Transforming Rhetoric to Reality', in S. A. White, S. Nair and J. Ascroft, *Participatory Communication: Working for Change and Development*, London: Sage, 1994, pp. 1–35.

White, S. A., Nair, S. and Ascroft, J. *Participatory communication: Working for change and development.* London: Sage, 1994.

## Chapter 13

The Future of Local Radio in the Digital Era: Opportunity or Threat?
The Case of Small, Local, Community Radio in the Flemish Community

Hilde van den Bulck and Bert Hermans

I n recent years, a range of new, digital applications have changed the radio landscape. These new media differ from traditional media as access is cheap, the number and geographical spread of users is unlimited and the audience rather than the producer decides to consume what, when, where and in what ways (Breen 2007). Particularly internet radio and podcasting have influenced traditional radio production as they allow for alternative content to be offered and for listeners to obtain a more active, selective role. Handheld media players further enable podcasts and internet radio stations to be listened to at any time and any place. These developments beg the question if and to what extent traditional radio stations still have a future ahead of them.

Indeed, traditional radio listening figures have dropped significantly in, amongst others, the United Kingdom, the United States and Canada (Berry 2006; O'Neill 2006). At the same time, major mainstream radio stations have cunningly incorporated these new applications in an attempt to accommodate changing listeners' demands. Yet, while big public service and commercial radio stations have sufficient financial means and logistical know-how to do so, the question is what these new media opportunities mean for small, local, community radio stations with their limited funds and know-how. Taking Flemish local, community radio as a case in point, this chapter studies the potential of technological developments for small, local radio stations. Do they consider these new media applications as an opportunity or a threat? Are they already using them and with what success?

## Local radio and the community ideal

'Local radio' is here equated with 'community radio', a term much used in the US and UK academic literature (Evens 2009). A central characteristic of community radio stations is that it operates on a non-commercial basis and aims at a local community. They are mostly run by non-professional volunteers. A close link with the local community influences programme policy: programmes have a local 'feel' with an emphasis on local and regional news. They are non-profit organizations but often rely on sponsorship and advertising to complement the limited funding from fees, donations and grants (Jauert 1997; Jankowski 2003; Evens 2009). As such, community radio differs markedly from commercial local radio. The latter's profit-based philosophy leads to networking and content based on the lowest common denominator in order to maximize profits (Evens 2009).

In Flanders, the Dutch-speaking half of Belgium with a population of about 6 million, radio stations based on the community ideal have become rare (Evens 2009). Local stations struggle to survive financially in the hyper-competitive Flemish radio market. First, lack of funds and volunteers make it difficult to maintain their duties to inform and engage the local community. Second, the overcrowded Flemish airwaves combined with the limited reach the Flemish radio legislation allows for are structural factors threatening the viability of Flemish local radio stations as they compete not just with national and syndicated but also neighbouring local radio stations. These problems, thirdly, can to a large extent be related back to a failing government policy. While the original 1982 local radio legislation was modelled along the lines of the community ideal (small-scale, non-profit, non-commercial, limited reach, to inform, stimulate and communicate with the local community), subsequent legislation progressively abandoned these ideals in favour of networks and commercialism (Van den Bulck 2009). As a result, today most local radio stations have severed their close ties with the community in favour of syndication or a more commercial profile. Although a considerable number are still independent and low budget, few adhere to a community ideal.

## Digital 'revolution' in the radio landscape

To investigate if and how new media applications can turn the tide for local, community radio, a brief overview of the main digital developments is in order. Menduni (2007) identifies four phases of radio innovations. The first, situated in the 1990s, consists of the development of digital music, the internet and software to play music from a personal computer in order to send music over the internet in a way that it can be played in real time (streaming). The second phase starts in the second half of the 1990s with the introduction of internet radio stations in the US, quickly followed the world over. Some internet radio stations are simulcasting, (that is being distributed at the same time as a terrestrial station and overcoming geographical limitations) while others are restricted to the internet. While internet radio has the potential for social empowerment, every extra listener is a cost to the broadcaster (Ala-Fossi 2005). It further lacks mobility and transportability. The third phase allows for file sharing, exchanging musical data via particular websites on the internet, which started with Napster in 1999. File sharing coincides with the rise of MP3 as a standard format and the development of the MP3 player. As a result, music can be produced, exchanged and transported beyond the reach of the home. The final phase is that of podcasting, described as a 'means of broadcasting listenership and increasing listeners' involvement' (Menduni 2007). Podcasting is an automatic or programmable distribution system via the internet that combines online sound data in MP3 or other formats with RSS feeds and portable, digital music players (Ala-Fossi 2005; Berry 2006; Breen 2007). Podcasting allows individual users to select content rather than to tune into a station with set programmes and recurrent formats; it enables time-shifting as opposed to linear radio and portable media players enable listening to podcasts wherever the user wants. Podcasts thus increase consumer freedom. It was expected that by late 2010, in the US alone there would be sixty million podcast users. Podcasts can be both a threat and opportunity for traditional radio. They can be real and significant competition for traditional broadcasters but at the same time the latter can incorporate these new applications quite easily, meeting the new demands of the listener with no extra costs for the station. Many public and commercial radio stations in the US and Europe have started to offer their regular programmes as podcasts. For instance, both the BBC and Flemish PSB VRT started podcast projects as early as 2005 (Ala-Fossi 2005; Digitale Radio 2005).

## What new media can (not) do for local, community radio

'Believers' maintain that new media platforms and applications provide interesting possibilities for small, local radio stations to move beyond geographically limited, one-way broadcasting over the airwaves and to improve audience involvement – a notion central to the community media ideal. According to Bailey, Cammaerts and Carpentier (2008) 'technological advances in terms of network-based communication tools, digital cameras and compression techniques have provided them (alternative radio) with new means to distribute alternative content worldwide'. They further maintain that small-scale, alternative media are a breeding ground for innovations which, in a later phase, will be copied by mainstream media. Tacchi (2000) stresses the potential of the new digital opportunities for community building and for the provision of alternatives to legal frameworks that inhibit traditional broadcasting over the airwaves. 'Non-believers' are rare but point to the fact that small, local, community radio stations lack the money and know-how to integrate these new applications.

Huntsberger (2008), Atton (2004) and Bailey et al. (2008) provide some interesting but anecdotal evidence of small-scale initiatives successfully embracing the new media, yet little is known about the wider potential and actual use of new, digital platforms and applications by small, local, community radio stations or about the opportunities and problems these radio stations face in implementation. Our aim is to contribute to this discussion by a case study of small, local, community radio stations in Flanders that aims to answer the following research questions:

- To what extent do local Flemish radio stations use new media applications, and which ones do they use?
- What are their motivations to move into these new media (or not)?
- How does it affect programme output?

## Methodological set up

The methodological set up was two-fold and involved different methodologies. First, the websites of all Flemish local radio stations were submitted to quantitative content analysis. During the second phase of this study, a selection of local radio producers were questioned by means of a semi-structured interview enquiring after their motives in using or not using these new digital media applications.

The quantitative content analysis started from VRM, the Flemish media regulator's, February 2009 list of all officially registered local radio stations. From this list of 294 stations, all local radio stations connected to a group or network were excluded. As they merely use a local frequency to broadcast general rather than local content, they do not meet the local requirement in Evens' (2009) definition of community radio. Next, special and unrepresentative cases such as a number of local or regional co-operations between local radio stations were excluded. They broadcast the same content over several local frequencies to reach an urban or other community and share the same website. As such, they do not qualify as independent local radio stations. Finally, FM Brussels was excluded from the list because it received funding from the Flemish government in the form of subsidies to strengthen the position of Flemish in the Belgian capital; it does not need to provide its own funding. The eventual list comprised ninety-seven local, community radio stations that fitted all of Evens' (2009) requirements.

All ninety-seven stations' digital media use was analysed for the existence of a website and, where they had one, for the use of digital applications: basic information, forum, RSS feed, chat or shout boxes, news flashes, podcasts, live streaming and listen-on-demand. Stations were segregated into four categories based on this data.

1. local, community radio stations with no website;
2. local, community radio stations with a limited website with regard to content;
3. local, community radio stations with an extensive website with regard to content; and
4. local, community radio stations with a live stream and/or podcasts

Limited websites with regard to content are websites consisting of one page with little more than a logo and/or contact details. Extensive websites have several pages with a variety of content. While categorization necessarily involves a level of arbitrariness, it allows for the development of a digital continuum on which local, community radio stations can be situated. This further allowed us to select a representative sample for the second part of this study.

In the second part the focus shifts to reasons for (not) using digital media applications and tools. A sample of radio makers was questioned about their motives in this regard by means of a semi-structured interview. A topic list provided a range of subjects to deal with, including why radio makers did or did not have a website, how they had come about their website and what (kind of) content the website included. They were asked about their thoughts on internet streaming and podcasts. Radio stations that provide live streams or podcasts were asked how they were set up and what their experiences were so far. Subsequently, interactive radio and contact with the audience members was discussed. Finally, they were asked about their views on the future of local, community radio.

A convenience sample of seven local, community radio stations was selected, including two radio stations from each of the categories two, three and four and one from the first category. The selected radio stations were Radio Mol from the village of Mol, Geel FM from Geel, Radio Christina from Heist Op Den Berg, Radio Apollo from Wiekevorst, Radio RL from Herenthout, Radio Lichtaart from Lichtaart and Capitol Gold from Tienen.

## Results I: Flemish local, community radio and new media – a question of status

First, all ninety-seven radio stations were checked for the availability of a website and, second, the existing websites were analysed using the above-mentioned coding schedule. Subsequently they were identified as belonging to one of four categories. It was found that fourteen out of all ninety-seven local, community radio stations do not have a website. Two of these radio stations (Spitsradio from the village of Gavere and Radio Meer Goud from Meerhout) have web addresses that were, however, offline at the time of analysis. Subsequent checks confirmed the offline status.

Only eight radio stations fit the second category of radio stations with a limited website. Three of these websites (Stadsradio Halle from the city of Halle, Radio RL from Herenthout and Radio Ariane from Kortessem) indicate that they are under construction. At the time of analysis, Radio Lichtaart from Lichtaart was building its first website and had a test site online that comprised several pages, none of which had any content at the time. Radio Eagle from Arendonk is the only website in this category with an online contact form where visitors can leave a message and contact information. All the other stations have an e-mail link where visitors can click to open a standard e-mail programme.

The third category comprises thirty-one stations with an extensive website but with no internet live streaming or podcasting. These thirty-one websites are not identical as they differ aesthetically and also in type and amount of information they provide. The most common types of content are programme schedules, overviews and announcements, photo pages, international, national and/or regional and local news, hit lists, contact information and links to other websites. Many provide an overview of their resident DJs and producers, including photographs and some personal information. Lists of events and activities occurred regularly, too. Nine of these websites have a 'now playing' function, indicating what number is being played on the radio at any given point in time. In some cases this application includes the last or next song, or which programme and/or DJ is on air. Five websites offer play lists of some of the programmes. Only two radio stations (Radio Canteclaer from the City of Deinze and Radio Noorderkempen from Turnhout) provide a search button for their play lists. Radio Canteclaer also provides RSS feeds with news.

Three radio stations explain which hit singles can be found in their play lists. Radio Diest from the city of Diest and Radio Christina from Heist Op Den Berg provide an online form for music requests. Interestingly, seven of these websites provide the stations' jingles via MP3 or MediaPlayer. Radio VRD from Diepenbeek and Sport FM from Hoeselt have a webcam allowing visitors to see what goes on in the studio. In terms of interactive feedback from listeners, four radio stations provide an online poll regarding local political issues or listeners' views on the station. Ten radio stations have a guest book where visitors can leave a message. Nine have an online contact form.

The final category is the biggest, with forty-four radio stations that broadcast live via the internet or offer podcasts. To a certain extent, this category partly overlaps with the previous one, as the majority of stations with live streaming or podcasts also have several of the applications mentioned above. Park FM from Brasschaat is the only exception, as the radio has a website which provides nothing other than a link to a live stream, with no additional information. Yet it is worth considering the use of streaming and podcasts as a separate category as these applications transgress and break through the traditional linear way of broadcasting. Interestingly, thirty-six of these forty-four radio stations broadcast via the internet. Eight of these stations also provide podcasts of programmes, interviews or documentaries. Radio Meetjesland from Ghent is exceptional as it only offers its daily musical request programme *De Muzikale Fruitmand* as a live stream. Eight radio stations have no live streams and only offer podcasts or MP3s of programmes, interviews, documentaries, newscasts or music mixes. The website of Radio Ham from Ham even offers PDF files of its fanzine. A number of radio stations provide interactive applications. Radio Stad from the city of Antwerp and Radio IRO from Izegem each have a chatroom. Furthermore, Radio Stad provides a forum where listeners can ask questions about playlists, while Radio IRO offers a shout box. The shout box service is provided by two other stations (Radio Geel from Geel and Urgent FM from Ghent), while three radio stations (FM Goud from Hechtel-Eksel, Thals FM from Herentals and Spits FM from Opwijk) provide a forum. There is only one radio station in this category with a webcam: FM Goud. Five radio stations organize online polls on issues ranging from current affairs to questions about the station. Eight radio stations have an online form to request songs. Radio Katanga from the city of Aalst, Crooze FM from Antwerp, Radio Tequila from Deinze, Urgent FM from Ghent and Radio Extra Gold from Ichtegem deliver RSS feeds that listeners can subscribe to. These feeds alert them to new content such as news flashes or new podcasts being put online. Other recurring types of content include programme schedules and overviews, lists of DJs and producers, newscasts, list of activities, chart lists, photo pages, 'now playing', guest books, contact information, online contact forms and links to other websites of sponsors and partners.

## Results II: radio makers discussing digitalization and the future of local, community radio

It appears that the majority of Flemish local community radio stations are well represented on the internet, which is an indication that they believe it is important to move beyond traditional radio formats by means of a supportive website. To probe explanations and motivations in this regard, seven local community radio makers, with representatives from each category,[1] submitted to a semi-structured interview. All interviewees indicated that a website provides added value for a radio station, pointing out advantages such as the fact that a website can attract new, additional listeners as well as additional advertising revenue.

> "It can function as a promotional tool for programmes, activities and events. It is a space in which to provide local news and, finally, it can give the station a face: pictures of DJs, producers, studios and activities can be put online. When you depend on an audience, you need to communicate, preferably on multiple platforms [...] A website offers gigantic opportunities in that regard."
>
> (Jean-Paul De Bie, Radio Christina)

> "Part of our target audience may not always listen to the radio but still wants to know what is going on in Geel. They can find this on our website. So, if they listen to the radio and they come across Geel FM (online), there is an immediate recognition. You can also provide information for people who want to know what is going to be on the radio next or soon. If somebody listened to the newscast but did not quite understand it, he can find it on the website. All this provides added-value for the listener."
>
> (Hans Claesen, Geel FM)

> "We want to use the website to make the radio better known, particularly with the younger generation as our audience members are relatively old [...] For sponsoring too it can be very interesting. A potential advertiser will be more eager to work with us if he is on the site as well."
>
> (Gerard Vissers & Linda De Prins, Radio Lichtaart)

Some radio makers believe their website to be outdated and are eager to update them, but both time and financial constraints result in delays. Moreover, maintaining a website is considered a lot of work and many radio stations lack the staff or technical know-how to do so.

> "We need to restyle the website urgently [...] but the economic crisis is hitting the radio sector as much as any, so it will have to wait."
>
> (Frank Hus, Radio Mol)

"We have not changed the current website for two years [...] Both privately and job-wise we had so much going on that there simply was not enough time to do it."

(Jean-Paul De Bie, Radio Christina)

"Our old website was online for about three years. We had designed it ourselves because we really wanted to but also to save money [...] You need someone who has the skills to do this and we are still looking for that person."

(Martin Lieckens, Radio RL)

Capitol Gold has been planning a website for several years, but here too, personal circumstances have delayed the project. Since this is a specialized station centred around golden oldies, listeners and programme makers feel the need for online play lists and live streaming. Such live streams are already available on the websites of Radio Mol and Geel FM, who also have an on-demand service. Geel FM allows for interviews to be revisited while Radio Mol makes available a number of live broadcasts on location. Making streams and downloads available is considered as a definitive plus point by the management. Yet, the extra costs make these applications less obvious an inclusion.

"We have been offering live streams for the past two years now. That was quite an undertaking, as we were hampered by government. We pay copyright to broadcast music and were expected to pay these rights again for the live stream. That has stopped us for quite a long time but at some point we felt we were lagging behind the competition and so decided we could not wait any longer. We want to be seen as a professional radio station and therefore cannot do without such a stream."

(Frank Hus, Radio Mol)

The other radio makers also take a positive attitude towards these new media applications and some of them plan to integrate them in the future. Some respondents consider this to be a necessary adjustment to innovations. Yet, here too the extra costs and necessary technical know-how are considered as obstacles. Some also doubt whether the quality of presentation on their station warrants such a live stream. Finally, one respondent believes that local, community radio should remain first and foremost local.

"We have talked about live streaming [...] Of course money is a key issue as is the absence of the technical knowledge required for it. Copyright fees could seriously increase and is the main reason we have not moved forward on this."

(Wil Heylen, Radio Apollo)

"We have a number of DJs that are well-fitted for a local audience but not for streaming. They love their work but the quality of their presentation is somewhat lacking and so you would simply lose people. You can afford to make little mistakes locally, but not on an internet stream that goes out more widely."

(Gerard Vissers & Linda De Prins, Radio Lichtaart)

"In the end we are a local station aimed at listeners in and around the village of Herenthout and so I do not think we should aim to be received all over the world."

(Martin Lieckens, Radio RL)

A number of radio stations use their website to interact with their listeners. For instance, Radio Apollo and Radio Lichtaart have a guest book on their website while on the website of Geel FM people can send messages in a shout box. Radio Mol, in turn, offers a list of activities where visitors can put up their own events. Radio Christina also wants to increase listener interactivity with its new website, while Radio Mol plans a guest book to create an extra channel for people to offer feedback. Yet, all interviewees state that most of their contact with the audience occurs via e-mail, telephone or personal contact.

"The guest book results from a request of visiting musicians that wanted to write something on our website. That way, listeners know who came to the studio. We also started it for people that may not find it easy to say something face to face or live on radio and find it easier to do it via the guest book. This way we can take into account the wishes of our audience members."

(Gerard Vissers & Linda De Prins, Radio Lichtaart)

"Originally we wondered whether to add a forum or guest book to our website. Yet, these things need constant monitoring in case people post things that are out of bounds. For that reason we have chosen to provide a shout box, a place where people can leave short messages […]Yet, most listeners still simply e-mail their reactions."

(Hans Claesen, Geel FM)

"I think a website compensates for things we used to do live and direct. Live, direct broadcast have become rare with most radio stations as we simply do not have the money or producers […] I am convinced that the interactivity that has become less powerful in local, community radio can be revived through these new means."

(Jean-Paul De bie, Radio Christina)

"Our online list of activities allows for people to put their events in the spotlights for free. It has been built in a very user-friendly fashion. We find this calendar very important as we believe that local, community radio has an important local function. We want to offer a platform to other local organisations to make their events known. This, in turn, encourages people to go to the website and that way we reach a wider audience that may listen to the radio every now and then."

(Frank Hus, Radio Mol)

Finally, respondents were asked to give their views on the future of the medium. Almost all of them expect that in the near future the internet will take up an ever greater role and position in the provision of content. Yet, some of them believe that broadcasting via the airwaves will not disappear completely due to the ease of use of the FM band. Two radio makers are more pessimistic and predict that in ten years time local, community radio will have disappeared due to the success of online media. Others claim that radio, in whatever form, is here to stay.

"The MP3 era has arrived and that will evolve, but the medium of radio as such will definitely survive. The new media that are added, like internet radio, must be seen as an addition, an extension of radio."

(Frank Hus, Radio Mol)

"I believe that we will see the arrival of more and more internet radio stations [...] On the other hand, I am sure the FM part will survive as it is always more easy to switch on a radio than a computer."

(Wim Heylen, Radio Apollo)

"Our view is that within five to ten years, there will not be a single local, community radio left. Radio as such will probably remain in one form or other, but not at local level. Computers will take over. The visual becomes ever more important and that means radio becomes outdated. Adolescents do not stay at home to listen to the radio anymore. They take the music they like from MP3 and they go."

(Gerard Vissers & Linda De Prins, Radio Lichtaart)

"I believe we are moving more and more to the online component, to on-demand. People become used to pressing the red button on their TV's remote control to revisit programmes and they expect the same from radio. As a local radio you must try as much as possible to offer what people want."

(Hans Claesen, Geel FM)

"I would not go as far as to state that the FM band has no future but I think that we will adjust to the new circumstances. Today we work with streaming, tomorrow some other application will show up and we will feel forced to go along, albeit delayed as we are financially unable to incorporate that immediately. If it would turn out that there is no more audience for the airwaves, something different will come along. Local radio in itself still has a raison d'être as it allows you to comment on events from close by, something national radio cannot."

(Jean-Paul De Bie, Radio Christina)

## Discussion

Local, community radio stations in Flanders have clearly entered the virtual world. More than 75% of all local, community stations each have their own website. The majority of these websites are more than a token presence as they provide a platform with an array of content and applications. Content commonly includes programme schedules, overviews, chart lists, local news, histories and information regarding radio makers and DJs. Many websites offer photos of activities and events and of the people behind the radio station. Almost half of all stations simulcast through the internet. Some allow for programming, such as interviews and documentaries, to be revisited on the website. Many of the radio practitioners being interviewed agree that today a website is essential for any organization or company. They recognize the potentially interesting synergies between both media to create added value for the listener. Information offered on the website provides extra services that radio practitioners hope will attract new listeners. A website can also be a way to attract additional advertising revenues as they create wider exposure.

Local, community radio practitioners try to strengthen their relationship with the audience members via their websites. Applications such as guest books and contact forms through which listeners can send in questions or comments make this possible. The station thus becomes more accessible and listeners feel free to react more than in a face-to-face or call-in situation. Local radio makers are keen to offer their listeners as many different contact options as feasible, because they are aware of the fact that they make radio for their community rather than for themselves.

The internet has only recently been adopted by local, community radio stations as the interviews reveal: apart from Radio Mol, no other station started their online activities until 2000 or later. So, contrary to the claim of Bailey et al. (2008) and Berry (2006), local, community radio stations in Flanders do not function as a breeding place for innovation but instead lag behind. Many offer internet streaming, but interviewees stressed financial cost of such a stream owing to copyright issues as a strong deterrent to start such an initiative. The examples of Radio Mol and Geel FM further show that financial restraints mean only a few listeners can listen to the live stream at the same time. In that regard, Ala-Fossi (2005) is right in claiming that, for the time being, the online applications are not sufficiently cheap for local radio stations to benefit from them. Podcasts and other audio-on-demand are also a marginal phenomenon in local, community radio. Contrary to Berry's (2006) claim, podcasting is not a typical grass roots phenomenon in Flanders – traditional broadcasting does not perceive it as a threat yet. Although the interviewees claim to be interested and might incorporate it in future, they have so far not felt a real need to actually do so. The integration of podcasting into local radio is mainly hampered by the financial costs of storage, lack of technological knowhow and potential copyright problems. Finally, and unlike the examples Huntsberger (2008) offers about public radio in the US, neither has the interactive potential of websites been fully exploited by Flemish local, community radio.

The main reasons are a lack of financial means and technological knowhow to implement interactive functions on the websites.

So, do new media options offer possibilities for local radio to better and more effectively realize the community (radio) ideal? Having a website and offering streaming or on-demand content are a clear aid in day-to-day operations of a radio station and create added-value for their listeners. Yet, these new media options are not miracle solutions for the difficult situation Flemish local community radio is facing at the moment. For local community radio to be really able to fulfil its community function, problems of a more structural nature need to be solved. Firstly, the Flemish government does not offer enough potential for growth. Flemish local community radio is subject to very strict rules with regard to reach and has to compete for space in too small a bandwidth. Despite the 2003 Frequency Plan, the FM band is still overcrowded (Van den Bulck, 2009; ECC 2009), making it hard for local community radio to see a future and therefore a reason to invest in infrastructure and knowhow. While applications such as streaming and podcasting offer possibilities to solve the bandwidth problem, there are many advantages to FM broadcasting that would be lost if they were to switch to online platforms only. Streaming and on-demand services are considered a means to better reach the audience but not as a substitute. The interviewees further indicate these online applications reach few additional listeners, in the case of streaming due to the financial implications of attracting larger numbers of listeners. In that regard, our data confirm the results of Ali-Fossi et al. (2008) study where radio experts claimed that, at the moment, FM is still the best option for local radio. Still, most of our interviewees expect these media applications to gain significance in the future as computers take up an ever more central position in peoples' lives. They refer to television where digital functionality and on-demand services gain in popularity.

Secondly, the application of new media is determined by the general economic viability of a station. Most of them have limited financial means. This means that some copyright costs are a concern that prevents many from including streaming and podcasting because they believe the trend is irreversible and will need to be picked up in future. Radio stations that do offer streaming have seen an increase in costs but consider it part of their professional image as a radio station to provide this service to their audience. Limited financial means are also behind time lags in the implementation of such new media and the maintenance and adjustment of websites. Some of the interviewees indicate that they are eager to start streaming or podcasting but have not as yet found the financial means to do so.

Other relevant factors include limited staff numbers and a lack of time to devote to radio making. Stations usually lack staff with sufficient technological knowhow to maintain and renew websites or enable streaming or podcasting. Contracting outside help stretches financial means. To survive, most radio makers have a full time job outside radio, leaving them with little time to keep websites up to date or to keep up with latest developments. To most of them, radio making is at the end of the day a hobby.

## Note

1. Management from Radio Mol from Mol (category 4), Geel FM from Geel (category 4), Radio Christina from Heist Op Den Berg (category 3), Radio Apollo from Wiekevorst (category 3) Radio Lichtaart from Lichtaart (category 2), Radio RL from Herenthout (category 2) and Capitol Gold from Tielen (category 1).

## References and further reading

Ala-Fossi, M., 'Mapping the Technological Landscape of Radio: Where Do We Go Next?' Paper presented at the First ECREA Conference. Amsterdam: December, 2005.

Ala-Fossi, M., Lax, S., O'Neill, B., Jauert, P. & Shaw, H., 'The Future of Radio is Still Digital – But Which One? Expert Perspectives and Future Scenarios for Radio Media in 2015', *Journal of Radio and Audio Media*, 15:1, 2008, pp. 4–25.

Atton, C., *An alternative internet: Radical media, politics and creativity*. Edinburgh: Edinburgh University Press, 2004.

Baily, O. G., Cammaerts, B., & Carpentier, N., *Understanding alternative media*. Berkshire: Open University Press, 2008.

Berry, R., 'Will the iPod Kill the Radio Star?' *Convergence*, 12:2, 2006, pp. 14362.

Breen, M. J., 'Mass Media and New Media Technologies', in E. Devereux (ed.) *Media Studies: Key Issues and Debates*, London: Sage, 2007, pp. 55–77.

Carpentier, N., 'The On-Line Community Media Database: Radio Stationswap as a Trans Local Tool to Broaden the Communicative Rhizone', *Observatorio*, 1, 2007, pp. 1–26.

Digitale Radio, 'VRT zet download- en podcastproject voort', http://www.digitaleradio.be/dab/hoeluisteren/pc/nieuws_20050905_proefproject_fase2.html. Accessed 10 April 2009.

ECC, Future Possibilities for the Digitalisation of Band II (87,5 – 108 Mhz). Copenhagen: ECC, 2009.

Evens, T., 'Less Is More. De leefbaarheid van lokale radio in Vlaanderen', Ghent: University of Ghent, 2009.

Huntsberger, M., 'Create Once, Play Everywhere: Convergence Strategies for Public Radio in the US', Paper presented at RIPE@2008, Mainz: October 2008.

Jankowski, N.W., 'Community Media Research: A Quest for Theoretically-Grounded Models', *The Public* 10:1, 2003, pp. 5–14.

Jauert, P., 'Local adio in Western Europe: Conflicts between the Cultures of Center and Periphery', *The Nordic Review*, 1, 1997, pp. 93–106.

Menduni, E., 'Four Steps in Innovative Radio Broadcasting: From QuickTime to Podcasting', *The Radio Journal – International Studies in Broadcast and Audio Media*, 5:1, 2007, pp. 9–18.

O'Neill, B., 'CBC.ca. Broadcast Sovereignty in a Digital Environment', *Convergence*, 12:2, 2006, pp. 179–97.

Tacchi, J., 'The Need for Radio Theory in the Digital Age', *International Journal of Cultural Studies*, 3:2, 2001, pp. 289–98.

VRM, 'Lijst van alle particuliere radio's', http://www.vlaamser,egulatormedia.be/documentatie/lokaleradio.html. Accessed 17 February 2009.

Van den Bulck, H., 'Media: Structuur en Werking', Antwerp: ACCO, 2009.

# Chapter 14

Slovenia and the Origins of its Community Radio

Mojca Plansak

## Introduction

Many scholars are exploring the question whether better and more equity-oriented state policy, especially policies addressing media, cultural policy and social mobility issues, could have avoided the series of tragic events that led to the break-up of Yugoslavia and the consequent series of ethnic battles that took place there in the 1990s (Ramet 1996). Other observers wonder whether and how the former Yugoslav republics will manage to mould themselves into European nation states – whether or not they will be able to address issues of nationalism, ethnicity, citizenship and multiethnic immigration that will necessarily contradict and challenge a sense of national identity built on a homogeneous language/culture model (Popov 2000).

Considering the media sphere, we should not forget the time and space we are living in. We live in the age of electronic technology. Actually, this new technology brings opportunities and threats to community radio. New communication forms can re-establish the composition and power of the message which is disseminated with the help of various speakers and mediators, such as the internet. However, 'the changes in the media industry are an integral part of the global transition from an industrial society to an information society, a development that is largely sustained by the evolution of digital technologies' (Nissen 2006). It appears that 'people currently living in the evolving information society tend to regard themselves more as individual consumers than citizens, and society more as a marketplace than a community' (Nissen 2006).

## Community radio in Slovenia and Macedonia

To be able to understand community media, one has to consider both the bonds which connect them and those which differentiate them, making them distinctive, not in the sense of one, single narrative, but in the sense of their plurality, openness, and heterogeneous quality. The development of community media links up with many of the leading issues in social sciences and the political sphere in the twentieth century – issues concerning a categorical differentiation between the state and civil society (of which the market is a part) and a third realm, the public sphere, which ideally mediates between the two. Furthermore, questions focus on the balance between the roles of technology, economics and public opinion in determining social developments; the mechanisms of political democracy and the role of public debate; community integration and culture; paternalism and social order and control; and the relative weight given to private versus public ownership in capitalist societies. All these issues coincide in the study of community media.

Today, the value of community media is finally getting some recognition. However government policy in Slovenia and Macedonia still does not recognize the importance of community media, despite the fact that 'Community media has proven again and again it is here to stay and it demands to be taken seriously' (Rennie 2006). A characteristic of community media is that they serve particular social groups within civil society. They have helped create crucial social changes, movements including student movements (as in the case of Radio Student in Ljubljana),[1] emancipation from the state (as in the case of Radio Mars in Maribor and Kanal 103 in Skopje, Macedonia) or after war and intercultural connection (such as Cross Radio in the former territory of Yugoslavia, www. crossradio.org).

Lately Slovene and Macedonian media came under attack from (re)nationalization and commercialization. Political elites are trying to use the media for their political purposes, but at the same time both the media and political elites are oriented towards the maximization of profit because a capitalist market economy is seen as the only way to legitimize political changes. The neoliberal rhetoric of deregulated media is championed on the grounds that the media are paralleled with party political pluralism and parliamentary democracy, and that democratic requirements for more communication channels and media can be met only under market conditions. Media debates reflected the key controversies of the general project of (political) democratization of the Slovene and Macedonian societies. A number of ideas in the discussions about the reorganization of the communication sphere were guided by the political agenda already established in Western countries, but there are still no clear results, as Kolar Panov explained:

'The Macedonian media is not much different from any other media in southeastern Europe. They have experienced a transformation from how things were during the socialist regime, to the euphoric creation of free and independent media, frequent funding from international institutions on which the media leant against up to today, when the market defines what and how to do. This means that the media today is facing a rough market of competitiveness and unfortunately some of them are not resourceful enough to work and survive under such circumstances. They are still and constantly waiting for someone to donate means for their existence. The tremendous number of Macedonian media is changing from day to day. On one day a medium is shut down and on the other day a new one opens up. Radio nevertheless managed to survive, despite television and the internet because it is nowadays also possible to listen to the radio via the internet and to use your computer to watch TV and listen to the radio. Radio is omnipresent as you are not obliged to watch it but instead you can listen to it in the car, the elevator, in short, everywhere. We still have to learn a lot but I think that the time, where the Macedonian media will have to crystallize itself on the basis of quality, is still yet to come. Only then, we will be able to speak differently about the media in Macedonia.'[2]

In Slovenia, there are Radio Student in Ljubljana (www.radiostudent.si), Radio Mars in Maribor (www.radiomars.si), Radio Romic in Murska Sobota (http://www.romic.si, broadcasting *for/with/about* Roma community in both the Slovene and Roma languages), the temporary project Radio for Contemporary Arts (the case of RadioCona[3] in Ljubljana, (http://radiocona.wordpress.com/) and some local community bulletins.

Kanal 103 in Macedonia (accessible at www.kanal103.com.mk/) was established by students in 1991. It represents a unique radio station, in that its diverse community radio programme can be heard in the multi-ethnic capital city Skopje. It is a so-called low power radio station, which functions within Macedonian public service (MTV). This represents a very specific example of a community radio scene in the former Yugoslav territory, because most community radio stations in former Yugoslavia (or Europe) do not operate under the patronage of public broadcasting services. Although the problem is that legally the frequency of Kanal 103 does not exist in the policy documents of the MTV, but rather, in the broadcasting law. What this means is that there is a frequency, but no one actually wants to legalize its status under the patronage of MTV. That is why the Macedonian authorities have abolished the frequency several times, the last occasion being in year 2004 for fourteen days, since Macedonia (in contrast to almost all European states) does not have a mass media act as their main and general media policy document. It has never adopted it, but instead it only adopted the law for radio broadcasting in 2005, yet it includes no inclusion or definition of community media (for further details, see www.srd.org.mk). Alternatively, as Trpevska says in her in-depth analysis of the broadcasting situation in Macedonia, which is symptomatic of the region generally:

'Financial instability leads to a lack of programming consistency in broadcasting. Even though pluralism has been achieved in terms of quantity, the same does not apply to content diversity. As broadcasters lack financial stability, they fail to produce or procure good quality programming. This means that overall programming is highly uniform; with a focus on soft news […] the quality of other programming is very low. Commercial TV stations (with rare exceptions) mostly run soap operas, telenovelas, games of chance, and entertainment-music talk shows. Contact shows often seize opportunities for additional profits by promoting use of premium phone services. Almost all entertainment programmes are sponsored, and one can hardly distinguish the content from the sponsorship. Public service programmes are also generally unsatisfactory. Analyses have shown that the public broadcasting service in Macedonia does not satisfy at least three of its five basic functions (universality, quality, diversity, nurturing cultural identity and giving value for cost).'

(2005)

## Community radio in the process of digitalization

Let us focus on community media, including radio in the age of the information society, especially on digitalization,[4] which will, especially dealing with the possibilities and plurality of media content, offer a great deal of choice and possibilities. The European Union Initiative i2010, 'which stakes on the vision of common and adjusted removal of limitations with regard to the spectrum use in all European member states, would, in this way, stimulate an open and competitive economy. The European citizens should acquire direct benefits with a faster access to the new technology and lower communication prices' (Ministry of Economy 2006). Dealing with the whole topic of the transfer to digitalization, the battle for the digital frequency spectrum is, in general, already over in the basin of the political European Union. The finished public consultation of the European Commission group for radio spectrum policy in Slovenia has already indicated some main obstacles to the possible fast transition from analogue to digital broadcasting, among which, the first one is the most obvious, stating that

> 'on a political playground with the absence of political decisions, such as the national shutdown of analogue broadcasting, and not setting the deadlines for the abolition of the analogue broadcasting and the lack of European hearing and policy, and due to the fact that numerous new technologies and services are dependent on the attainment of the users' critical mass on the European level, they are more attracted to the enlargement of the basic technology in Europe.'
>
> (Ministry of Economy 2006)

However, we agree that the main question posed is what are the possibilities of other states, which are not yet in the European Union? Such as, for example, in the neighbouring state of Croatia, where the transition from analogue to digital is, surprisingly, almost successfully finished. The whole spectrum of digitalization is in the hands of the European Union and its capital and technical development, in short, in the hands of capitalistic and politically powerful people, without considering the rest of the European members and those who are still on the waiting list, and their technological development. Slovenian radio activists have pointed out that the majority of the Slovenian people, especially in villages, still do not have internet access at home. How influential will community media be and what kind of accessibility will they have if they should support minorities, marginal groups, ethnic groups, and in short, those whose roots are suppressed and who only have limited media communication access, if their accessibility is slim or non-existent and their technology is underdeveloped?

The second indisputable fact is that the deadline for the transition from analogue to digital is strictly defined by the European Union only for television (stating the year 2012), and not for the radio spectrum, or as the Slovenian strategy for the transition from analogue to digital broadcasting claims:

the strategy for the transition also takes into consideration the needs for the digital radio T-DAB and DRM, including the fact that the present analogue radio frequency zones are still operating, meaning that the transition to digital radio broadcasting represents merely another alternative to the analogue way of broadcasting. There is no deadline until when the providers and users of radio programmes should switch and cancel the current analogue way of broadcasting and receiving (2006).

Another worrying fact in Slovenia is that the 'final and sufficient spectrum and programme diversity in the radio media is still missing, however, it is in the process of being finalized in the near future' (Ministry of Economy 2006), and that 'the strategy has been adopted too late, with the authors having taken up an exceedingly technical approach in creating it (its main occupation is peculiarly technical and economical concerning broadcasting digital signals, and it does not deal with programmes, new services and the accessibility of the media content); also the lack of concrete proposals, initiatives and estimations of costs and social consequences of digital transition are missing' (Kucic 2006). Furthermore, a third instance of absence in the realization of the transition from analogue to digital broadcasting emerges from the fact that 'every spectrum part on the national level will be very much dependent on the number of the neighborhood states, which have already cancelled analogue broadcasting and will be wholly realized on the European level only in the event of entirely cancelling analogue radio broadcasting in the European Union and the neighbouring states' (Ministry of Economy 2006). How, then, will Slovenia transparently provide an assurance for all the promises over digital transition, considering neighbouring Austria, which assumes its transition to be complete in the year 2010, neighbouring Italy, where the transition was already finished on the 21st of July 2006 and Hungary, where the transition to the digital broadcasting shall be finished by the year 2012? These are the questions, which the current government, being led by Prime Minister Borut Pahor, should soon be able to answer, especially the authoritative Ministry of the Economy – Directorate for Electronic Communication and the Post and Electronic Communications Agency of the Republic of Slovenia. Furthermore, as is seen from the report of the European Commission 'in contrast to TV digitization, which is gaining pace across Europe, the digitization of broadcast digital radio is – apart from very few countries – still stagnating at a very low level or even at a trial stage' (DG Information Society and Media 2006). The report of the European Commission also warns that DAB, the standard originally designed to replace FM, is outdated and other, newer standards, such as DAB +, DRM (+), DMB, DVB-H are superior in terms of quality and efficiency of the individual states. Most of the European community media today are already using the possibility of online radio; also, they are using podcasting as a way of broadcasting. However, as stated before, the actual solution, how, in which way and to which extent the community radio-media platform will change and rearticulate is not yet clear.

By all means the era of the information society brings especially to community media the possibility to act within the internet space, and can with its knowledge and creativity develop various participatory forms and broadcasting platforms, which the public and commercial media are perhaps not aware of. The future, at least considering information technology of the community media, would in any case be worth developing and exploring within the internet and with MP3 players; on the open market we can already buy wireless internet digital transmitters,[5] which make data transfer possible without a computer. The problem of such developing projects again appears at the financial level. There also exists the possibility of visual radio: Nokia and Hewlett-Packard started their service in March 2005 in collaboration with the Finnish Radio station Kiss FM (named 'Uusi Kiss today'). As sound is received analogically via traditional FM radio, visual radio is not a digital radio solution. Additional visual content synchronized with the radio programme is streamed to the phone via data connection (GPRS or UMTS), for which the user is charged.[6] This again leads us to the fact that those developed projects are strongly connected with big capital investments and profitable earnings of media and technological conglomerates, from whom community media do not gain anything. As Preston and Kerr said, they 'continue to be marked by very specific "market" boundaries on the demand and consumption fronts, based around distinct national, ethnic, etc. formations of taste, culture, habitus, community and other identities, whatever the global reach of the new technologies of content production and distribution' (2001: 115). However, 'the overcoming of distance requires more than technology and indeed more than the creation of a public sphere' (Silverstone 2004: 444). After Silverstone the content that media are distributing through the internet 'is still seen to be essentially technical, and is rarely approached as requiring more sophisticated skills' (2004).

## Conclusion

Slovenian and Macedonian broadcasting and media policy need further development considering community media/radio. Especially when the *European Recommendation of the Committee of Ministers* to the member states on media pluralism and diversity of media content says, that

> '[M]ember states should encourage the development of other media capable of making a contribution to pluralism and diversity and providing a space for dialogue. These media could, for example, take the form of community, local, minority or social media. The content of such media can be created mainly, but not exclusively, by and for certain groups in society, can provide a response to their specific needs or demands, and can serve as a factor of social cohesion and integration. The means of distribution, which may include digital technologies, should be adapted to the habits and needs of the public for whom these media are intended.'
>
> (Rec (2007)2))[7]

As Rennie argues, 'our political institutions are antiquated, not community media' (2006), and Hamilton stresses that 'their collective value is in their exploration of new forms of organizing more participatory techniques of media and more inclusive, democratic forms of communication' (2000). It can be concluded that not only Slovenia, but also the whole European Union should 'today elaborate mechanisms, which would assure, that also in private infrastructures there will stay a fixed number of programme contents (content in the interests of public) available to all viewers – under the same conditions and for the equal price. On the contrary the digital technology can instead of promised greater media plurality only bring new, more solid media monopolies' (Kucic 2006).

## Notes

1. The very beginnings of community media in Slovenia were in the year 1969, when Radio Student in the capital city of Ljubljana was established from the Association of Students of the University of Ljubljana. Radio Mars in Maribor, the second biggest city in Slovenia, was established later as a 'younger brother' in 1990 as a base for criticism of the mainstream media's musical selections with an emphasis on the absence of creative contemporary music. However, the initial idea of Radio Mars dates back to 1984. Since its inception, Radio Student has been one of the few local bastions of alternative independent journalism, and the only form of electronic media open to the 'new waves' in various fields of culture.

   In the 1970s it was widely listened to mostly because of the music it broadcast. It was also the first wider regional radio station with DJs who presented and reviewed the latest alternative music releases. The explosion of punk rock and the independent musical production of the late 1970s coupled with the burgeoning economical and political crisis in Yugoslavia in the early 1980s gradually shifted the primary attention of Radio Student to social and political issues.

   The 1980s marked the establishment of the highly and widely respected Radio Student practical school of journalism, which not only puts an emphasis on breaking taboos and the limits on freedom of speech, but also on journalist's ethical principles. The reputation of Radio Student in the wider region near Ljubljana has been always high, in part due to its specific school of announcers and sound technicians who give a specifically personal touch to the creation of radio programmes and the station's classic and unrivalled radio jingles.

   Both Radio Student and Radio Mars's primary objective is to promote and investigate the generally ignored issues faced by the student community as well as marginalized social and cultural groups; in so doing, they also educate their listeners. Since its inception, Radio Student has promoted tolerance, respect for differences of opinion, freedom, truth, solidarity and multiculturalism. The promotion of these values is carried out at two levels: the educational (not just of listeners, but authors as well) and the practical, as Radio Student acts as a mirror to Slovene society, in which it can check to what extent it is really ready to accept these widely proclaimed values.
2. Manuscript, Skopje, Macedonia, June 2006.
3. The need to rearticulate the use and abuse of the radio-frequency space in both social and artistic contexts has arisen recently. The abuse of radio for exclusively propaganda purposes (for politics or the economy) is slowly but surely undermining this space. History stands witness that the radio is interpreted as a forerunner of the Internet, mobile communication and other two-way communication technologies. Artworks employing communication technology relate to locative media and to placing events in artistic and social contexts. Through a series of FM and online broadcasts and the formulation of a radioCona platform, the project uses radio frequency space

in artistic and broader social contexts. Legally and without any major procedural complications (such as those that marked 2008, the first year of its operation), radioCona has occasional access to a frequency band. For this it was necessary to define the domain and find an interlocutor (the national administrator of frequency space) in order to realize the project on FM frequencies. The local FM broadcast is also streamed live for the sake of wider distribution. The project is set up and activated periodically at relatively short intervals. The mobile audio studio changes location in accordance with the content and logistics of the individual broadcast, captures sounds from the environment and maps active spaces. Therefore radioCona works as a platform for processing, producing and exhibiting contemporary art projects that can be distributed by radio. Its programme also comprises accompanying events: talks, panel discussions, guided tours of exhibition projects, with an important part being radioCona's own sound-art projects and sounds capes. RadioCona also focuses on projects that think two-way, radio-frequency-based transmission of information, not one-to-one communication but rather social systems of communicating, social protocols and temporary communities originating there from, and the interactions within a community as the source of basic information.

4. In Slovenia, on 16 March 2005, the project group was appointed by the previous Minister of Economy, mag. Andrej Vizjak, and has prepared the starting-points of the Slovenian Strategy for the Transition from Analogue to Digital Broadcasting, finally adopted in February 2006. The proposal of the Strategy was finally adjusted and prepared at the Directorate for electronic communications; the Ministry of Economy. The Strategy (Ministry of Economy 2006) is founded on the action plan e-Europe 2005 and Slovenia has adopted the Commission proposal that the digitalization process will be initiated in the year 2012. The Strategy forecasts octuple covering (eight equal networks) and three areas (West, Centre and East) and is founded on mutual adjustments with the neighbouring states.

5. See http://www.freecom.com/.

6. For details, see DG Information Society and Media (2006).

7. For further details, see Rec (2007)2 – Recommendation of the Committee of Ministers to member states on media pluralism and diversity of media content, adopted by the Committee of Ministers on 31st January 2007 at the 985th meeting of the Ministers' Deputies, available at https://wcd.coe.int/ViewDoc.jsp?id=1089699&BackColorInternet=9999CC&Back.

## References and further reading

B. Hrvatin, S., 'V Sloveniji brez javne razprave o novi medijski direktivi', *Media Watch Journal*, 28, 2007, pp. 21–22.

DG Information Society and Media, *Interactive Content and Convergence: Implications for the information society. A study for the European Commission. Final report*, October 2006, http://ec.europa.eu/information_society/eeurope/i2010/docs/studies/interactive_content_ec2006_final_report.pdf. Accessed 8 August 2009.

Hamilton, J., 'Alternative Media: Conceptual Difficulties, Critical Possibilities', *Journal of Communication Inquiry*, 24:4, 2000, pp. 357–78.

Kucic, L. J., 'Neznanke digitalne televizije', *Media Watch Journal*, 25:26, 2006, pp. 39–40.

Ministry of Economy – Directorate for Electronic Communication and the Post and Electronic Communications Agency of the Republic of Slovenia, *Strategy for the transition from analogue to digital broadcasting*, 2006 http://ec.europa.eu/information_society/policy/ecomm/doc/todays_framework/

digital_broadcasting/switchover/si_s_mekicar_strategija_a_d_prehoda_12_1_sm_lektorirano.pdf. Accessed 8 August 2009

Nissen, C. S., Public service media in the information society. Report prepared for the Council of Europe's Group of Specialists on Public Service Broadcasting in the information society (MC-S-PSB), Media Division, Directorate General of Human Rights, Council of Europe (2006).

Popov, N., *The road to war in Serbia*. Budapest: CEU Press, 2000.

Preston, P. and Kerr, A., 'Digital Media, Nation-States and Local Cultures: The Case of Multimedia "Content" Production', *Media, Culture and Society*, 23, 2001, pp. 109–31.

Ramet, S. P., 'Nationalism and the "Idiocy" of the Countryside: The Case of Serbia', *Ethnic and Racial Studies*, 19:1, 1996, January, pp. 70–87.

Rennie, E., *Community media – a global introduction*. Lanham: Rowman & Littlefield Publishers, 2006.

Recommendation of the Committee of Ministers to member states on media pluralism and diversity of media content (Rec (2007)2), adopted by the Committee of Ministers on 31st January 2007 at the 985th meeting of the Ministers' Deputies, https://wcd.coe.int/ViewDoc.jsp?id=1089699&Back ColorInternet=9999CC&Back. Accessed 5 March 2007.

Silverstone, R., 'Regulation, Media Literacy and Media Civics', *Media, Culture and Society*, 26:3, 2004, pp. 440–49.

Trpevska, S., 'The Business of Ethics, the Ethics of Business', in M. Preoteasa (ed.), Bucharest: Centre for Independent Journalism, 2005.

Woodward, S. L., *Balkan tragedy: Chaos and dissolution after the cold war*, Washington DC: The Brookings Institution, 1995.

### Web pages

www.crossradio.org.
www.radiostudent.si.
www.radiomars.si.
www.srd.org.mk
www.romic.si
www.kanal103.com.mk/.
www.crossradio.org.
http://radiocona.wordpress.com/.
www.freecom.com/.

**Chapter 15**

The Community of Radio Listeners in the Era of the Internet in Africa:
New Forms and New Radio Content, the Fan Club Zephyr Lome (Togo)
as a Basis for Analysis

Etienne L. Damome

## Introduction: African radio and ICT

African radio stations are increasingly facing the challenge of new technologies that require changes in radio practice. After the introduction of FM and then distribution via audio sub-carriers of television satellite channels, radio is currently undergoing another transformation with the development of increasingly complex new information and communication technologies (NICT) and the convergence of broadcasting, computing and telecommunications. ICTs (information and communication technologies) in fact widen the opportunities of radio broadcasting, including via the internet. The opportunities offered by this mode of broadcasting induces significant changes to African radio in that it creates new patterns of production and reception and includes new content and more diverse audiences. But we can see yet another level of change in radio, which takes place at the level of the relationship between a radio and its audiences, and within the community of listeners. Most FM radio stations in Africa have active groups of fans and faithful listeners and radio clubs. They have specific activities in radio broadcasts and outside it. Internet broadcasting has reconfigured these groups by introducing new parameters of belonging and new uses and new radio content to provide for distant listeners and offer something different to these new listeners who embrace the radio with their affection and their activism.

It is difficult to obtain data on new technologies across the whole continent of Africa. The disparities are considerable. Moreover, the fact that development in this area is so steep does little to facilitate the task. That is why we refer to West Africa, which we know best and for which, fortunately, there is a recent study. However, projections can be made regarding other areas of the continent. These data show that the internet is developing rapidly and significantly and that the media no longer hesitate to use it as a preferred means of dissemination and communication.

## Increasing **development of connectivity**

An IPAO (Institut Panos Afrique de l'Ouest) study conducted in 2008 on the connectivity of radio and ICT (internet, satellite, computer, digital storage tools and so on) in West Africa, which concentrates on seven countries (Ghana, Benin, Senegal, Mali, Sierra Leone, Burkina Faso and Niger) and which concerns 220 radio stations (public, community, commercial and religious radio stations), shows that the average rate of internet access to the radio stations in the seven countries is 51.8%, with large disparities among the countries and radio types. Indeed, while the rate of connectivity is 72.2% for private commercial radio on the one hand, it is limited to 31.5% for community or non-profit radio stations on the other hand. While Ghanaian radio stations have a 93.5% connectivity rate, Senegalese radio stations have 89.7%, and only 20% of radio stations in Sierra Leone are connected. In Ghana and Senegal, nearly all commercial radio stations are connected to the net. In addition, 72.7% of Senegalese community radio stations have access to the internet (75% have an ADSL or broadband connection), in contrast to only 8.3% of Nigerien community stations.

The rate of connectivity for all radio stations in Burkina Faso, Benin and Mali is 61.5% , 55% and 34% respectively. Thanks to ADSL technology the majority of stations in the sub-region are connected, in particular Senegal, where more than 92% of stations have access to the worldwide web. As might be expected, this study concludes that 'as illustrated by the cost of internet access, in certain countries internet use has become more and more accessible, but is limited to regions with good infrastructure'.[1]

## Internet as a window and a communication space

Radio stations have various uses of the internet. For those who do not have an internet connection, the relationship to the internet is manifested by the possession and use of an e-mail address. Another 2001 study by a team from the University of Bordeaux (Lenoble-Bart *et al.* 2001) reiterates this observation. Each of the 90 stations covered in this study has at least one e-mail address. Having an e-mail address has become the easiest way to contact neighbours within the same region and in the country. Even if we need to go to the closest city to send an e-mail, it is often cheaper than the phone. The usefulness of the internet for African broadcasters cannot be doubted. For the majority, it has become an essential tool of communication and documentation. The internet allows them to save time that they can spend searching for information for their broadcasts. This reveals an evolution in the uses of the internet because several previous studies emphasize that 'among the three possible uses of the internet radio (e-mail, web pages and broadcasting live), it is the first that is the most common' (Paré 2000).

People with internet connections can create websites. These sites are like radio logs, a written version of what is said orally through the FM band. Many radiobroadcasters prefer the web page, which allows them to present the radio, its administration, its leaders, its technicians, its programme schedule, a photo album, its relationship with listeners – in short everything that was previously presented on pads and flyers. Sport FM's page has such features as 'Overview', 'Administration', 'Presenters', 'Technicians', 'Journal', 'Programme', 'Dedications', 'Photo Album' and 'Archive'. However, the Nostalgie-Abidjan's website is even more developed. It is divided into four sections of which the radio is only one component. This component, 'Radio', offers visitors many choices: 'News', 'Events,' 'Programmes', 'Animation' (entertainment), 'Nostagag' (jokes) and 'Radio Life'. In 'Nostazik' (music section), there is a 'Playlist of the Hits of the Week', of the 'Clips of the Week', the 'Retro Clips' and 'Your Dedications'. The 'Games' section offers 'Vocalis', 'Games Online' and 'Games on the Radio'. If visitors go to the press releases section, they find, surprisingly, 'Love and Intimacy', 'Meeting' 'Fan Club', 'Horoscope' and 'Partnerships'. In this way, with the exception of Radio Okapi and Radio Méditerranée Internationale, which give equal importance to the audio and the written presentations on their website – that is, radio stations logs coexist with the written news – in most other radio stations, broadcasting on the internet remains an additional feature. However, the option of archiving can address this shortcoming. Archives allow downloading of radio news bulletins, broadcasts and reports. Sometimes these records are better kept than those on the premises of the radio stations.

The presence of such topics as 'Meeting', 'Dedications', 'Games', 'Love and Intimacy' and 'Fan Club' shows that the sites are also areas of communication and friendship. Radio Canal Angola proves this fully: its motto is *O verdadeiro ponto de encontro* ('the real meeting point'). Radio Méditerranée Internationale gives advice of all kinds, such as employment offers and advice concerning interpersonal contacts. The advertising on this site, as well as on the websites of other radio stations, shows that the internet also offers opportunities for e-business. Radio Canal Angola also provides counselling in project management. The IPAO study cited above has identified around seventy websites in the seven studied countries, the majority of which have domain names matching the names of the stations, but regrets that their presence on the internet remains limited. In addition, a large number of websites have very little content – or even none at all. Nonetheless, several radio stations extend their offer by streaming on the internet. It is these stations that this chapter is interested in.

## Podcasting a minority activity, webcasting an extension of FM

As shown by connectivity data, African radio is indeed present on the internet. Public and private media of all types (community, voluntary, commercial, religious, educational, municipal, etc.) are there. Podcasting and webcasting possibilities are also available. The distribution of audio or video online in the form of podcasting is not a widespread practice in Africa. The few internet radio stations that are actually employing this mode of dissemination are situated in South Africa, Nigeria, Kenya, Ghana and North Africa. However, the most surprising example is Radio Kankan (http://radio-kankan.com) in Guinée Conakry. This site, managed locally in Conakry, allows users to download sound and images posted there. In addition, several sites offer general or thematic sounds and programmes for downloading. That is the case of CongoKulture.net, of republicoftogo.com, Abidjan.net and others. There is usually at least one such website for many countries, but these websites are not related to the podcast sites of local radio stations. Moreover, most of these podcasting sites are generally located in the West, where there are many possibilities to accommodate them. However, we can say that several FM operators have seized the opportunities offered by the new technologies to extend their radius of broadcasting beyond their territorial roots and to export themselves to wider audiences.

Webcasting is not fundamentally different from podcasting except that it uses streaming, which reminds us of classical radio technology. In fact, it is often the stations on FM frequencies that broadcast all or part of their programme on the internet. Obviously the FM band is not incompatible with broadcasting online and those who are capable of sending programmes online do not hesitate to do so. Using podcasting and the webradio does not require great skill as long as there are the necessary technical and material resources. One just has to be able to create digital files, put them on air and provide for the fluidity of webcasting. In Africa, there is now interest among existing FM radio stations in this type of broadcasting, whether streaming or podcasts. As many as 149 African radio stations were broadcasting on the internet in 2006. But a glance at the web helps us to realize that it is a constantly evolving sector. Again, it is in South Africa and Nigeria that the largest number of radio stations of this type are operating: ten in each of these countries in 2006. Following the example of Channel Africa, the 'Voice of the African Renaissance' of South Africa, which broadcasts on short wave and on satellite is also one of the most visible ones among the African web platforms. Ghana, similar to Madagascar, Senegal, Angola and Benin, has nine web radio stations. Six Tunisian and Congolese radio stations are available on the net and five in Togo, Kenya, Uganda and Zimbabwe. Cameroon has four, along with Mali and Zambia. There are three channels of the Algerian national radio and two additional channels – the regional Oran and the local Sidi Bel Abbes – next to Radio Dzaïr, which was the first private radio in Algeria and in all likelihood is also the first online radio in the country since it started broadcasting in June 2006. Most national channels of different countries participate in the trend of internet radio broadcasting.

In this way, several African radio stations have liberated themselves from constraints of all kinds, ranging from limits imposed by the use of terrestrial frequencies to political constraints created by financial problems. Besides which, the African broadcasters give two fundamental reasons: the internet ensures an international audience and allows you to reach the expatriates. Just as the transistor had 'saved' the radio at the advent of television, new digital technologies will certainly give a new dynamism to this medium. Unfortunately, live broadcasts on the internet are still rare (and sometimes missing, despite being advertised), and the existing ones are often very unstable (in that streaming is usually inaccessible).

## What content?

The major developments in broadcasting allow us to consider several new features: customization of the programmes, more detailed content, invention of new formats, and so on. Are some new aspects already operating in radio broadcasting at present? Are the resources provided by digital materials employed to produce new content and more varied programmes? New technologies offer ample possibilities to all African radio stations, those which broadcast on FM as well as those which broadcast on satellite and online. In addition to freeing them from the grip of local situations, facilitating professional exchanges and synchronizing the media with world events, the internet enriches media content and enables better access to diverse information. New possibilities are made through the convergence of digital technology, writing, broadcasting and telecommunications. All the components of the life of the radio and its reports to its public are better integrated. Through offering articles, video reports or clips in addition to the sound, the content becomes more dense and new programme formats emerge (consisting of sound and associated data). One also notes an increase in supplying information in more specific areas and the customization of programmes, providing an opportunity to share one's tastes in diverse communities of listeners. If most radio sites offer opportunities in travel and tourism, possibilities to meet people, local and ethnic music, and even some interactive programmes, it is because they target the diaspora. Radio stations broadcasting on the web improve both their content and also their relationship with their audiences. Even if the radio stations only broadcast a selection of their programmes online instead of the whole lot, the internet option is always an important addition because it involves the integration of new possibilities.

Thus an FM radio, such as Zephyr, which offers some of its programmes on the web (only five programmes), will be forced to find new content specifically for the online version. Indeed, the additional content consists of various other services for the benefit of the listeners, not only advertising: 'Useful Numbers', 'Pharmacies Guard', 'Horoscope', 'Travel Agencies', 'Entry Formalities', 'Togolese Embassies', 'Hotels & Bars' and 'Attractions'. It also contains, as an extension of the broadcast, a page called 'Artists' as an extension of the music played on the radio, offering a 'Bibliography', a 'Discography', 'Album Releases' and 'Hits of the Month'. There is also an agenda in which the audience is made aware, on a daily basis , of 'Traditional Festivals' celebrated in all regions of Togo, and the 'Shows' on tour. The website also offers files related to 'World Days', 'Culture', 'Sports News' and 'Politics'. Similarly, Radio Canal Angola has had the idea of offering videos. A radio station that broadcasts the entire FM programme schedule online – as is the case with Sport FM, Radio Okapi or Radio Méditerranée Internationale – is not free from the need to adapt the programmes for broadcasting through the internet. The specific needs of the internet platform require additional elements. The spread of online radio programmes therefore always requires additional work, resources and skills.

## What formats?

As for classical radio stations, there are thousands of web radio stations in the world with a general orientation as well as thematic web radio stations because technically anyone can create their own station. However, the practical issues involved in the production of these broadcasts require appropriate technology and properly mastered techniques. It is for this reason that there are not many web radio stations in Africa. As they are the extensions of their counterparts on FM, the majority of African web radio stations have a general orientation. They produce and broadcast programmes covering all areas (news, politics, economics, sociocultural and educational development, environment and so on). The radio stations seem to share the same objectives, so that one can say that there is a homogenization of programmes. Religious radio stations are thematic radio stations but they incorporate local development dimensions to the point of becoming duplicates of community and associative radio stations. Commercial radio stations also provide a religious service on a par with confessional radio stations. Associative and community radio stations are all educative and school radio stations are community radio stations. Political radio stations are also commercial.

However, this is normal. We should admire the ability to adapt and change that radio stations have demonstrated at this stage of their evolution. Many among the first private radio stations, from the 1990s, have simply disappeared because they failed to achieve the 'conversion' that proved vital to their survival. Created with the ambition to be alternative media to the media of the state, particularly in the production and dissemination of news, they quickly realized that the freedom granted to them did not cover politics. They are mostly oriented towards the areas of music and miscellaneous information. They have also managed to integrate a number of areas of the social sphere (health, environment, local development, religion). This means that they were able to legitimately set foot in the political field. The impression that they all do the same thing is therefore less a sign of poverty than of resilience.

Furthermore it should be noted that the priorities and the contexts are not conducive to great specialization in terms of programme options. In Africa, listeners' needs have equal importance and urgency; they need to be taken into account with the same priority. In semi-urban and rural areas there is often only one radio that is obliged to provide a public service. Even in cities where there are sometimes a large number of radio stations, specialization remains very difficult because at the moment there are no strong trends in the habits of the listeners. They move easily from one frequency to another. The multiplicity of programmes seems to cause a real 'voracity' and the listeners 'swallow' anything they find. The only specialized audience is perhaps that of religious or sports programmes and of international political news. Editors are therefore obliged to propose 'everything' in the hope of attracting a certain audience. The particular context of Africa seems currently to exclude the possibility of too extensive specializations. Strictly musical radio stations could not even choose a specific genre to follow!

As radio stations with a general orientation on FM, African radio stations also retain their general orientation on the internet. The most obvious examples (beyond public radio stations) are Radio Méditerranée Internationale and Radio Okapi, which aspire to be 'general and popular'. Méditerranée Internationale (Medi1) offers cultural programmes, broadcasts on energy, on sustainable development, on the economy, politics and sport. Okapi, in addition to fulfilling its essential objective (to mediate peace communication in the Congo), provides development news, awareness of the environment, hygiene and health, sports, music, other cultural agendas, exchange rates and even a library. All this allows the radio stations to reach a wide audience and especially to please their loyal listeners. To ensure that the expectations of all the listeners are taken into account, the community formed by these listeners is consulted regularly, so that their relationship with the radio station is strengthened further.

## The community of radio listeners

Several radio stations have promoted the creation of groups of radio listeners or fan clubs, so that those with an interest in radio can meet. They gather, organize demonstrations in support of the radio station, make contributions and participate in various aspects of the life of the radio station. Often they are also the ones who provide feedback, and for the radio stations, these are indeed the best places to meet their listeners and discuss issues with them. At the Radio de l'Alliance Chrétienne in Burkina Faso the meetings of the club are called 'graine' (seed). The club meets every month in the presence of the director of the station for a drink and talks about the radio station. The community of listeners of Radio Maria in Togo and the Radio de l'Immaculée Conception in Bénin also meet regularly. For them, it is truly a 'family' surrounding the radio stations. There are people of all demographics but very few young people. Because of the objective of 'providing help to the radio station', assumed by these groups, the members are mostly adults and seniors. For example, 80% of the members of the Radio Maria Association are over forty-five years old. Among them, women are slightly in the majority. Most of them have a job or another paid activity. Almost all of these members are also members of the various groups and parish congregations (choirs, charismatic renewal and so on). The groups are also a source of young people who are active in radio associations. This does not mean that young people are a minority among the fans of the radio, quite on the contrary, but they have their own *modus operandi* and their own interests.

## Young fans in the era of the internet

African listeners of web radio stations, except for journalists, are mostly relatively young. If we look at the case of a group of Lomé, Kouvé is 17 years old and most of his friends – about the same age as him – like him, prefer to listen to Zephyr online rather than on a FM receiver. They are attracted to the possibility of interaction offered by this radio on its web page. Instead of calling by telephone to participate in a show, they prefer posting e-mails. According to Kouvé, for example, "beyond listening to Zephyr for its music, it is the exchanges with other radio fans that are important". These youths are part of the Fan Club Zephyr at their college. Listening to the radio with a delay virtually compels them to go for the internet option. Yet "it is a choice" according to Jean-Paul, who furthermore noted that "this listening mode is best for students". Except for some favourite overnight programmes, others, especially music, are broadcast in daytime when the students are in the classroom. Fortunately, libraries, media centres and computer rooms in their establishments, which have internet connections, are a great help: "When we have a break, we go straight to the computer room of our college to download the programme of our choice. We listen to it at noon or in the evening and then we discuss it on the blog until the closing hours of the centre", said Elom. Anani, who is not as fascinated by discussion forums, said he is rather a fan of the karaoke online, another space dedicated to the fan club. To participate in it, he registers himself and posts the song on the radio though he is not sure whether he will be able to listen to his song when it is on air. He will know the effect produced by it after reading the comments the next day! Everybody enjoys the online dedications, because for them, it is the place for 'birthday wishes' or 'winking at friends'.

It is true that blogging can produce a new dynamic interaction with the public and be a place of sharing, mobilization and organization of fan clubs. The case of Radio Futur Média cited above shows how these forums stimulate real excitement. It is also true of Radio Nostalgie Abidjan which has a public space on its site. It is therefore probably in this way that radio stations can provide for larger audiences and will be able to expand their listenership in Africa. Even though these spaces dedicated to the listeners are rarely updated, without a moderator or effective webmasters, they still open up a new dimension in the relationship between production and reception. It also shows that the strong penetration of the mobile phone on the continent allows stations to use it as an indispensable tool for relating to and communicating with listeners; this has contributed to today's large number of radio listeners. Mobile phones, especially text messages, are used by many stations. This usage is very popular among the local population. The new services are considered important tools of interaction between radio stations and listeners and are a potential source of substantial revenue for radio companies. In this connection we should note the role played by the young fans of Radio Ocean FM in Benin in text testing in interactive programmes. Knowing that adult listeners prefer using the landline telephone or the post, while young people are more willing to use modern technologies, especially the e-mail, developers have tested loyal listeners with respect to the use of texts, and it has worked. Within the same groups of fans, the ability has been developed to contribute to their enjoyment of their favourite shows. When information about meetings and events is posted on the fan club web page, the members receive or send each other text messages. Therefore we can say that new technologies contribute significantly to the running of these groups.

## What change?

Since the advent of the internet, radio is in control of groups of its listeners. Indeed, before the creation of blogs reinforced the websites of the radio stations, which provided a clear station perspective on fan club life, these groups were managed independently. They were developing activities of which the radio station could be informed without automatically participating in them as an institution. Also external members, in particular those in the diaspora, have been integrated into the radio community. Thus the fan club no longer consists of just a few friends but embraces anyone willing to share the family atmosphere around a broadcast or around the radio station. There are also new parameters of participation. To be member of a fan club one needs to know how to use a computer, surf the net and send texts. With new technologies, a sectorization of the radio community takes place. Rather than radio stations having fans of their station overall, fans tend to be of particular programmes and even of aspects of the station. There is also a multiplicity of allegiances. A fan of a broadcast of a specific radio station can also be a fan of a broadcast of another station. Finally, surprising as it may seem, this form of activism is more virtual than the traditional forms. Besides the price of text messages, which provides financial support to the radio station after the mobile operator has deducted its share, the new fan clubs are not subject to 'obligations' vis-à-vis the radio. Fortunately, traditional clubs have remained. They contribute towards sustaining the radio with donations, meetings, offers to help with cleaning and so on.

## Conclusion

It is certain that digitalization is now inevitable and is a positive factor, given the benefits it brings and the opportunities it offers. However, the internet does not seem to have solved all the challenges. It has not improved the quality of programmes nor increased local production. The dependence pointed out by André-Jean Tudesq (1998) and Renaud de la Brosse (1999) in this area is also a cultural allegiance. It does not encourage real autonomy of production or differentiation of programmes from one channel to another. By receiving daily satellite programmes to cover international news or cultural and educational issues, African radio stations forget local realities. African radio stations should therefore better identify the needs of their listeners. They have been able to diversify their audiences by engaging with people: urban and rural populations, intellectuals and the illiterate, managers and workers, students and apprentices, men and women, young and old, believers and unbelievers. The radio stations reach almost all social categories. But it is unclear whether they know precisely who the beneficiaries of their activities are. The general character strengthens the effects of mass communication. Combining programmes that attract wide audiences and more specialized programmes, the radio stations can mobilize audiences but just how anonymous or otherwise are these large groups of individuals? By completely covering all the areas of social life they can have the certainty of being heard. The challenge is to identify the programme which does not contribute towards audience retention at all. A smörgåsbord approach, with many dishes to choose from, certainly seems friendlier to visitors

Diversification of programmes and a prudent choice of formats is also important. Competition and the paradoxical homogenization it generates leads to the assumption that audiences are the same and they have the same preferences. However, surely they do not choose a station randomly, much less a programme. The enthusiasm for the generalist model shows that it will work for a while yet, it is the thematic model which will gradually come to prevail, as can be concluded on the basis of an observation made in Togo, where radio audiences began a gradual reversal in the general trend since the moment when a sports radio station was created in Lomé. Our interviews with listeners in that city in August 2008 revealed that of the thirty-five respondents, twenty-two reported listening to Sport FM at least once a week between the first and the fifteenth days of the month. The second reason why a thematic radio station is the radio of 'the future' in urban Africa is the inevitable weariness brought about by the current homogenization of programmes. In most of the countries we visited, listeners have mentioned that they got bored of roaming across frequencies in search of an original programme. Radio stations are likely to evolve towards target groups defined either by interest or by language, by sex or age. Maybe radio will then exploit all the possibilities offered by new technologies.

There remains, however, one peculiarity with regard to rural areas. Stations broadcasting in these areas need to take into account various concerns affecting the daily life and immediate environment. The media concerned are obliged to maintain a general format if they want to fulfil their function as local media.

## Note

1. See http://www.panos-ao.org/ipao/spip.php?article15211&lang=fr.

## References and further reading

de la Brosse , R., 'Uniformisation médiatique des sociétés d'Afrique subsaharienne', in S Prouls & A. Vitalis (eds), *Vers une citoyenneté simulée*: Médias, réseaux et mondilaistion, Paris: Apogée, 1999, pp. 250–54.

Lenoble-Bart A., Cheval J.-J., Tudesq A.-J., 'Médias africains et Internet', in Internet *en Afrique subsaharienne: acteurs et usages, MSHA Publication en ligne*, http://www.msha.fr/msha/publi/en_ligne/netafriq/index.htm (rubrique Médias), 2001. Accessed 7 September 2009.

Malick Ndiaye, Kwami Ahiabenu II, Abdourahame Ousmane, Hippolyte Djiwan, & Al, 'Radio and ICT in West Africa: Connectivity and Use', Panos Institute West Africa, October 2008.

Paré C., 'Enjeux des nouvelles technologies de l'information et de la communication en Afrique', *Marchés Tropicaux*, June 2000, pp. 108–14.

Paré C., *Médias et société de l'information en Afrique de l'Ouest. Enjeux, discours et appropriations*, thèse de doctorat, Université Bordeaux 3, 2007.

Tudesq A.-J., *L'espoir et l'illusion : actions positives et effets pervers des médias en Afrique subsaharienne*, Talence, MSHA, 1998.

# Contributors to this Volume

**Avelino Amoedo** holds a Ph.D. in Journalism from the University of Navarra (1998). He is Associate Professor for Radio Production at the Department of Journalism Projects, University of Navarra. He is also the Academic Secretary of the Department of Journalism Projects of the School of Communication. His research focuses on radio production, both communication and technical aspects, and on the structure of the radio stations in Spain and in Europe (history, legal regulation, programming, listeners), and he has published several articles in different publications. He is a member of the Asociación Española de Investigadores de la Comunicación and of ECREA. His curriculum vitae may be viewed at http://www.unav.es/fcom/profesores/amoedo.htm.

**Tiziano Bonini** holds a Ph.D. in Media and Communication from Siena University (2008). He is a researcher in media sociology at IULM University in Milan, where he teaches radio communication. He wrote a book on web radio in Italy (2006) and edited a book on the history of Radio Popolare, the most important Italian community radio. His last book, published in 2010, is about media, migrants and the sense of 'home'. As a student at Siena, he was among the founders of the first Italian college radio. He worked as freelance features producer and as assistant radio play director for RTSI. In 2005 he won the special prize of RTSI (Italian-language Swiss public radio) for the best radio documentary. He worked as freelance producer for Radio2 RAI from 2006 to 2009. Actually he is a freelance author for Radio24. In 2009 he was invited as a speaker at EBU conferences on radio and new media.

**Frank Byrne** trained as a teacher and spent most of his working life in primary and secondary schools, and in the 16 years prior to retirement as principal, in a large, working-class city comprehensive school. During those years he also trained as a radio producer and worked as a freelance contract producer for 2FM – the popular music arm of RTE (the state PSB station) mostly at night, at weekends and over the summer. In 1991 he was conferred with a Masters in Media, Communication and Culture at DCU – his final dissertation examining the provision of radio drama for young people. On retirement from teaching he embarked upon a Ph.D. programme at DCU researching the connection between phone-in radio and the democratic process. He has a particular interest in rehabilitating the status of the radio professional as co-citizen in the public sphere. In addition to working with communications students at DCU, he also delivers the core module on Contemporary Irish Society at the Dublin Internship Programme of Boston University.

**Etienne L. Damome**, Ph.D., is a researcher of MICA (Mediation, Information, Communication, Art) doctoral education team in information and communication sciences at the University of Bordeaux 3 in France. In 2007 he presented a doctoral thesis on radio and religions in Africa using the example of four countries in West Africa, and this year he is about to publish a book on religious radio stations in Africa at Presses Universitaires de Bordeaux. He is now working on the contemporary changes to radio in Africa by analysing the effects on the radio and its audiences of adopting new information and communication technologies. He is a member of GRER (the francophone radio research network).

**Rosemary Day** is the Director of the Radio Research Centre based in Mary Immaculate College, University of Limerick, where she is a senior lecturer and Head of the Department of Media and Communication Studies. She was a founder and the first Chair of the Radio Research Section of ECREA and of RRI (Radio Research Ireland). She was one of the founders of IREN (The International Radio Research Network) and her research is primarily in the following areas: community radio, public participation in the mass media, the relationship between radio and identity and broadcasting in lesser-used languages. She was one of the founders of Raidió na Life, the Irish language community radio station in Dublin, Wired FM, Limerick's cross-campus student community radio and of Wired Luimnigh, a community radio project for Irish speakers in Limerick. She was also one of the founders of Craol (The Community Radio Forum of Ireland) and was an elected council member of AMARC Europe (The World Association of Community Radio Broadcasters) for two terms.

**Angeliki Gazi** is a visiting lecturer at the Department of Communication and Internet Studies of Cyprus University of Technology. She is a psychologist and holds a Masters Degree and a Ph.D. in Psychology of Communication, focusing on the media psychology of radio communication, from the Department of Communication and Media Studies of the University of Athens. She was a founder and a vice chair of the Radio Research Section of ECREA and one of the founders of IREN (International Radio Research Network). She is member of the International Editorial Board of the *Journal of Radio and Audio Media*, a member of the International Editorial Board of *The Radio Journal* and a member of the International Scientific Board of GRER (Group de Recherches et d'Etudes sur la Radio). She is in charge of the organization, functioning and programme flow of the university radio at the Cyprus University of Technology. She has participated in various academic research projects and has published several articles relevant to her research interests.

**Maria Gutierrez** is a lecturer in Audiovisual Communication and Advertising. She has a doctorate in Communication Informationand Journalism specialization. She has taught subjects related to broadcasting programming (including language, conventional and thematic radio, speciality contents, strategies in the digital age), courses in journalism and audiovisual communication and on several Masters courses. She also works as an adviser for el Consell de l'Audiovisual de Catalunya (CAC) on radio programming content and is a member of the Radio Observatory of Catalonia Autònoma University. Her publications are connected with broadcasting strategies and politics on conventional and analogical radio. Her research work focuses on analysis of the programming of the main Spanish broadcasters, and also on the reception process of the migration of the radio audience.

**Bert Herman** obtained a Masters in Communication Studies from the University of Antwerp. His field of expertise is media culture. He worked as a researcher for the Media, Policy, Research Group focussing on the feasibility of local radio in the current media landscape.

**Susana Herrera Damas** has a degree in audiovisual communication (University of Navarra, 1998) and in sociology (UNED 2004). She also has a Ph.D. in audiovisual communication (University of Navarra 2002). Holder of the Extraordinary Doctoral Award, she is the author of three books and over fifty articles published in prestigious academic journals. Having worked at the Universities of Navarra and Piura, currently she works at the University Carlos III at Madrid. Her research is oriented towards the study of journalistic genres in radio and to the analysis of the different possibilities for public participation in the media.

**Stanislaw Jedrzejewski** is a graduate of the Institute of Sociology at the University of Warsaw and has an MBA from Kozminski University, Poland. A professor of Media and Social Communications at Kozminski University and the John Paul II Catholic University of Lublin, he is currently a researcher at the Communication and Society Studies Centre of Minho University in Braga, Portugal. He was a member and vice chairman of the Radio Committee of the European Broadcasting Union from 1995–2007. He has been a member of the board of the public broadcaster Polski Radio (1994–1998) and the Programme Director of Polish public radio between 1990 and 1993 and from 1998 to 1999. The former Controller of Polish public broadcaster Radio 1 from 2003 to 2005, he was also a member of the supervisory board of Polish Radio and a member of the National Broadcasting Council in 2005. A member of the International Radio Research Network (IREN), Vice Chair of the Radio Research Section of ECREA, he also serves on the editorial boards of *The Radio Journal: International Studies in Broadcast and Audio Media* and the *Central European Journal of Communication*. The author of numerous studies, articles and reports on radio, his publications include *Public radio in Europe in Digital Age* (Universitas 2010), 'Digital Radio: Problems and Dilemmas of Radio Development' in *Transformaciones de la radio y la television en Europa* (Penafiel Saiz ed., Universidad del Pais Vasco 2007), *Radio in Social Communication: Radio Role and Trends Development* (Profi-Press 2003) and as editor *The Medium with Promising Future: Radio in Central and Eastern European Countries* (KUL 2007).

**Vesa Kurkela** is Professor of Popular Music Studies at the Sibelius Academy (Helsinki) and at the University of Tampere. His main research interests include Finnish popular music history, music media in the Balkans and elsewhere, processes of folklorization and radio music.

**Josep Maria Marti** is Lecturer in Audiovisual Communication and Advertising. A graduate and Doctor in information sciences of the Universitat Autònoma de Barcelona (UAB), he combines his teaching and research work with a professional career in radio. He is a member of the Image, Sound and Synthesis Research Group (GRISS), a consolidated research group attached to UAB and created in 1980, acknowledged by the Catalan Autonomous Government of la Generalitat de Catalunya (Grup 2009SGR1013) and part of the Department of Audiovisual Communication and Advertising I. He is Dean of the Journalists Association of Catalonia, Director of the Catalan Radio Observatory and a member of the board of the European Broadcasting Union Radio Committee and the Forum Éuropenne de la Radio. He also runs the Masters in Management and Radio Administration Companies, jointly run by the UAB, Cadena SER and Santillana Formación. He has taught courses and has given papers in several cities in Europe and America. His research focuses on radio media.

**María del Pilar Martinez-Costa** holds a Ph.D. in public communication from the University of Navarra. She is the current Associate Dean for Students of the School of Communication of the University of Navarra. Since the mid-1990s, she has been researching the introduction of digital radio systems in Europe and the changes brought about by digital technology in the way radio content is conceived, produced and managed. Her book *La radio en la era digital* (El País Aguilar, Madrid 1997) was a pioneering work on this subject. She has published many articles and some of her books are *Reinventar la radio* (Eunate, Pamplona 2001), *Información radiofónica* (Ariel, Barcelona 2002), *Programación radiofónica* (Ariel, Barcelona 2004), *Lenguaje, géneros y programas de radio* (Eunsa, Pamplona, 2005) and *La crónica radiofónica* (IORTV, Madrid, 2008).

**Luisa Martinez** is an associate lecturer, a graduate in communication sciences from the Universidad Veracruzana in Mexico, of the Masters in Creative Documentaries at the UAB and Doctor of Audiovisual Communication from the UAB, with a doctoral thesis on cultural identity in fiction series in Catalonia. A member of the Image, Sound and Synthesis Research Group (GRISS), she has directed the documentaries *Por amor a la Trova* and *Los Decires de la Huaca*, and has taught courses on this audiovisual speciality and new technologies in various Mexican Universities.

**Belén Monclus** is an assistant lecturer in Audiovisual Communication and Advertising. A graduate in journalism, she also has a Masters in Audiovisual Communication at the UAB and is the Coordinator of the Catalan Radio Observatory. A member of the Image, Sound and Synthesis Research Group (GRISS), she has worked in the media, such as Barcelona

Televisió, Televisió de Catalunya and Localia and in companies such as Hi-Media. She has also participated in the organization of such events as Open Radio, the Ondas Media Awards and the Second and Third Radio Congress in Catalonia. She develops her research task chiefly in the television and radio environments. In the radio broadcasting sphere, her main focus is the radio broadcasting system, more concretely, in the Catalan sector, young people, audience and programming.

**Elsa Moreno** is a journalist and holds a Ph.D. in Public Communication from the University of Navarra (1998). She is Associate Professor for Radio Programming at the Department of Journalism Projects, University of Navarra. She researches the concept of 'radios' and content management of multi-channel radio, together with the evolution of programming criteria and techniques: specifically, management strategies, content design, means of production and direction, commercialization and the promotion of radio programmes. Her research also covers trends in the Spanish, European and American radio market. She is the author of several studies on talk radio stations, specialized news stations and music radio stations.

**Maria Papadomanolaki** is a Greek artist working primarily with sound in the context of phonography, audience-centred performance pieces and radio art. Her background in language studies and her interest in environmental sound inform her artistic practice. Papadomanolaki often combines these two elements in her work to amplify the intrinsic physical and psychological qualities of an experienced time and space. In 2006, she marked her transition from French language and literature to the sonic arts with *Stoma* – an interactive voice piece based on Samuel Beckett's *Not I*, exhibited with great success in the United Kingdom and Greece. She received grants to pursue studies in Digital Music and Sound Art in the UK – most notably the Alexander S. Onassis Public Benefit grant for emerging artists. Her work has been awarded by respected panellists like the Nagoya University of the Arts in Japan. She has presented her practice-based research on experimental radio at international conferences, and many of her collaborations with fellow artists have been exhibited at European and international festivals. She currently resides in New York where she works as a freelance artist and is involved as a volunteer in a variety of free103point9's activities.

**Carmen Peñafiel Saiz** holds a Ph.D. in journalism and she has worked as Professor of Broadcasting Technology at the University of the Basque Country (UPV/EHU) since 1987. She worked as an editor and radio broadcaster at SER, COPE and RADIO EUSKADI from 1980–87. She is a founding member of the Group IREN (International Radio Research Network), a member of the francophone research group GRER, a member of ECREA and a member of the AE-IC. She is responsible for Ph.D. courses and co-director of a Masters degree for radio and TV professionals as well as a lecturer on the Masters in Multimedia Communication and Radio Broadcasting Production. She often takes part in international fora and conferences on radio and television broadcasting and she has been a visiting professor in mass media in many European and North American Universities. She has written more than fifty scientific articles and she has also authored eight books, five of them published by UPV/EHU, *Las radios autonómicas y transformaciones de la radio entre 1980–1990* (1994); *Tecnología de la televisión. Del disco de Nipkow a la revolución numérica* (2000); *La tecnología en radio: Principios básicos, desarrollo y revolución digital* (2000); *Claves para la era digital: Evolución. hacia nuevos medios, nuevos lenguajes y nuevos servicios* (2002) and *Transformaciones de la Radio y la TV en Europa* (2007) as well as *Odisea 21.La evolución del sector audiovisual* (Fragua 2004) and *La transición de la TV digital en España* (Bosch 2005).

**Mojca Plansak** is an independent media and cultural researcher, living in Maribor, Slovenia. She received her MA in the area of comparative studies of ideas and cultures in Ljubljana, Slovenia at the University of Nova Gorica. She is a founder and board member of the Community Media Forum Europe (www.cmfe.eu) and a founder and member of the So0gledi group (http://soogledi.blogspot.com/). From 2003 until 2005 she was editor-in-chief of an independent radio station (Radio Mars) in Maribor, Slovenia. From February 2008 until February 2010 she was Assistant Director at Maska Institution in Ljubljana/Slovenia. She was also assistant lecturer at the University of Maribor, Faculty of Electrical Engineering and Computer Science at the Institute of Media and Communications from February 2008 until March 2010. In 2009 she was a Member of Expert Committee for the Media Content Programme at the Ministry of Culture of Slovenia. Her main field is journalism, but lately her work is more dedicated to media and cultural policy research. She works in Slovenia and abroad.

**Pedro Portela** is currently a Ph.D. student at the Communication Science Department at the University of Minho. From 1987 until 1992 he worked as a music journalist in *Blitz*, a weekly music newspaper. In 1988 he was part of the team that founded RUM – Rádio Universitária do Minho, a university-connected commercial radio station, where he still runs a weekly show and is member of the editorial board. In 1994 he graduated in systems and computers engineering at the University of Minho. In 1996 he founded Sensoria, a multimedia company devoted to the production of interactive software, both online and offline. In 2004 he started teaching at the Communication Science Department at the University of Minho, where he still works as an assistant. In 2006 he obtained a Masters in Communication Science at the University Of Minho.

**José Luis Requejo Alemán** holds a degree in information sciences (University of Piura 1997), a Ph.D. in communication (University of Navarra 2001) and an MBA in communication business management (University of Navarra 2008). After working at the University of Piura, at the moment he works at the University Carlos III of Madrid. His research focuses on the analysis of the diverse Web 2.0 applications and on the study of new financial support forms for investigative journalism.

**Xavier Ribes** is a lecturer in Audiovisual Communication and Advertising. He holds a doctorate in Communication Sciences, and has taught subjects linked to new technologies in journalism and audiovisual communication and on several Masters courses. A member of the Image, Sound and Synthesis Research Group (GRISS), he has also lectured at the Universitat Politècnica de Catalunya and on postgraduate courses and Masters courses organized by the Instituto Universitario de Postgrado and the Universitat Oberta de Catalunya, where he has also written papers. His publications are connected with electronic media, interactivity, digitalization, the internet and multimedia communication. His research is currently focused on analysis of the main Spanish online communication media and the use of sound in the net.

**Pascal Ricaud** holds a Ph.D. in Communication and Information Sciences (University of Bordeaux 3 2000). Working on community radio and alternative media, he has published chapters in edited collections and articles in academic journals. His research is oriented towards the study of the impact of media on territories and on recompositions of identity. He has been a senior lecturer at the University François Rabelais (Tours) since 2002. He was member of CEDP (Studies Centre for Public Debates, Tours) between 2001 and 2006. Working on 'media and public space', and more specifically, on the emergence of new participation spaces on the internet, he has published several articles in books and academic journals, and co-edited a book on deliberative forms of public debates (two volumes). A member of GRER since 1999, he is a researcher in the UMR CNRS 6173 CITERES, COST laboratory (Political and Social Construction of Territories).

**Blandine Schmidt** is a Ph.D. student and Research Fellow in Information and Communication Sciences in the University of Bordeaux 3 (France). In her research team, the MICA (Médiation, Information, Communication, Art), she focuses her work on radio and its history. More particularly, she studies interactive broadcasts and listeners' participation. She is engaged in associative activities in GRER (Groupe de Recherches et d'Études sur la Radio www.grer.fr) as a member of its administration council and on Est-ce que t'entends ce que je vois ? (www.estceque.blogspot.com) as president.

**Guy Starkey** is a former radio practitioner on the Voice of Peace, Radio Nova International, Radio West, BFBS Gibraltar, Beacon Radio, Marcher Sound, MFM and City Talk. He began presenting in hospital radio, co-produced a documentary for BBC Radio Four while a student and volunteered at University Radio Bath. From Senior Producer at Radio City, he went into teaching in 1991, managing temporary student radio stations until Utopia FM became the full-time community station 107 Spark FM. He has been closely involved in developing and assessing national media qualifications for Edexcel, and his book *Radio in Context* (Palgrave Macmillan 2004) combines practical instruction with underpinning knowledge of most aspects of production and presentation. His other publications include *Balance and Bias in Journalism: Representation, Regulation and Democracy* (Palgrave Macmillan 2007) and *Radio Journalism* which he co-authored with Professor Andrew Crisell (Sage 2009). The Chair of the Radio Research Section of ECREA, he is also a member of the steering committee of the Radio Studies Network within MeCCSA, as well as Professor of Radio and Journalism and Head of the Department of Media and Communication at the University of Sunderland.

**Heikki Uimonen** is an Academy of Finland post-doctoral researcher at the School of Social Sciences and Humanities at the University of Tampere, Finland. His main research interests are radio, music, media, acoustic communication and changes in the sonic environment.

**Hilde van den Bulck**, Ph.D., is a senior lecturer and head of the research group Media, Policy and Culture of the University of Antwerp. She obtained a Ph.D. in Social Sciences with a study on the historical role of public service broadcasting in modernity. Her expertise is situated, firstly, in the field of media policy, focussing on a political-economic analysis of structures and processes, including digitization, and secondly, on media culture, analysing the role of media culture in collective identities.